SPECIAL GUEST

SPECIAL GUEST

Recipes for the happily
imperfect host

ANNABEL CRABB

WENDY SHARPE

MURDOCH BOOKS
SYDNEY · LONDON

Love in a Cold Climate
G. DURRELL
Julian Barnes Letters from London

For Jeremy: weapons-grade speed tidier and the best co-host in the business *AC*

For Gwen Bennett, who was a marvellous and generous host *WS*

Contents

Happily imperfect hosting	9
Maximum effect, minimum effort recipes	14
Early bird breakfasts	16
Stay for lunch	42
Here's one I prepared earlier	72
Salads for all	112
Bring back afternoon tea	138
Crowded house	168
Pudding club	194
The happy hour	214
Index	235

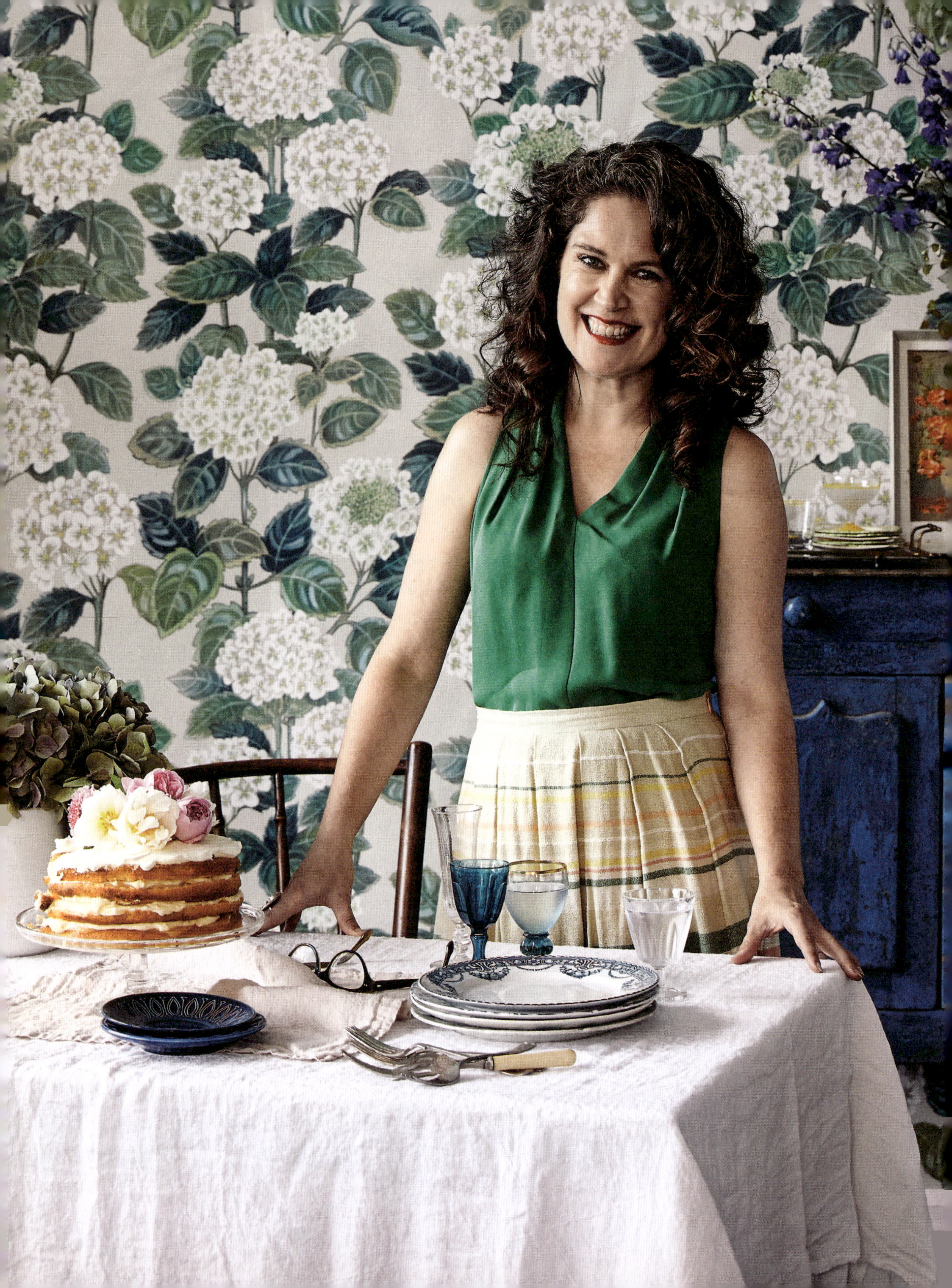

Happily imperfect hosting

I wish I could be one of those hosts who opens the door to reveal an oasis of tasteful tranquillity; flawless mise en place, flowers arranged, children tucked away out of sight reading something improving, and kitchen surfaces clean as a whistle.

Tragically, this never happens at my house. A dinner party will almost always involve a major uplift of clutter from the dining room table, for starters. School bags will be shoved swearingly into cupboards. (I actually have a special word for that panicky, edge-of-tears, shoving-things-into-cupboards tidying you do when you've left not quite enough time before guests are due to arrive: 'crydying'. I've done a lot of crydying in my time. Not to be confused, of course, with 'procrastibaking', which is when you make a cake in order to avoid cleaning out the fridge.) It will suddenly be discovered, five minutes before the guests arrive, that there is no ice. I'll gaze at the kitchen walls in an idle moment and realise how hellishly grubby they are. And the three elegant courses I planned and prepared never flow as smoothly as I pictured; suddenly I'll realise that a whole bag of herbs need picking over, or the dressing isn't done, or it's 9pm and I've forgotten to serve any food at all yet.

I once decided to cook slow-roast lamb for a large group of friends and realised, at the end of four hours, that the oven had malevolently switched itself off at the sixty-minute mark. I baked a dessert tart for Penny Wong that collapsed entirely, covering the floor of the oven with lemon curd. Why? I still don't know why that happened. I've made possets that curdled. Pasta that congealed.

Here's a tip: never try to make fresh pasta for more than six people.

(Here's another: once you've published a cookbook, your friends' pleasure in your kitchen disasters will soar exponentially skyward.)

I've come to terms with being an imperfect host. Dinner parties are great, but they are largely governed by a dreadful rule. In general, the better time the host is having, the higher the likelihood that militaristic order in the kitchen will break down. Culinary disaster may ensue.

But here's the thing. You don't have to stage a three-course full catastrophe to achieve the real point of hospitality, which is to have a nice time and be generous to your friends. And over time, Wendy and I have realised that the most satisfying way of cooking for friends is to catch them when everyone's expectations are low. Throw together a last-minute lunch or dinner when your friends just drop in and fail to leave again. I know that even the term 'throw together' is annoying when you can't be expected to have all the right ingredients on hand for something fancy. But there are some ingredients with a good shelf-life that can be kept on hand to make easy dishes that will delight a guest who's not expecting much.

Or maybe do one thing – just one, like a cake – and make it incredibly fancy or just very generous, like a big slab cake. Ask your friends around for a cup of tea and surprise them. Ask them around for a meal that isn't usually an entertainment proposition, like breakfast or a late supper. Ask friends who genuinely don't care that your house is a mess. And instead of labouring over an intricate feast, show your thoughtfulness for your friends in other ways; if they're vegan or gluten-free or Muslim, cook something that works for them but isn't obviously an afterthought.

Cooking for people in your home isn't about showing off. It's about delighting the people you love, while also remembering to actually spend time with them, not weeping in the kitchen as you espalier a dozen quail or whatever. (And yes, I know that's not even the right verb.) My dear old friend and partner in cookery writing, Wendy Sharpe, is an odd cocktail of kitchen impulses. On the one hand, she will not hesitate to cater a friend's entire birthday party/wedding/child's christening, even if it involves three days' work and a million canapés. On the other hand, she will routinely declare herself too lazy to grate cheese.

But isn't that what cooking's about? It's entirely subjective. Wendy has worked out the things she finds stressful (fancy birthday cakes, for instance) and hit on ways to avoid them. She has also utterly convinced me that there is no disgrace in serving the same dish more than once. If you're good at cooking it, and your guests like it, then keep on serving it!

So don't be menaced by expectations of multiple courses and pressed linen and children who waft off to bed at 7.25pm. Look after your friends, be generous, and trim the sails of your culinary ambition. In the end, cooking for others is an act of generosity. And that means knowing their needs, and being able to cater for them in a way that doesn't feel like you're making a great effort; that's the ancient principle of hospitality.

We've made this book largely vegetarian (with some seafood), because that's how we both eat. But there are plenty of opportunities for the addition of meat, and we've included lists in the index to help locate recipes that can be made vegan or gluten-free. Most recipes in the book are halal, or can be made so, but much will depend on the antecedents of the ingredients you buy (the source of rennet in cheese, the fermentation process of vinegars, and so on), so be sure to check your shopping basket and read labels carefully when cooking for Muslim guests.

Often, it is assumed that an omnivore-type dish is standard, with any vegetarians or gluten-avoiders present expected to eat the main dish, but with the offending elements omitted. And, as a guest, I'm always more than happy with that. But if you stop thinking of a guest with a particular dietary requirement as a problem, and start thinking laterally, what emerges is an opportunity to cook something new. And if your omnivore friends get something exciting and a night off from meat and three veg, and your vegan friend gets to eat the same as everyone else for once, then that sounds like a recipe for a good night.

So many cookbooks published today are about how to take care of yourself; how to get leaner or less depressed, or how to achieve a more smoothly functioning gut. This one is about how to look after other people. We hope it brings you joy.

Annabel Crabb

I have some lovely early memories of dinner parties at my grandmother's house. The men wore ties, the ladies wore chiffon and guest arrival was heralded by a gorgeous mix of Nina Ricci perfume and Old Spice. My own excitement really started when my grandmother clipped on her earrings, ready for the evening ahead. It was always the same four couples - friends for decades. They ate in the separate dining room with the special plates (warmed!) and silver placemats. They had three courses, with the proper rows of cutlery laid out. I could hear from my bedroom at the top of the house, laughing and clanking of plates. I drifted off to sleep happy and hopeful about the prospect of leftovers for me in the morning.

If my grandmother found cooking for ten people and looking after a small grandchild for the evening stressful, she didn't show it. The formal table settings, the ironed linen, the ever immaculate house, it all seemed effortless. She dressed for dinner, for goodness sake!

But my hosting looks nothing like those sparkly dinner parties from the mid seventies. Houses have changed shape, walls have been knocked through and separate dining rooms have melted into vast eat-in kitchens. The food we eat has changed; the smells of garlic and cumin chickpeas might have replaced the wafts of roast lamb. And you rarely hear the swish of chiffon when guests drop by these days (more is the pity, we would contest). Your crockery will more likely be whatever you find (hopefully) clean in the dishwasher, not the Royal Doulton carefully lifted out from a shiny chiffonier.

But does it matter? Not a sausage! At the heart of why we invite people to our house for food is that we want to spend some time and share food with them. The shape and smell and look of how that takes place is mere peripheral detail. The most essential ingredient for a meal with friends is not, paradoxically, the food, nor the perfect house to host in, but the sentiment that you convey to guests when you open your home and carve out some time to share with them. It says: *I like you and I enjoy your company*.

But even knowing this in our heads, with so many threads to weave in to a week - home life, work life, children, caring responsibilities and probably more - a lunch table full of guests won't seem like fun. It will just look like hard work.

Since I became busy with the job of caring for young children, my enthusiasm for hosting does, at times, drop off a cliff. Cooking just for myself sometimes feels like a stretch. And since most friends have also partnered up, and had a string of children too, inviting two friends over now means a table of fifteen, once partners and children are added to my own brood. Help! Plus... one of them is coeliac and another has just signed on to veganism. TOO HARD!

Annabel and I both have a past in the business of ambitious, extravagant and outré cooking (I have borne witness to some of her most ridiculous culinary fripperies and she to my silliest menu follies). Those adventures were fun at the time, but just the thought of that kind of cooking and hosting now starts a terrible thick pain right behind my eyes.

So, feeling the frustration of no longer being able to entertain as we once loved to do, we have sometimes intentionally and sometimes by accident found ways to take what might be thought of as shortcuts and concessions in cooking for others at home. Inviting people for breakfast instead of dinner - hey, it's one course, no one will notice if I don't cook meat, and it's all over by 10 am! We have also come to lean in to the adrenaline rush of a spontaneous invitation – asking the fellow parent you chat to in the park to come home for lunch. All you need are a few basics in your larder and the courage to stare down the breakfast dishes that are exactly where you left them six hours ago. Since their lunch otherwise would have been the crusts from their toddler's sandwich, even a pasta with frozen peas can register as a great meal and a splendid time.

Do you know anyone who works from home? Someone who lives alone? Someone who is new in town? A person with their thesis due in three weeks? Someone in the business of caring for older relatives or young children? Anyone who regularly feels the four walls of their house closing in on them? (Or maybe that person is you?) Ask them over for a quick lunch break, an early dinner, or a drink after work. The flood of relief at a change of scenery, a bit of conversation and food that someone else has made will completely eclipse any concerns you might imagine your guest to have about the food you serve, your tiny house and stunningly messy kitchen.

Stick with a drinks hour for a tiny group and just one snack if that is all you feel like doing. Or return multiple invitations at once by having two dozen friends over for cake and mugs of builders' tea. Content yourself with knowing that, these days, a hearty salad is a perfectly acceptable midweek dinner.

There are so many ways to combine food and friends at home without finding yourself bare-knuckle punching a wall behind the scenes with the stress and frustration of it all. Hospitality comes in all shapes and sizes and what you can manage one year might be impossible the next. Offer only what you feel is achievable and what will make you happy too.

Most importantly, know that your friends or family or friends-in-waiting will love and welcome any gift of hospitality, complex or otherwise, because people just love to be cooked for. While the message might be easier to utter than implement, do believe that there really isn't any need to be stressed or trepidatious about hosting. The crowd is on your side!

Some of the recipes in this book are fiddly; some are them are hardly more effort than reaching for a takeaway menu. Whatever you choose to make, our hope is that when it comes to cooking for friends, we might convince the hosting-shy or hosting-fatigued or the hosting-frazzled that near enough really will be good enough.

Wendy Sharpe

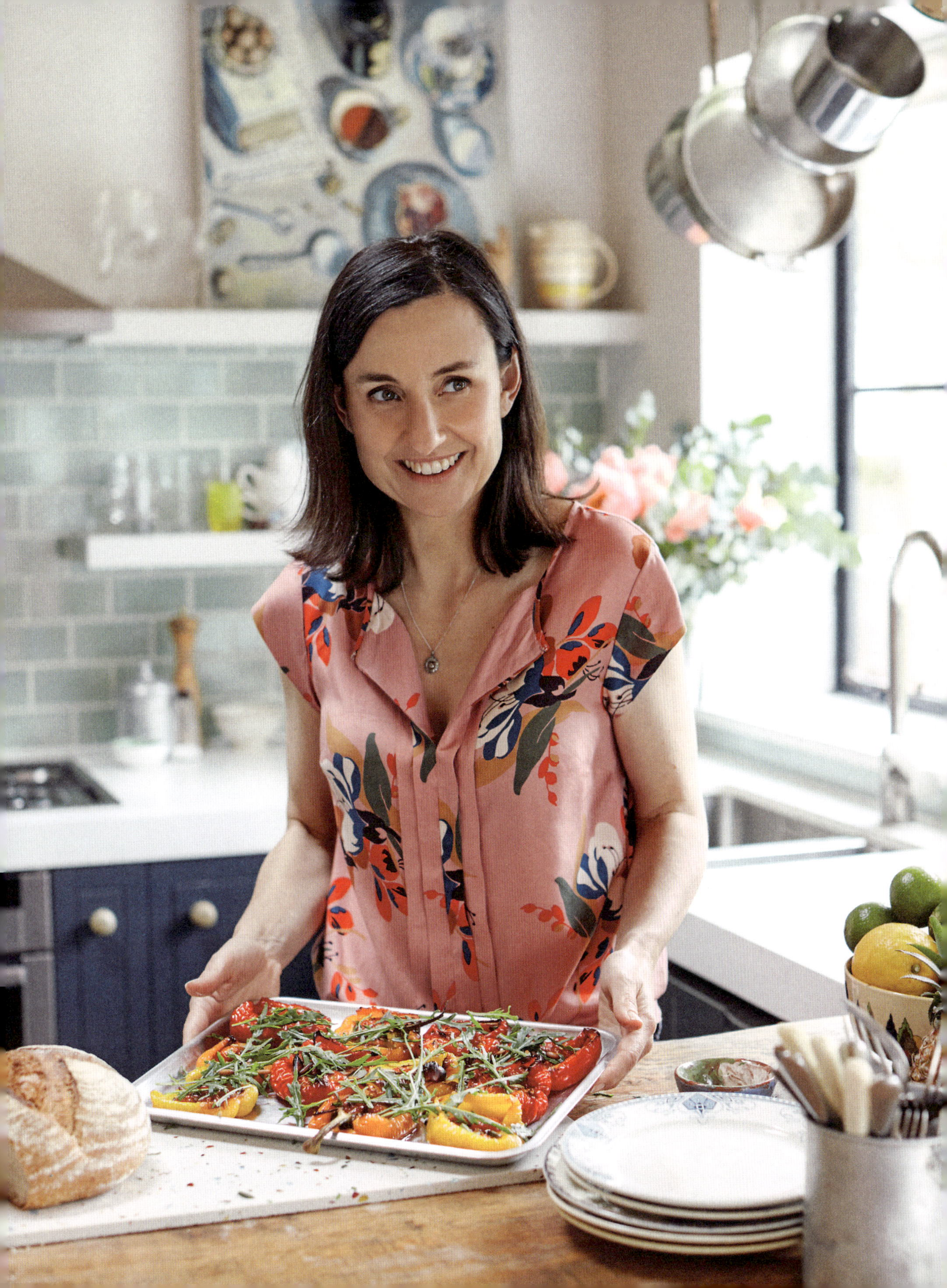

Maximum effect, minimum effort recipes

Here we're operating on the premise that sometimes the inclusion of one homemade element is the way to achieve maximum effect with the least-possible effort. Imagine a tomato salad transformed by a spoonful of pesto from your fridge, avocado on toast with a drizzle of lemon-infused oil, or a little harissa stirred through cream cheese to bring an everyday salad sandwich to life.

GLUTEN-FREE SHORTCRUST PASTRY

Bought gluten-free pastry somehow manages to combine unworkability with cardboardiness and tastelessness to a riveting degree. Which is strange, because it's actually not that hard to make a flaky, light and workable gluten-free pastry. This shortcrust works for everything from quiches to sweet tarts (add 50 g caster sugar and perhaps a teaspoon of vanilla paste to the mix, and omit the salt). It rolls out just fine, as the egg helps to keep it workable.

To make enough pastry for one 25 cm tart crust, whizz 120 g almond meal, 60 g tapioca flour, 60 g gluten-free plain flour and 1 teaspoon salt with 125 g cubed cold butter in a food processor until it resembles coarse breadcrumbs.

Add 1 lightly beaten egg and pulse, gradually adding up to a teaspoon of iced water, until the dough starts to clump together. Scrape onto a sheet of plastic wrap and press into a disc, then wrap and refrigerate for half an hour.

When you're ready to roll, preheat the oven to 180°C (160°C fan) and grease and line a 25 cm tart tin. Tear off two sheets of baking paper, dust with tapioca flour and place the dough between them, then roll out until you have a circle of about 35 cm in diameter. Remove the top sheet of paper and gently roll the pastry around the rolling pin, then unroll the pastry over the tin. Press it into the corners of the tin, then chill for 15 minutes. Line your tart shell with baking paper and ceramic baking beans (or dried beans) and blind-bake for 10 minutes, then remove the beans and paper and bake for another 5 minutes. There you go: gluten-free tart crust!

HARISSA (SORT OF)

This harissa-like paste is easy to make, adaptable and delicious. If it isn't complex enough for you, add some rosewater or dried rose petals, coriander seeds, fennel seeds, finely grated orange zest... you get the picture. To make enough to fill a small jar, put 200 g peeled roasted peppers (capsicum) - from a jar is fine, but give them a quick rinse then pat dry - with ½ teaspoon caraway seeds, ½ teaspoon ground cumin, ¼ teaspoon sweet paprika, 4 thin slices of fresh ginger, 5 sun-dried tomatoes in oil, 3 garlic cloves and a pinch of sea salt into a robust blender, and blitz to a paste. Add chilli powder or pepper to taste; if you have roasted your peppers from fresh, you might also need a dash of lemon juice for zing. Stored in a clean jar and covered with a film of oil, this will keep in the fridge for a week or two. Use to pep up tagines, salads and sandwiches.

HUMMUS

The secret to a good fluffy hummus is a powerful blender. Start with 2 tablespoons each of tahini and lemon juice, plus 2 crushed garlic cloves, and whizz until smooth. Drain a 400 g tin of chickpeas, reserving the liquid, then tip the chickpeas into the blender and pulse briefly. Add a good pinch each of ground cumin and salt and blend for 1 minute, then loosen with chickpea liquid as needed before blending on high for at least 3 minutes. Swirl the hummus into a bowl and cover - it will keep for a couple of days in the fridge, but is best served at room temperature, drizzled with olive oil and sprinkled with sumac and toasted pine nuts.

LEMON-INFUSED OIL

Zest 2 large unwaxed, organic lemons directly into a small saucepan. Add 150 ml olive oil and place over low heat. When the oil is just about to start bubbling, take off the heat and let it cool slightly before adding 50 ml extra virgin olive oil. Carefully transfer to a clean jar and leave to infuse for at least a day. Strain, if you like, and refrigerate – the oil will keep for several weeks. Use anywhere you want the taste of lemon without the acidity, such as salads, pasta, risotto.

MAYONNAISE

To make about ¾ cup (185 g) mayonnaise, put 1 room-temperature egg yolk into a small high-sided bowl and set it on a folded damp tea towel. Using a hand whisk, stir the yolk for a few seconds and then carefully, drop by drop, start adding 150 ml room-temperature, neutral-flavoured oil (not extra virgin olive oil, as it splits more easily and can taste bitter), whisking well between each addition. Once about 2 teaspoons of oil have been incorporated, drizzle in the rest from a jug in a slow but steady thin stream, whisking constantly. When you have a billowy mayonnaise, whisk in 1-2 teaspoons of lemon juice, ½ teaspoon dijon mustard and salt and pepper to taste. Serve right away, or cover and keep in the fridge for a couple of days.

Variations include anchovy mayonnaise, to have with cold roast beef or seafood (add 5 crushed fillets to the mayonnaise); tartare sauce (add finely chopped gherkins, capers and dill); aioli (add as much crushed slow-roasted garlic as you dare, starting with 6 cloves); or rouille for fish soups and stews (add a pinch of saffron strands, white pepper and a dash of tabasco to aioli).

PESTO

Don't worry about digging out the food processor or mortar and pestle – this pesto is chopped. For a small jar of pesto, wash and dry a large bunch of basil and pick the leaves. Take 2 garlic cloves and set to chopping them finely – when you are about halfway there, add half of the basil leaves. Once it starts to reduce a bit, add a few tablespoons of pine nuts (or other nuts) and keep chopping, adding a couple of tablespoons of finely grated parmesan and the rest of the basil as you go. When everything is chopped and combined, pat the pesto mixture into a few balls, transfer to a small, clean jar and cover with olive oil. This will keep in the fridge for up to a week, ready to use on toasted sandwiches, tomato salads, pizza, pasta, or be dropped into a bowl of tomato soup – simply stir as much as you need into some of the oil.

ROASTED GARLIC

Take a whole bulb of garlic, scuff off any floaty layers of skin and then run the bulb under the cold tap for 10 seconds. Shake off the excess water, transfer to a sheet of baking paper and rub all over with olive oil, then sprinkle with salt and wrap in the paper, twisting the top to seal. Roast at 180°C (160°C fan) for 30-40 minutes, until squishy and slightly golden. Leave to cool, then keep, wrapped, in the fridge for up to a week. Roasted garlic is a mighty handy thing to have on standby for weeknight cooking or spontaneous entertaining: press the cloves out of their skins with the back of a fork or your fingers, warm gently and spread on toast; crush into mashed potatoes, mayonnaise (see left) or softened butter with chives to make garlic bread; or simmer with tinned tomatoes for 10 minutes to make a quick and delicious pasta sauce.

Early bird breakfasts

The first meal of the day is a lovely one to share with others. But more than that, the logistics of breakfast entertaining can really fall your way. Great breakfast dishes can be easy to prepare and are more pliable than other meals to work around dietary restrictions. Also, a bright start means you can be all done by 10.30, with the rest of the day to yourself. For parents of very small children (who often begin their day about three hours earlier than they would like), the prospect of big pots of tea and plungers of coffee with breakfast they didn't have to make is a proposition so much greater than the sum of its parts. Likewise, early doors invitations are just the spot for dawn dog walkers and people involved in rowing (heaven help them).

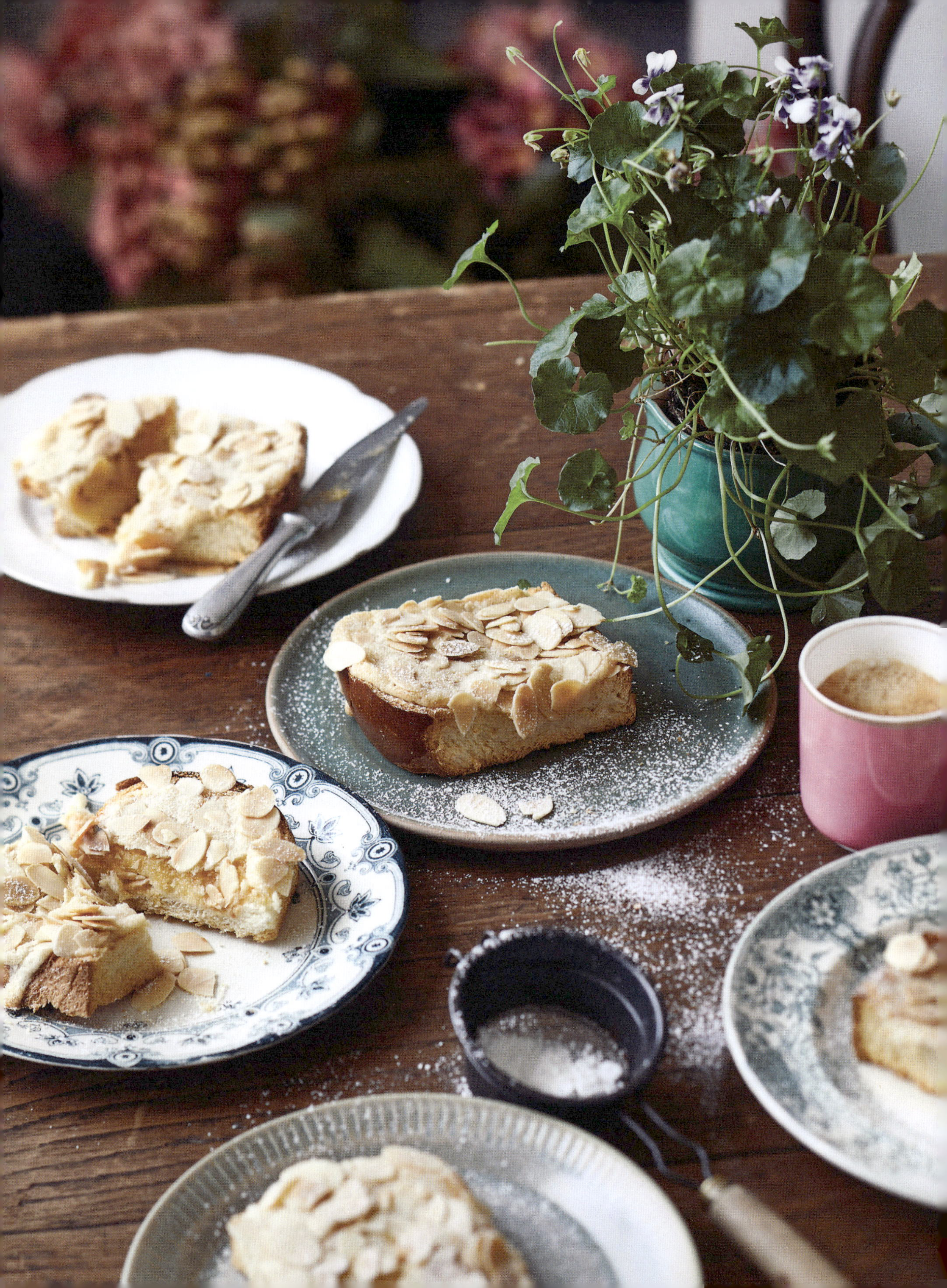

BOSTOCK

SERVES 8-10

If you like French toast AND you like those sweet, sugar-dusted almond croissants, then put a little bookmark on this page right now. Because a Bostock is a cross between the two – slightly stale brioche topped with jam and frangipane. The dish is *supposed* to have come from France, but my money is on it being one of those smart Yankee inventions. If the various components are stockpiled or made in advance, assembly is a pretty quick job in the morning. Crowds are easily catered for, since it isn't important to serve it hot, and it works as a hand-held cutlery-free treat. In my opinion, marmalade or a jam with some tartness to it, such as apricot, work better here than the really sweet options. But you will know your own mind. Lemon or passionfruit curd also works well as the middle layer.

---

1 loaf brioche, challah or similar enriched sweet bread
4 tablespoons jam or curd
4 tablespoons flaked almonds
icing sugar, for dusting

FRANGIPANE
100 g butter, softened
100 g caster sugar
100 g almond meal
1 teaspoon cornflour
1 teaspoon plain flour
1–2 large eggs
a few drops of orange flower water or the finely grated zest of ½ orange

The night before, cut the loaf into super-generous doorstep slices, then leave wrapped in a tea towel overnight, so the bread dries out and becomes slightly stale.

To make the frangipane, beat the butter and sugar together until creamy (in a stand mixer or by hand is fine). Sprinkle the almond meal and both flours over the top and mix well, then add 1 egg and the orange flower water or orange zest and mix again. The frangipane needs to be quite easily spreadable, so add another egg if the mixture seems too stiff. Stow the frangipane away in the fridge overnight.

The next morning, take your frangipane out of the fridge and let it come to room temperature. Preheat your oven to 180°C (160°C fan). Place your slices of stale bread on a few baking trays, and spread each one with a thin layer of jam or curd, then frangipane. Without being too fussy about it, try to spread the toppings right to the edges. Scatter generously with flaked almonds and bake in the oven for about 15 minutes or until golden brown.

Leave to cool slightly, then dust with icing sugar. (And pow! Instantly these look like you picked them up at the expensive bakery you couldn't be bothered to line up at/be fleeced by/drive to/all of the above.) Serve just warm or at room temperature.

TURKISH SCRAMBLED EGGS

SERVES 4

Rich and full of flavour, this is the dish everyone falls in love with when they visit Istanbul. Luckily it is easy to make at home, and avoids completely the fool's mission of cooking eggs to order for a crowd. Much of this dish can be thrown together the night before, and is then simply served in the pan, with plenty of warm Turkish bread alongside. If you can find pul biber (Aleppo pepper) chilli flakes, so much the better; regular chilli flakes will generally be more fiery, so add to taste.

---

about 50 ml olive oil
2 small brown onions, finely chopped
2 green peppers (capsicums), cut into 1 cm squares
1 garlic clove, finely chopped
5 tasty tomatoes, chopped
pinch of ground cumin
½ teaspoon mild chilli flakes, plus extra for sprinkling
½ teaspoon paprika
¼ teaspoon dried oregano
8 eggs
handful of chopped coriander and/or dill
Turkish bread, lemon wedges and sumac, to serve

ASIAN SCRAMBLED EGGS

If you like this, do try the terrifically more-ish Asian version, where the spices and peppers are replaced with soy sauce, rice vinegar, fresh ginger and garlic chives.

MAKE IT GLUTEN-FREE

Serve these eggs with gluten-free toast, or just as is.

Pour a generous glug of olive oil into a large frying pan and fry the onions and peppers over low heat for about 8 minutes – you want them to soften and cook slowly, without browning. Add a sprinkle of salt and the garlic and cook for 2 minutes, then add the tomatoes, along with another glug of olive oil. Once the tomatoes start to break down (use the back of a wooden spoon to help crush them), add the spices and oregano, and keep cooking until you have a glossy and fragrant stew. Season with salt and a lot of pepper. (If you are preparing this in advance, cool and keep in the fridge, then gently reheat before continuing.)

When you are almost ready to eat, preheat the oven to 160°C (140°C fan) and put the Turkish bread in to warm up.

Break the eggs into a bowl with a pinch of salt and use a fork to beat them very lightly. Scoop about three-quarters of the tomato mixture out of the frying pan and set aside. Add a bit more olive oil to the pan containing the rest of the tomato mixture and turn the flame to low-medium. Pour in the beaten egg, then sprinkle over the chopped herbs and a few extra chilli flakes. Once the egg has started to set, move a spatula around the pan, dragging some of the tomato mixture through the egg. Do this a few more times until everything is mixed, but not combined: there should still be distinct curds of egg. While the egg is still runny, gently fold in the reserved tomato mixture. The trick here is to take the pan off the heat *before* the egg looks completely cooked – the residual heat means you will end up with perfectly scrambled eggs. If you keep the pan over the heat too long, you risk the eggs becoming rubbery.

Take the pan to the table and grind over even more black pepper, followed by a squeeze of lemon juice and a sprinkle of sumac. Don't forget the bread in the oven, then let people serve themselves.

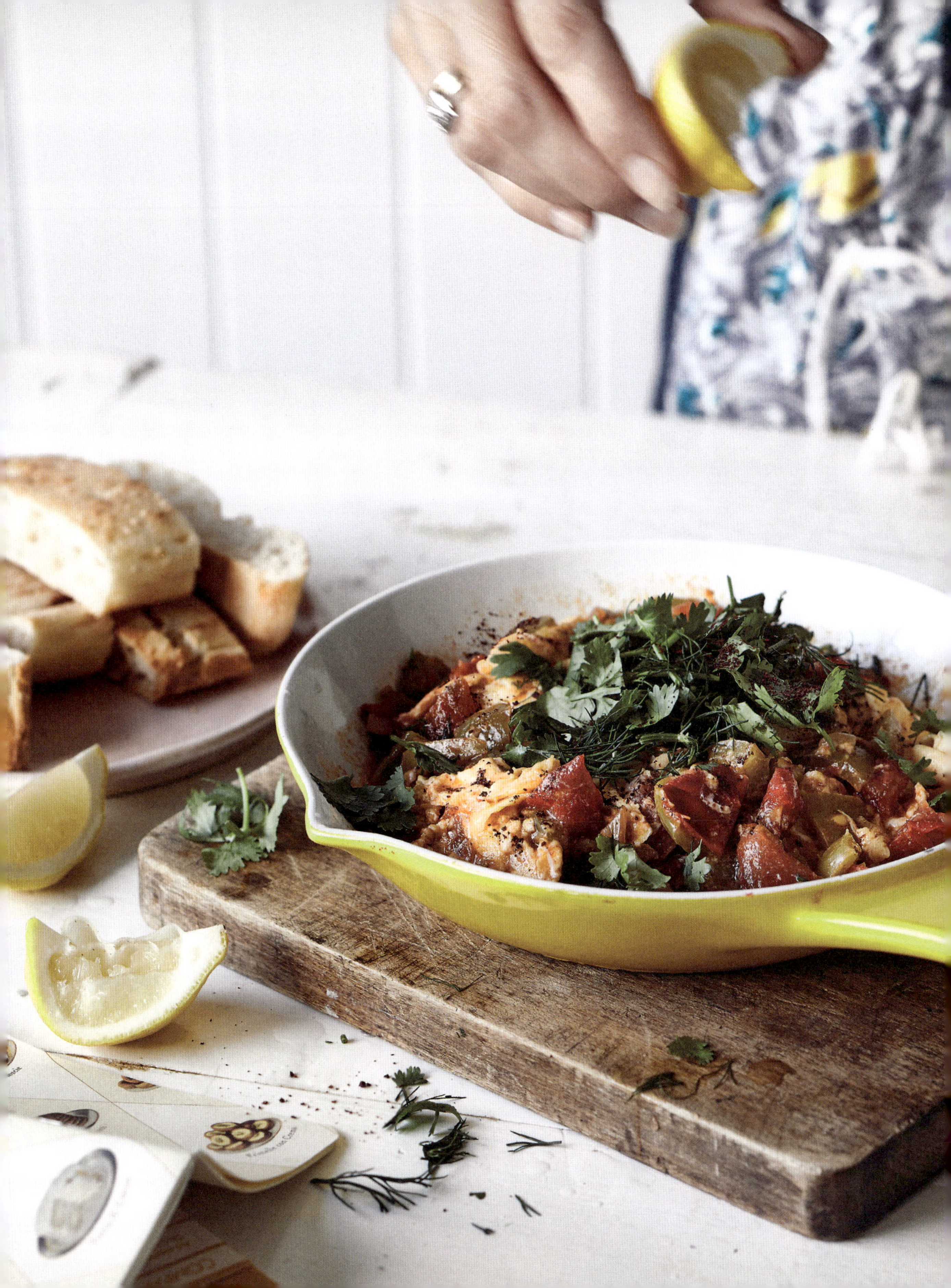

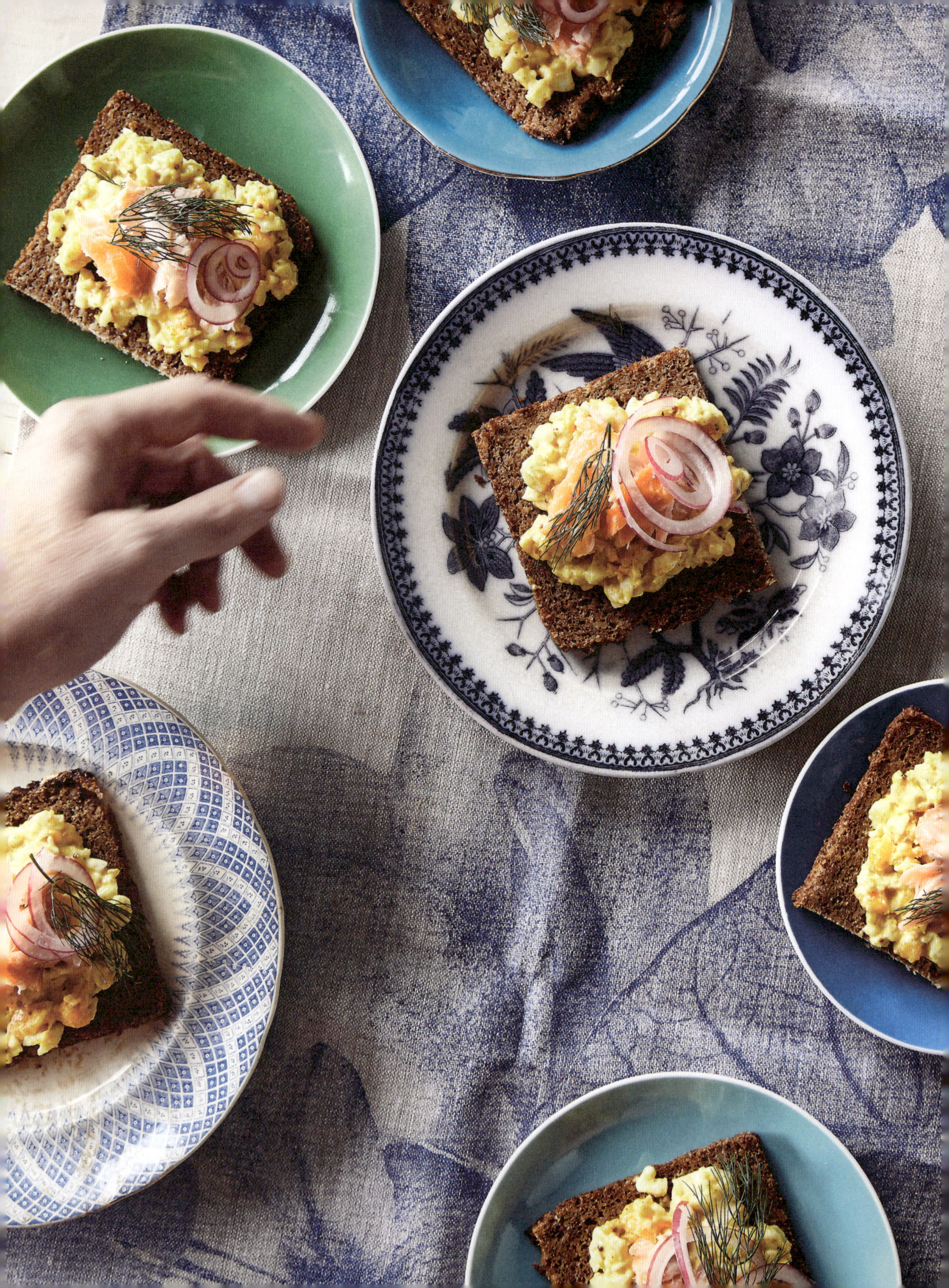

EGG & SALMON ON RYE BREAKFAST SQUARES

SERVES 6

I love eggs royale - poached eggs with salmon and hollandaise - as much as the next person. But what a faff to get all those elements ready at the same time for your guests at home! Here is a Danish take, using much the same ingredients, that offers a super-easy plan-ahead format. Make the hot-smoked salmon, eggs and pickled onions the night before, then in the morning, it's a ten-minute job to get everything together.

---

8 eggs, at room temperature
1½ tablespoons mayonnaise
1½ teaspoons wholegrain mustard
½ teaspoon curry powder
6 slices of rye bread
300 g hot-smoked salmon (see page 184)
dill (or parsley) sprigs
lemon wedges

QUICK PICKLED ONIONS
½ small red onion, thinly sliced
½ teaspoon caster sugar
2 pinches of salt
2 teaspoons cider vinegar

Place the eggs in a large saucepan and pour in enough hot water to cover them by about 5 cm, then set over high heat and bring to the boil. Immediately reduce the heat to as low as possible and simmer the eggs for 12 minutes (allow another minute or so for large eggs). Drain, cover with cold water and leave to cool for a few minutes. This no-boil method keeps the yolks a perky yellow and avoids the dull grey that sneaks its way into yolks that have been too hot for too long.

Peel your eggs, then mash roughly with a fork. Add the mayonnaise, mustard, curry powder and a pinch of salt and keep mashing until everything is just combined. Cover and refrigerate for up to 24 hours.

For the quick pickled onions, put the onion in a small glass or ceramic bowl. Sprinkle with the sugar and salt, then leave for 10 minutes. Drain off any liquid, add the vinegar and leave for at least 10 minutes, or overnight in the fridge.

To serve, arrange your rye bread on the biggest platter or chopping board you have. Spread each slice with a handsome amount of egg salad and then flake some salmon on top, followed by a sprig of dill, a few rings of pickled onion, a squeeze of lemon juice and a generous grinding of pepper.

EVEN EASIER
Use bought hot-smoked salmon.

MAKE IT GLUTEN-FREE
Exchange the rye bread for a slice of gluten-free toast.

COFFEE, BANANA & OAT SMOOTHIE

SERVES 1 (SCALE UP TO SUIT YOUR NUMBER OF GUESTS – AND BLENDER CAPACITY)

Not everyone is on Team Smoothie. They can be trouble-prone (too sweet, too thick, too thin, too sickly). However, of all the conceivable smoothies, this is one that you should consider trying: an unusual, grown-up iced coffee with oats.

Guests can be delivered their first caffeine dose without delay, and you are released from the work and tedium of turning out a half-dozen different coffees to order.

---

1 ripe banana
200 ml milk
1 shot of coffee, cooled (or 2, if needed)
2 tablespoons rolled oats
a few large ice cubes

Pile everything into the most powerful blender you have and whizz the hell out of it. The banana will give the drink some sweetness, so hold off on adding any honey or maple syrup until you've had a taste – the deep, earthy coffee flavour should be the hero here.

MAKE IT VEGAN
Use almond milk or soy milk.

A SMALL BUT MIGHTY BLENDER
Marketed for smoothies and juices, these small bullet-shaped blenders with a large-capacity cup and a crazy-strong motor (try for at least 1000W) are also great for crushing ice and nuts, whizzing up sauces, pestos, dips (every type of hummus), even making pancake batters. What's more, they take up very little space on the bench and – hallelujah – are easy to wash.

ST NIKLAS GRANOLA

MAKES 12 GENEROUS SERVINGS

The inspiration for this sprang from a bag of St Niklas biscuits (pepernoten), seasonal little spicy gingerbread biscuits. Dutch tradition has it that they are supposed to be thrown from the sack of a Spanish sailor who comes to Holland with a band of small helpers every December. If you look into the detail, the story is ethically flawed and morally suspect; however, the deliciousness and more-ish nature of the biscuits cannot be questioned.

Having a batch of this similarly flavoured granola on hand will either make your own mornings a bit more exciting, or equip you for spontaneous breakfast guests. There are no downsides. Pears or stewed plums would be just right to go with this, alongside a generous spoonful of thick yoghurt.

---

50 ml black treacle
100 ml runny honey
50 g soft brown sugar
50 g neutral-flavoured oil
50 g butter
1 teaspoon ground ginger
½ teaspoon ground cloves
1 teaspoon ground cinnamon
½ teaspoon ground coriander
¼ teaspoon white pepper
500 g rolled oats
50 g pecans
50 g flaked almonds
50 g whole almonds
25 g pumpkin seeds
a few pieces of crystallised ginger, finely chopped – optional

AN IMPROMPTU DESSERT

I absolutely would not hesitate to fry up a few sliced ripe pears in butter, top them with a scoop of ice cream and a sprinkle of this (perhaps with extra crystallised ginger) and call the result an excellent dessert.

Preheat the oven to 200°C (180°C fan). Line a large baking tray with baking paper.

Combine the treacle, honey, sugar, oil and butter in a small saucepan over medium heat. Bring to the boil, stirring every so often, then let it bubble a bit and stir again to make sure the sugar is dissolved. Set aside to cool for a minute or two. Mix together the ginger, cloves, cinnamon, coriander and pepper, then add to the treacle mixture.

Tip the oats into a large bowl and then pour in most of the spice and treacle mixture, keeping back about 4 tablespoons in the saucepan. Use a spatula to work the treacle mixture into the oats to coat them. Spill out onto the baking tray and bake for about 10 minutes. Because the treacle is so dark, it is difficult to judge from the colour when the oats are turning toasty, so keep an eye on them.

Use your fingers to break the pecans in half lengthways and add them to the leftover spice and treacle mixture, along with the flaked almonds. Stir to coat, then scatter over the oats and return the tray to the oven for another 5 minutes. The oats won't go crispy until they've cooled, so don't worry if they are still a bit soft.

Meanwhile, toss the whole almonds and the pumpkin seeds in a dry frying pan over medium heat for a minute or so, until they smell toasty. When the granola is cool enough to handle, break up any large clumps with your fingers, then add the toasted almonds and pumpkin seeds and the crystallised ginger, if using.

Store in an airtight container. This is best eaten in the first few days after it's made, but will last a good week or two no problem.

Early bird breakfasts

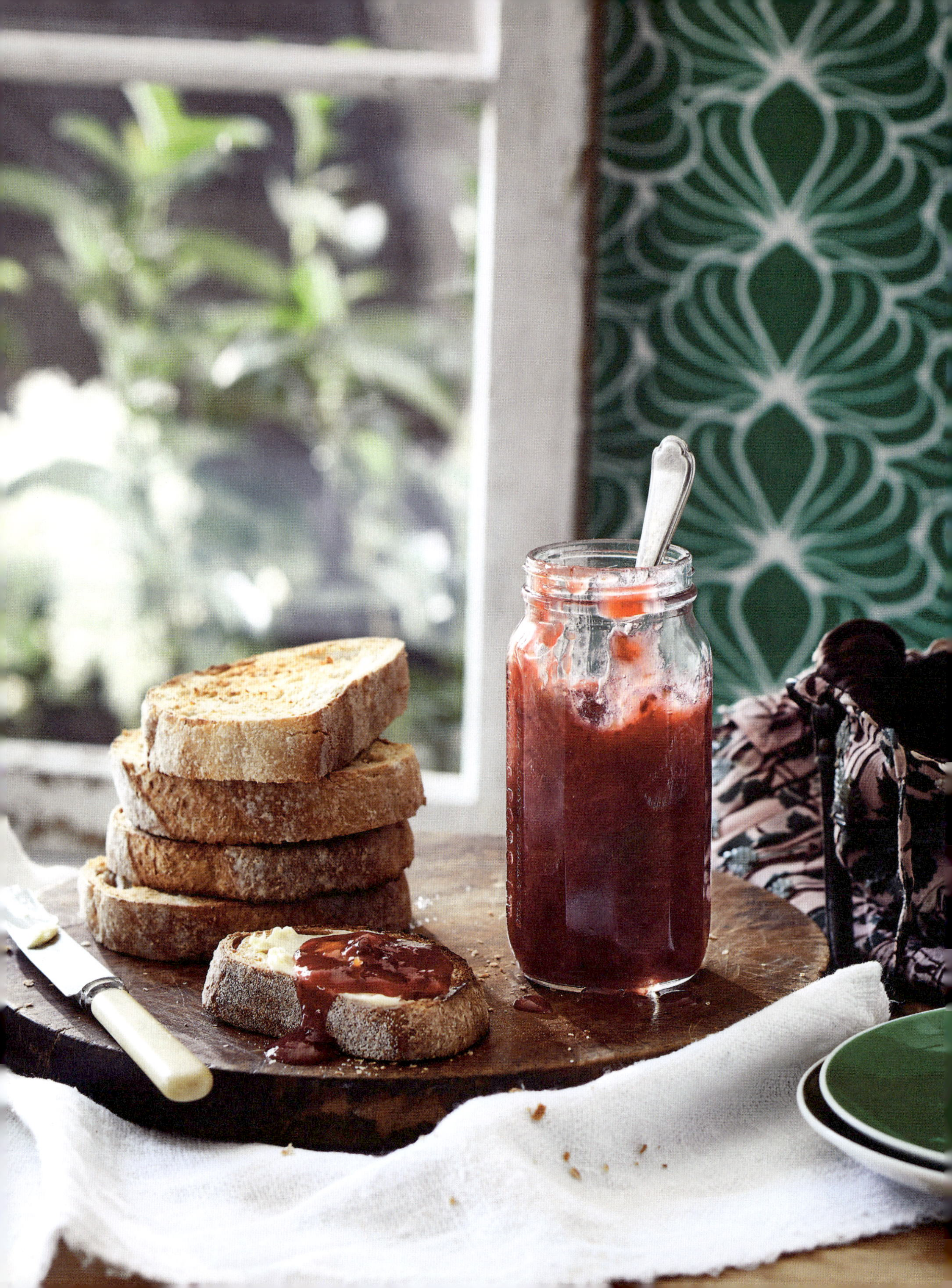

HEART-STARTER PLUM JAM

MAKES 500 ML

A fresh-tasting plum jam like this one is all you need to convert ordinary toast into a first-class breakfast for visitors. This method is miles from the Adelaide Plains traditions of our youth, when all the stonefruit would ripen at once and in vast quantities, necessitating an all-hands-on-deck industrial-scale jam making and preserving session.

Now living in small city houses with small city kitchens, it is difficult for either of us to imagine housing the huge Vacola-style preserving pan and kit, let alone knowing where to store the rows and rows of tall elegant preserve jars and the irregular ranks of filled and wax-sealed jam jars. Wendy keeps up the jam making with small batches here and there – mostly these quick jams that yield just one or two jars. They have much less sugar than other jams, and so need to be kept in the fridge. But on the upside there is less pressure to perfect your technique with such small batches, and they can be whipped up in a jiffy with whatever fresh fruit seems good and cheap that week. Campari found its way into this jam as an emergency replacement in some plum and sloe gin jam. If you don't like bitter stuff, then swap out the Campari for something more traditional like a vanilla pod, or a sprig of lemon verbena. But the Campari does give the plums an unusual flavour twist and a quite splendid colour.

---

750 g plums
150 g sugar
2 cm strip of orange zest
juice of ½ lemon
1 tablespoon Campari

STERILISING JARS

Our preferred method is a hot wash (ideally in a dishwasher) followed by 10 minutes in a 160°C (140°C fan) oven.

Wash the plums, then cut into eighths, discarding the stones. Put them in a saucepan with a tablespoon of water. Set over low heat and cover. Keep an eye on the pan and give the plums a stir occasionally – if you keep the heat low, they should get to the point of releasing their juices before they catch on the bottom of the pan. However, if you are worried, add another tablespoon or so of water.

Once the plums are starting to get soft and have yielded a bit of juice, add the sugar and orange zest. Bring to the boil, with the odd stir here and there, then reduce the heat to low and cook at a respectable simmer for about 15 minutes.

After this time, the jam should be, well, jammy: free-running, but not runny. Stir in the lemon juice and Campari and simmer for just another few minutes.

Carefully pour into a 500 ml sterilised jar (or two 250 ml ones) and seal. Once it's cool, keep in the fridge and use within 2–3 weeks.

CHEAT'S PIADINA

SERVES 6

All I really want in a breakfast, if I'm honest, is some combination of bread, tomato, cheese and basil. With the cheese - or at least some of it - given a fighting chance to get crusty and bubbly and brown. When I was pregnant with my first child I visited Bologna, where one night I had a dinner that consisted entirely of ten different kinds of hard cheese, served with a pot of honey. I think it was the very next morning (after what must presumably have been some very odd dreams) when I had piadina for breakfast - that lovely Italian flatbread of the region, served folded over and toasted with various treats inside. Lazily researching piadina afterwards, I made the galling discovery that the flatbread I'd eaten was very probably made with lard. Nevertheless, a sort of piadina is now a regular breakfast item in my house - though to the children it's known as 'flatbread toastie', and I see no reason to bother them with any mention of adipose tissue of the pig.

If you're hosting for breakfast, make the flatbreads the night before; they will be fine in the fridge overnight and can be folded, stuffed and toasted in the morning. But please don't deny yourself or your guests this breakfast just because you aren't up for making the flatbreads yourself. To be entirely honest with you, I much more frequently use store-bought Greek pitta bread. (Please don't mention this to any real Italians, obviously.) Greek pitta bread is paler, chewier and more bready than its yeastless Middle Eastern relative. It is found in most supermarkets and freezes very well in its bag, and can be requisitioned at short notice to make this extremely pleasing dish. Making the flatbreads is entirely pleasurable, but only if you've got time the night before or you fancy rising at baker's hour. If not, go Greek and no-one will know.

---

6 flatbreads (see opposite) or Greek pitta breads
butter, for spreading
1 x 250 g ball of smoked (or fresh) mozzarella, sliced
6 ripe tomatoes, sliced
100 g fat kalamata olives, halved and pitted
6 generous sprigs of basil

If you're making your own flatbreads, tip the flour into the bowl of a stand mixer fitted with the dough hook. In a small bowl or jug, whisk the honey and yeast into the warm milk. Stir in the yoghurt, then leave to stand for 5 minutes to activate the yeast - when it's ready, it should be frothy and bubbling.

Pour the yeast mixture into the flour and mix until it comes together raggedly. Add the warm water, salt and olive oil and knead on medium speed for about 5 minutes until you have a smooth dough. (Or you can hand-knead the dough until it's smooth and pliable - it will be a bit messier at first, but you'll get there!)

Sit the dough in an oiled bowl, cover with oiled plastic wrap and leave in a warm place until doubled in size, about 1-1½ hours.

Punch the dough down and divide into six equal pieces. Roll into balls, then leave to rest on a floured board for about half an hour.

Special Guest

FLATBREADS
350 g (2⅓ cups) strong white bread flour, plus extra for dusting
1 teaspoon honey
7 g dried yeast (1 standard sachet)
150 ml lukewarm milk
2 tablespoons Greek-style yoghurt
3 tablespoons warm water
1 teaspoon salt
2 tablespoons olive oil, plus extra for frying

Now you're ready to roll and cook. Take a ball and roll it out into a disc about 20 cm in diameter and about 6 mm thick. Set a large frying pan over medium-high heat. Add a glug of olive oil to the hot pan and swirl it around. Lay the flatbread in the pan - you should soon notice pleasing little air bubbles forming in the dough. Cook for about 1½ minutes on each side or until nicely blistered and golden in spots. While it cooks, roll out its successor and have it waiting its turn. Remove and stack, then repeat, re-oiling the pan after each flatbread is cooked.

Once you have your puffy fresh flatbreads (or have gone to the freezer for your shameless cheat's substitute), you're good to go. Take a flatbread and administer the teeniest scrape of butter on one side: this will become the outside of your piadina (the bit that will encounter the pan), and the butter will give it a nice golden touch. Lay slices of mozzarella and tomato, some olives, basil leaves and a grinding or two of black pepper over one half, then fold over the flatbread to sandwich the filling. Carefully transfer your piadina to a frying pan over medium heat and cook on both sides until the cheese is melted and spilling out of the sides to get a bit crusty and delicious on the hot pan: don't be shy of pressing down on the piadina with a spatula to assist the cheese to escape. If you have a sandwich press (WHY do I not have one of these things, when I've always wanted one so badly?), you'll be able to do several at once, keeping the finished sandwiches warm in a 160°C (140°C fan) oven until all six are cooked. If you're working with a frying pan, it helps to have two on the go at once.

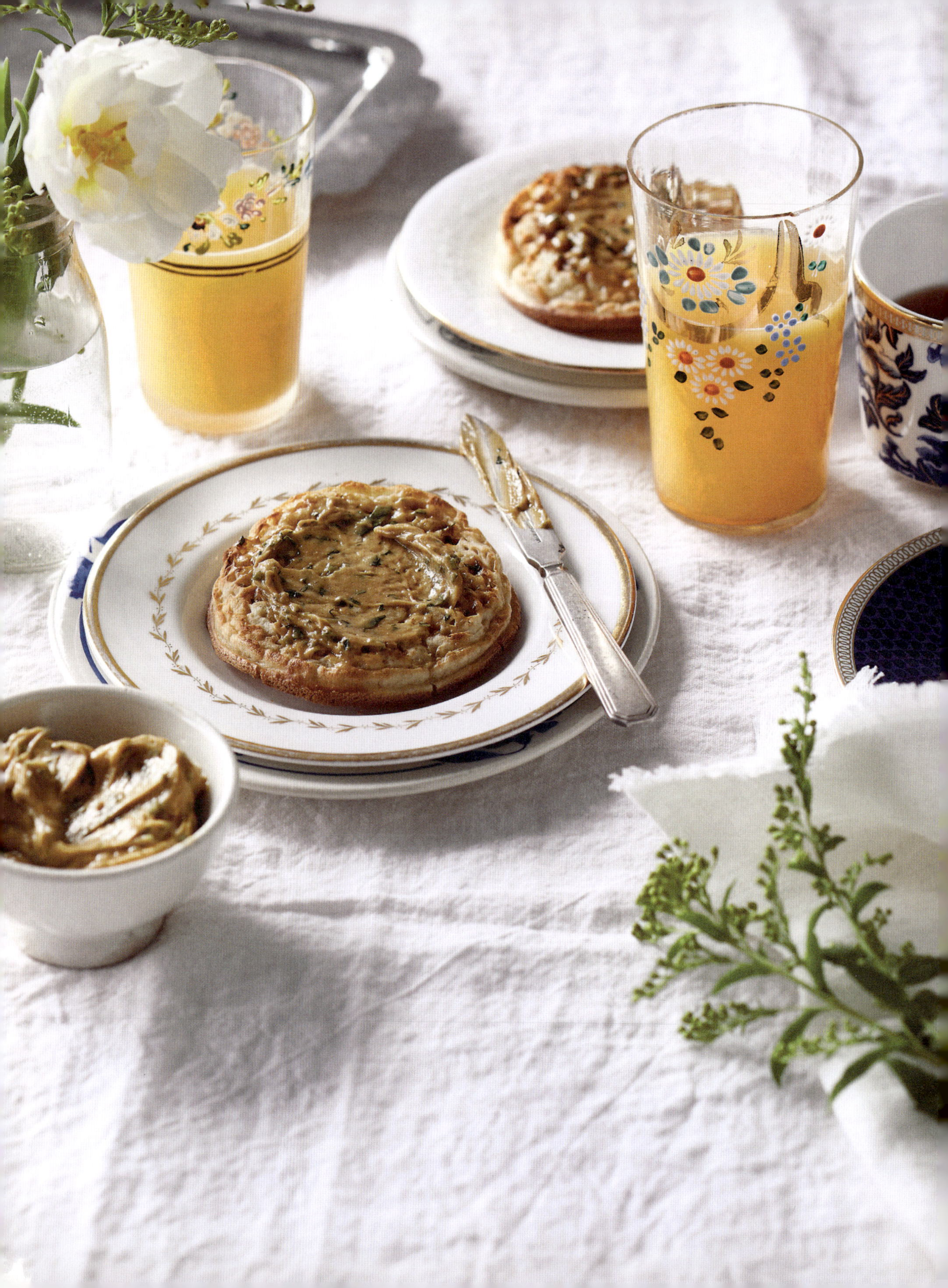

CRUMPETS WITH VEGEMITE, MUSTARD & PARSLEY BUTTER

SERVES 6

This isn't going to be to everyone's taste (well, you have to like Vegemite, to start with), but it will likely appeal to those who hanker for 'gentlemen's relish', 'bloater paste' and other niche delicacies that Jeeves might serve to Bertie Wooster alongside his morning tonic. One should also weigh up the cost of sacrificing a crumpet to a savoury topping, meaning one less opportunity to saturate a porous toasted thing with butter and honey.

BUT: the dish has pedigree. Wendy encountered a version of it (with Marmite, of course) at The Ivy, famed London purveyors of the sort of food you might easily make at home for Sunday night dinner - shepherd's pie, welsh rarebit, omelette and so on. Initially sceptical, she was, however, titrating doses of yeast extract and mustard into a slab of butter before the sun was down. As well as being a perplexing combination of flavours, this butter is notable for its make-ahead properties and long fridge-life.

---

100 g unsalted butter
2 teaspoons Vegemite (or Marmite)
4 teaspoons English mustard
1 teaspoon finely chopped flat-leaf parsley
6 crumpets

Soften the butter by smearing it around the sides of a bowl with a rubber spatula. Gradually add the Vegemite and mustard and work into the butter, tasting as you go and stopping when it tastes just right to you. Stir in the parsley and refrigerate until ready to serve.

Toast the crumpets and slather with the Vegemite, mustard and parsley butter. Smashing with a glass of juice and a big pot of tea.

FOR THE MEAT-EATERS
If, post-crumpets, you find yourself with left-over Vegemite, mustard and parsley butter, keep it in the fridge or freezer for your next barbecue: apparently it works a treat on a chargrilled steak.

Early bird breakfasts

CHOC-HAZELNUT MILK BUNS

MAKES 8 DECENT-SIZED BUNS

Pictured over the page, this is, granted, a pretty appalling breakfast food in a lot of ways. A feather-soft, buttery brioche stuffed with a certain well-known chocolate-hazelnut spread – a substance of dubious nutritional value and probably disreputable origins that boasts a rap sheet of Category A offences like the Cronut Shake and the Dessert Pizza.

Nevertheless. Sometimes a soft, sweet roll full of hazelnutty chocolate paste is EXACTLY what you feel like on an event morning. Like your eighth birthday. Or your forty-fourth. Or when excellent friends are bringing takeaway coffee around to pick up their children who slept over at your house. If you're expecting a crowd, it's probably worth doubling the recipe below.

If you get up extra-early you can make this all in one hit. The whole process will take about three hours (obviously you will not be busy all that time - there will be a lot of lulls while gluten and yeast are doing their thing); I mention this purely so you know when to get cracking. An easier option is to make the dough the day before, shape the buns and then leave them to prove in the fridge overnight and bake in the morning. The buns need to return to room temperature before being baked, so make sure they get at least an hour in a warm place while the oven heats.

---

150 g (1 cup) strong white bread flour
150 g (1 cup) plain flour
2–3 tablespoons honey
½ teaspoon active dried yeast
150 ml lukewarm milk
1 egg, plus 1 extra yolk
60 g salted butter, at room temperature
1 x 400 g jar of choc-hazelnut spread (you won't need it all – entirely your business what you do with the rest)
5 ice cubes

Tip both flours into the bowl of a stand mixer fitted with the dough hook. In a small bowl or jug, whisk 2 tablespoons of the honey and the yeast into the warm milk. Leave to stand for about 5 minutes to activate the yeast – when it's ready, it should look foamy.

Pour the yeast mixture into the flour, add the egg and mix until you start to notice that magical thing where a smooth, elastic dough forms. You can also do this step by hand: it will just take longer and you'll get messier hands. Now add the butter and keep mixing. After 6-7 minutes, you should have a shiny, elastic, slightly sticky dough. Cover the bowl with plastic wrap and leave in a warm place for 1½–2 hours or until roughly doubled in size. Once the dough has risen, punch it down and scrape out onto a lightly floured surface. Shape into a fat sausage and cut into eight equal pieces.

Grease and line a 20 cm cake tin or similar – I like something with sides because that way the buns will rise tall and noble. Roughly flatten each piece of dough into a disc and place a teaspoonful of choc-hazelnut spread in the middle. Fold the dough over, sealing the spread inside, then pull it into a sausage again. Twist it gently, then coil into a knot-like shape. Arrange these little bundles around the sides of the tin, with the last one in the middle; charmingly, it will look like a daisy. Cover with plastic wrap.

Special Guest

Now. If you are making these the night before, put the tin in the fridge and leave the dough to prove overnight, then the next morning, take the buns out of the fridge and allow them to return to room temperature before baking. If it's the early morning and you're smugly on track and planning to do fifty push-ups or whatever, your next step is to let the buns rise in a warm place until they are plumply fighting for space in the tin, about 1 hour.

When you're ready to bake your buns, preheat the oven to 200°C (180°C fan). Whisk the egg yolk with 1 teaspoon of cold water, then brush the buns with this egg wash and slide them into the oven. As you do so, throw the ice cubes into a roasting tin and place in the bottom of the oven – this will generate steam as the buns cook, helping to give them a good crust. Bake the buns for 3 minutes, then reduce the oven temperature to 180°C (160°C fan) and bake for another 15-20 minutes. When they're done, they should be shiny and golden-brown on top, and starting to pull away from the tin.

Leave the buns to cool in the tin for 10-15 minutes. If you want a super-shiny finish, heat the remaining tablespoon of honey in a small pan until it's bubbling, then use a pastry brush to glaze the top of the buns. Now turn them out of the tin and let your guests tuck in.

DIY CHOC-HAZELNUT SPREAD

If you don't fancy buying the much-adored and equally abhorred choc-hazelnut spread, or are worried about palm oil, you can make your own: blitz 135 g (1 cup) toasted, skinned hazelnuts with 2 tablespoons caster sugar, 1 tablespoon cocoa powder and 2 tablespoons rice bran oil in a food processor, then mix with 200 g melted dark chocolate – et voilà!

Early bird breakfasts

< CHOC-HAZELNUT
MILK BUNS

PUFFY PANCAKE
WITH HONEY &
ORANGE SYRUP >

PUFFY PANCAKE WITH HONEY & ORANGE SYRUP

SERVES 4-6

Traditional pancakes, hotcakes, pikelets and crêpes will always have a special and dear place in both our hearts, but there is no denying that making multiple batches is a faff. All too often, the host is a slave to the stove, swearingly juggling pans and preoccupied with turning out individual pancakes for guests, who eat them as fast as they're cooked and - fair enough - never stop wanting another one. Wendy loves pancakes so much that this was a sacrifice she was prepared to make... until, that is, she discovered the baked pancake, which leaves the host sipping tea and chatting instead of pouring batter and flipping. The puffy pancake employs a similar modus operandi to the Yorkshire pudding, puffs up more than you would think possible, and can be sliced into wedges for everyone to enjoy at the same time. No excuse for not giving it a go, whether for breakfast, or - since it feels quite a celebratory dish - a weeknight treat to mark a good spelling test, a viola exam passed, or just getting to Friday unscathed.

---

3 large eggs
180 ml (¾ cup) milk
100 g (⅔ cup) plain flour
pinch of salt
1 tablespoon caster sugar
30 g unsalted butter
berries (or a more old-school mix of banana, apple and orange) and Greek-style yoghurt, to serve
icing sugar, for dusting – optional

HONEY & ORANGE SYRUP
3 tablespoons runny honey
25 g unsalted butter
2 tablespoons pulp-free orange juice

Whizz up the eggs, milk, flour, salt and sugar using a blender, or just whisk well by hand. However you do it, keep going until you have a nice smooth batter: it should be pourable and quite thin. Set the batter aside for at least an hour at room temperature, or overnight in the fridge.

To make the syrup, put all the ingredients in a small saucepan and set over low-medium heat until the butter is melted and the mixture starts to froth, then pour into a heatproof jug. (The syrup will keep for a few days in the fridge.)

It is best to have your batter at room temperature, so take it out of the fridge an hour or so before you start to cook. Preheat your oven to 220°C (200°C fan), and put a 22-26 cm ovenproof skillet or frying pan with reasonably deep sides over high heat. When it is hot, add the unfeasible amount of butter prescribed and swirl it around until it starts to bubble; the butter might even get a slight nuttiness and start to brown. Don't sweat - the most important thing is to have a blisteringly hot pan. Quickly and carefully, pour the batter right into the middle of the pan: the batter should sweep the melted butter out to the sides of the pan to prevent any sticking and also give delicious crisp edges - a small pool of browned butter will gather in the middle of the batter and that is fine. Give the pancake about 30 seconds over high heat for the base to set and then transfer to the oven and bake for about 15 minutes or until puffed and golden. (If you don't have

Special Guest

an ovenproof frying pan, you could make this in a Pyrex dish with reasonably high sides: heat it in the oven, add the butter, return the dish to the oven so the butter gets really hot, then add the batter and bake in the same way.)

Meanwhile, have the syrup poised for action. Place a bowl of berries or other fruit on the table – and another bowl of yoghurt, if you like. (Or, if a guest asked on accepting the invitation 'what can I bring?' and you answered 'a giant fruit salad thanks', then you're all set.)

Get everyone seated and have a big chopping board or plate ready to go. Use your thickest oven gloves to remove the skillet from the oven and, with a bit of a tilt and jiggle, the pancake should slip right out onto your serving board or plate. A dusting of icing sugar is an option here, but that would be mostly about looks rather than necessity – you are about to douse it in syrup, for goodness sake. You have about 30 seconds before the thing starts to deflate, so hurry it to the table and use a bread knife to cut it into wedges (like a pizza).

Let people help themselves to fruit and yoghurt, and pass the syrup around. This is the kind of thing where you should not wait for others to start. Get stuck in!

EVEN EASIER

The honey and orange syrup came about when Wendy realised she was splashing more than ten dollars' worth of maple syrup on every family-sized puffy pancake at home, so looked for a less spendy option. But if you want to buy yourself a few extra minutes in bed, by all means go with maple syrup.

FRESH CORN POLENTA WITH BAKED EGGS & SMOKY TOMATOES

SERVES 6

We're so used to thinking of polenta as something dry and grainy that needs to be rehydrated slowly over heat, that it comes as a surprise to learn you can actually start with fresh, juicy corn and eliminate the moisture. This is the epiphany I had when reading Yotam Ottolenghi's sweetcorn polenta recipe. He teams his with eggplant (aubergine) pickle. I've borrowed the idea and made it into breakfast by adding eggs and chipotle tomatoes. This is designed to be prepared the night before, when you've got time for pottering, stirring and slow-roasting. Note that the tomatoes are three hours in the oven! If you have an oven timer, you can set it and go to bed, then all you need do in the morning is assemble and bake. And if you have left-over polenta, spread it on toast for lunch.

---

10 roma (plum) tomatoes
2 tablespoons chipotle sauce (see below)
1 tablespoon salt
1 teaspoon cracked black pepper
1 tablespoon caster sugar
butter, for greasing and dotting
6 eggs
basil leaves, to garnish
sourdough toast, to serve

FRESH CORN POLENTA

6 ears sweetcorn (as yellow as you can find), kernels sliced from cobs
50 g butter
200 g feta, crumbled
3 spring onions, thinly sliced

HOT STUFF

I use the sauce from a tin of chipotle peppers in adobo; if you're using bottled chipotle sauce, test for head-blowing-offness first and adjust the quantity if necessary.

FOR THE MEAT-EATERS

Sigh. I imagine there are people who would really, REALLY like some crispy bacon with this.

Preheat your oven to 120°C (100°C fan) and line a baking tray with baking paper.

Cut the tomatoes in half lengthways and lay on the baking tray, cut sides up. Mix the chipotle sauce with the salt, pepper and sugar and smear it over the tomatoes, then slow-roast in the oven for 3 hours or until sticky and slightly collapsed.

Next, the polenta. Stick the corn kernels in a heavy-based pan with the butter and 500 ml (2 cups) water and simmer for 15 minutes or until tender. Strain off the cooking liquid and reserve, then tip the kernels into a food processor and blitz for about 5 minutes until you have a smooth purée, adding some of the cooking liquid if needed. Return the whizzed-up corn and its cooking liquid to the pan and cook, stirring constantly, until the liquid evaporates and you have a thick paste. Just like polenta! Stir in the feta, and pepper to taste.

Now it's time to bring everything together, so if your pals are coming around tomorrow, refrigerate the tomatoes and polenta overnight.

When you're good to go, preheat the oven to 200°C (180°C fan). Stir the spring onions into the polenta, then divide between six buttered ramekins (if you don't have ramekins, just put all the polenta into a buttered casserole dish). Make six deep indentations in the polenta, crack an egg into each one and dot with butter. Bake for 10-15 minutes or until the egg whites have set but the yolks are still soft. Scatter with basil and serve with toast and a couple of tomatoes on the side.

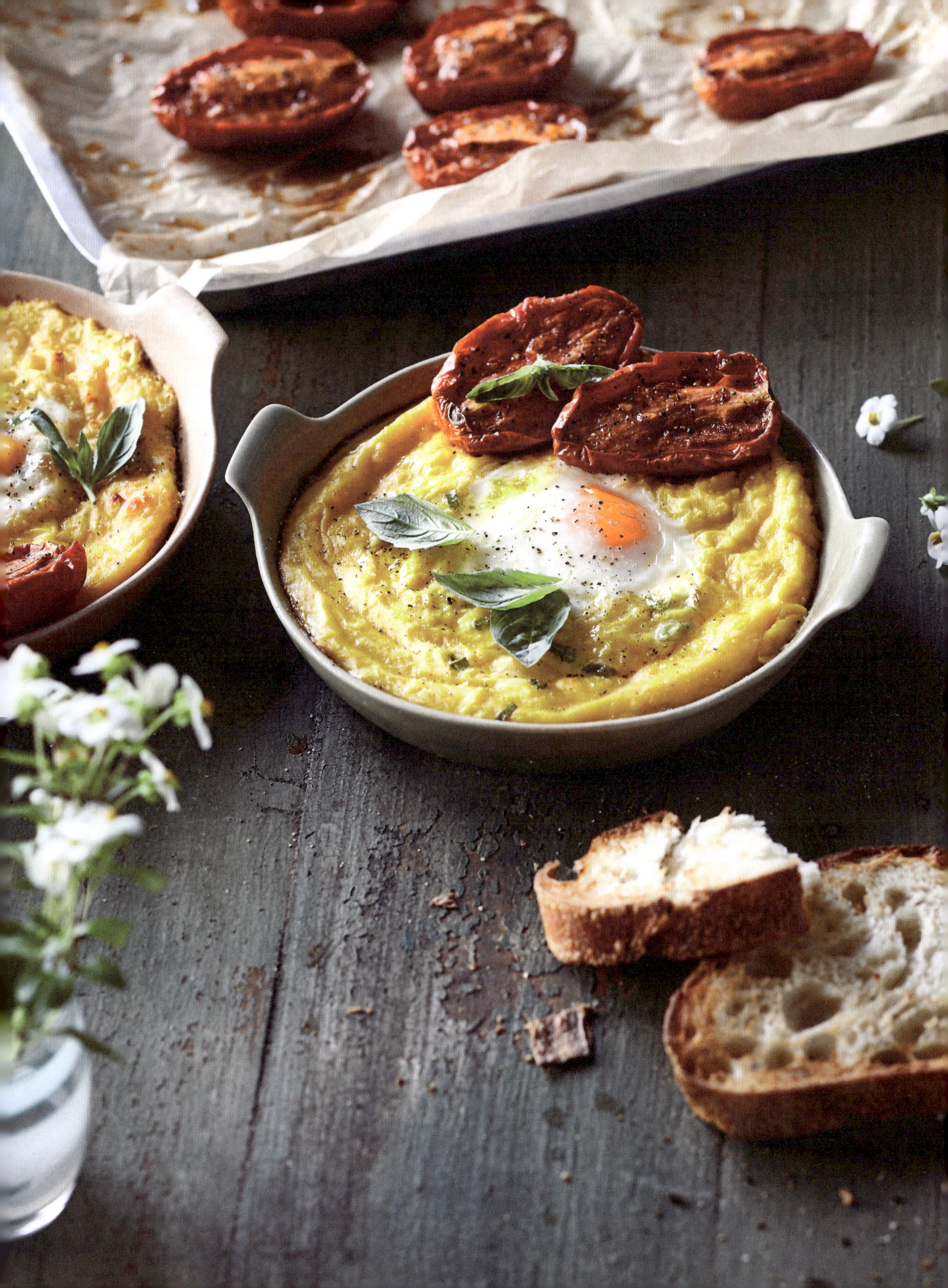

SMOKED SALMON WITH SODA BREAD & SPECIAL BUTTER

SERVES 4-6

If you are time-skint, baking bread probably isn't the first item on your to-do list. But soda bread is worth making an exception for, because it is so easy, and because it is best eaten very fresh. Shop-bought versions tend towards the cardboard end of the texture spectrum. And there is one role for soda bread where it really shines above all other breads: with butter and smoked salmon. A board of sliced smoked salmon, a couple of fancy butters that can be made ahead of time, and freshly baked soda bread – you need nothing else on your kitchen table. If you made damper as a kid, this recipe may be familiar, but without the obligation to wrap the dough around a dirty stick and hold it endlessly over a campfire. (And if you're feeling less time-poor, try hot-smoking your own salmon – see page 184.)

300–400 g smoked salmon
lemon wedges, to serve

SODA BREAD
250 g (1⅔ cups) wholemeal plain flour
250 g (1⅔ cups) plain flour
2 teaspoons bicarbonate of soda
1 teaspoon salt
200 g Greek-style yoghurt
250 ml (1 cup) full-fat milk
1 tablespoon lemon juice
oil, for greasing

HORSERADISH & CHIVE BUTTER
125 g unsalted butter, softened
3 teaspoons grated horseradish
4 tablespoons finely snipped chives

LEMON & PEPPER BUTTER
125 g unsalted butter, softened
½ teaspoon lemon juice
½ teaspoon finely grated lemon zest
freshly ground pepper, to taste

For the soda bread, preheat your oven to 200°C (180°C fan) and lightly oil your cooking vessel of choice. Most traditional would be a large lidded cast-iron casserole or Dutch oven that mimics the cooking conditions of yore; I love the shape of the resulting round loaf, scored with a cross. However, a 900 g loaf tin works fine too, and is probably more practical when it comes to cutting slices. Or, if all else fails, you can just use a baking tray lined with baking paper.

Put both flours, the bicarbonate of soda and salt into a large bowl and stir together. In a small bowl or jug, mix together the yoghurt, milk and lemon juice, then pour into the bowl of flour and use a knife to cut through the mixture until it starts to come together into a rough dough. Get your hands in there (or direct very willing young hands) to bring the dough together into a coherent ball.

Plonk the dough inside your cast-iron pot and use a knife to make two slashes in the shape of a cross in the top of the loaf. Traditionally, this was done to let the bad spirits out of your bread, should it happen to be harbouring such things. More pragmatically, it also means that the bread cooks more quickly and is easier to divide up afterwards. Cover with the lid and bake for 45 minutes, removing the lid for the final 10 minutes.

If you are using a loaf tin, ease your ball of dough into a rough sausage shape before dropping it into the lightly oiled tin. Or, transfer your slightly flattened ball of dough to a lined baking tray for a freeform loaf. Bake for about 30–35 minutes.

Meanwhile, for the butters, simply add the flavourings to the soft butter and combine well with a rubber spatula. Roll the butter in plastic wrap or pat into ramekins and chill until ready to serve.

Check your soda bread for doneness: when it's ready, the bottom of your loaf should sound hollow when tapped. Once the loaf is cool enough to handle, turn it out onto a wire rack to cool further. It's best eaten while still slightly warm or at room temperature. Cut into generous slices, then serve with some flavoured butter, smoked salmon and a few lemon wedges on the side.

EVEN EASIER

Skip making the flavoured butters and splash out on some fantastically expensive artisan (or French) butter. It really does taste nicer.

Stay for lunch

A spontaneous invitation is the best invitation: the ratio of effort to effect is weighted very much in favour of the host. If you invite someone for a meal today, as in right now, there is such little time for expectations to be fostered that they will be low. Your guest will expect the house to be in disarray and the meal to be simple. They will almost certainly pitch in and help. You can only delight a guest who would otherwise be heating up leftovers. So, when you're having a day when you feel optimistic about life, take the risk and ask someone for lunch. Another freelance worker who's also bored of their home office? Text them for lunch in 30 minutes. That person you see on Saturdays at your child's art club and never want to stop talking to? Suggest they follow you home. Fellow dog-walkers, gym-goers or the friend two streets away you've been meaning to have over for a year. Ask them now!

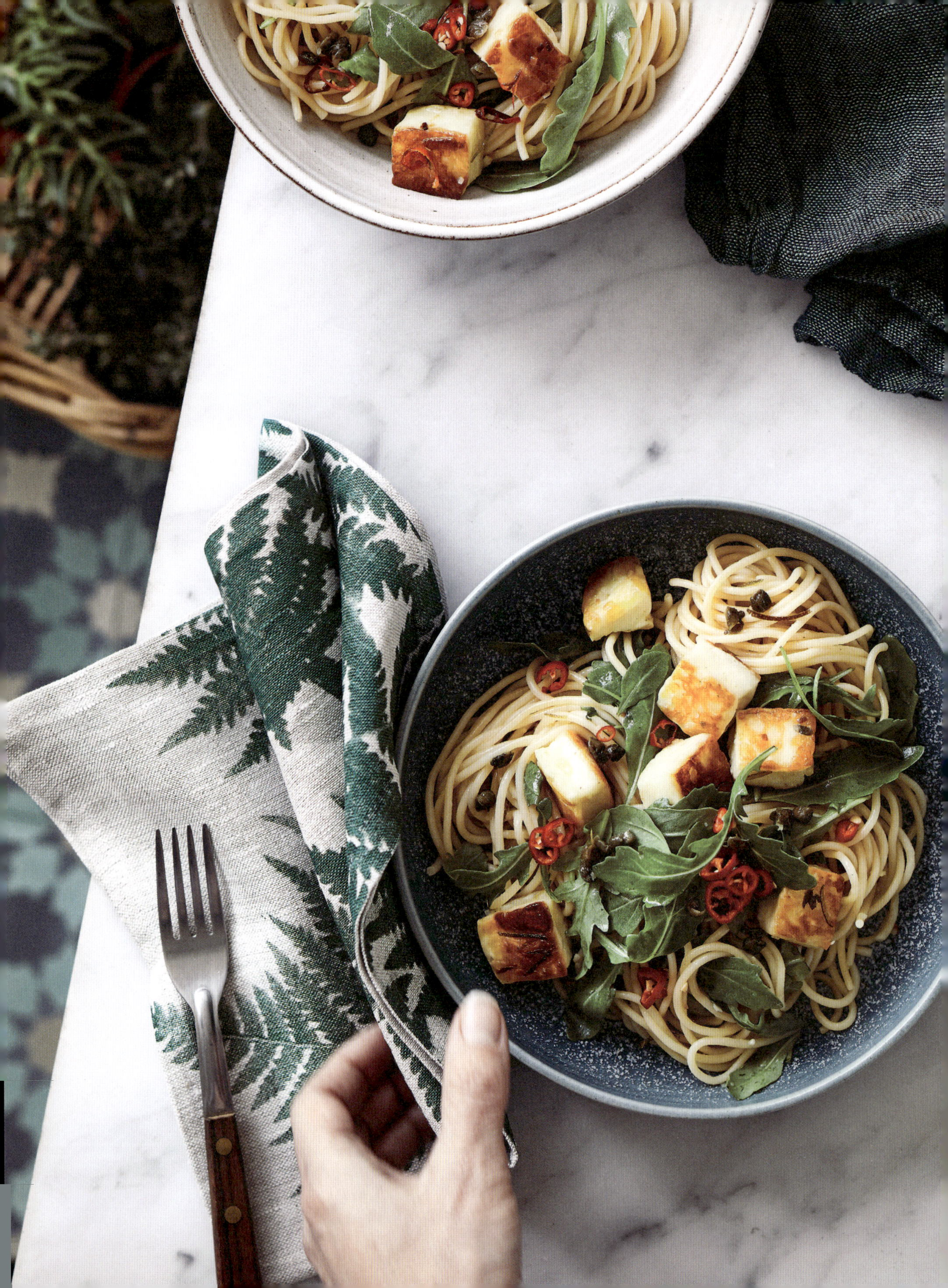

HALLOUMI, LIME & ROCKET SPAGHETTI

SERVES 4

I know it's shockingly predictable for a non-meat-eater to return so often to halloumi, but it really is such a useful cheese. It's sort of like the vegetarian peacetime equivalent of pemmican: it keeps for ages and is both tasty and easy to use. This recipe was first made for me in Canberra by my friend Zoe, who used to host viewing sessions of *The West Wing* for a small group of political staffers (and Jeremy and me). The staffers all loved *The West Wing*, but did tend to roll their eyes a bit about how unrealistic it was. A decade later, when Aaron Sorkin made *The Newsroom*, I finally understood their frustration.

In any event, this has – ever since – been my go-to weeknight pasta when I'm pushed for time, and a popular last-minute dish for drop-ins. It's got heat, salt, acid and pepper and a good helping of greens to make you feel a bit less gluggy. Lord, it's delicious. I feel like a bowl of it right now.

---

250 g halloumi, cut into 1.5 cm dice
2 tablespoons extra virgin olive oil
2 tablespoons small salted capers, rinsed then drained well
1 garlic clove, finely chopped
1 medium or 2 small red chillies, thinly sliced
1 juicy lime
100 g wild rocket leaves
500 g dried spaghetti

First step: tip the halloumi, olive oil, capers, garlic and the chilli into a bowl and stir about. Using one of those zesters that takes off the zest in long thin strips, add the zest of the lime. (If you don't have such a contraption, use a potato peeler to take the zest off and then cut it into thin strips, or alternatively you could do whatever you please and ignore my excessively controlling views on the subject.)

Squeeze the lime and reserve the juice. Arrange your rocket in a large serving bowl.

Cook the pasta according to its packet instructions. Now you're ready for the final assault.

While the pasta is cooking, heat a heavy frying pan over medium heat and tip in the contents of your bowl: the halloumi will become golden, so turn the bits over regularly and keep a sharp eye on it. It's done when all your halloumi is nicely browned. This should take about 5 minutes, so when it's done you'll be ready to drain your pasta. Dump the spaghetti into the pan and swirl it about to mop up every little bit of sauce. Working quickly, dress the rocket with the lime juice, then add the pasta to the bowl and give the whole lot a toss.

Serve straightaway!

SALMON & MUSTARD RICE PAPER ROLLS

SERVES 3–4

There are a million delicious things you can put in rice paper rolls, but these require only a few basic store-cupboard items and can be whipped up in a jiffy when you need lunch inside ten minutes. Your guests also have the fun of rolling their own meal.

The mix of mustard and salmon in a spring roll is a concept we first encountered in a Fitzroy restaurant called Kazen (long since closed, sadly). The mustard and salmon with fresh apple and light soy sauce is an irresistible combination whose taste belies its ease of assembly. In London - where Vietnamese food is still not such an everyday option as it is in Australia - there is still a rich seam to be mined of golden guests who have never seen soak-and-go rice paper rounds, nor really encountered much south-east Asian cuisine beyond Thai. Delighting such guests is a simple pleasure. But even in Australia, where rice paper rolls are more familiar, the mustard and salmon combo should pique some interest.

---

1 x 213 g tin of red or pink salmon
1 teaspoon dijon mustard
1 teaspoon chopped herbs
　(dill, tarragon or coriander –
　whatever you have to hand)
1 tart crisp apple
handful of watercress or a few iceberg
　lettuce leaves
handful of pumpkin seeds
12 small rice paper wrappers

DIPPING SAUCE
3 tablespoons tamari sauce
1 tablespoon lime or lemon juice

Drain the salmon and stir in the mustard and chopped herbs. Cut the apple into long, thin matchsticks. Arrange all these ingredients on the biggest chopping board you have, together with the lettuce or rocket, pumpkin seeds and rice papers.

Make the dipping sauce by combining the ingredients in a small bowl, then place it on the table.

Give each diner a dish of warm water and a dinner plate. The idea is to dunk the rice paper for 10 seconds, then spoon a stripe of salmon down the middle and add a few matchsticks of apple, some watercress or lettuce leaves and pumpkin seeds. Parcel up your roll, then get dipping and eating!

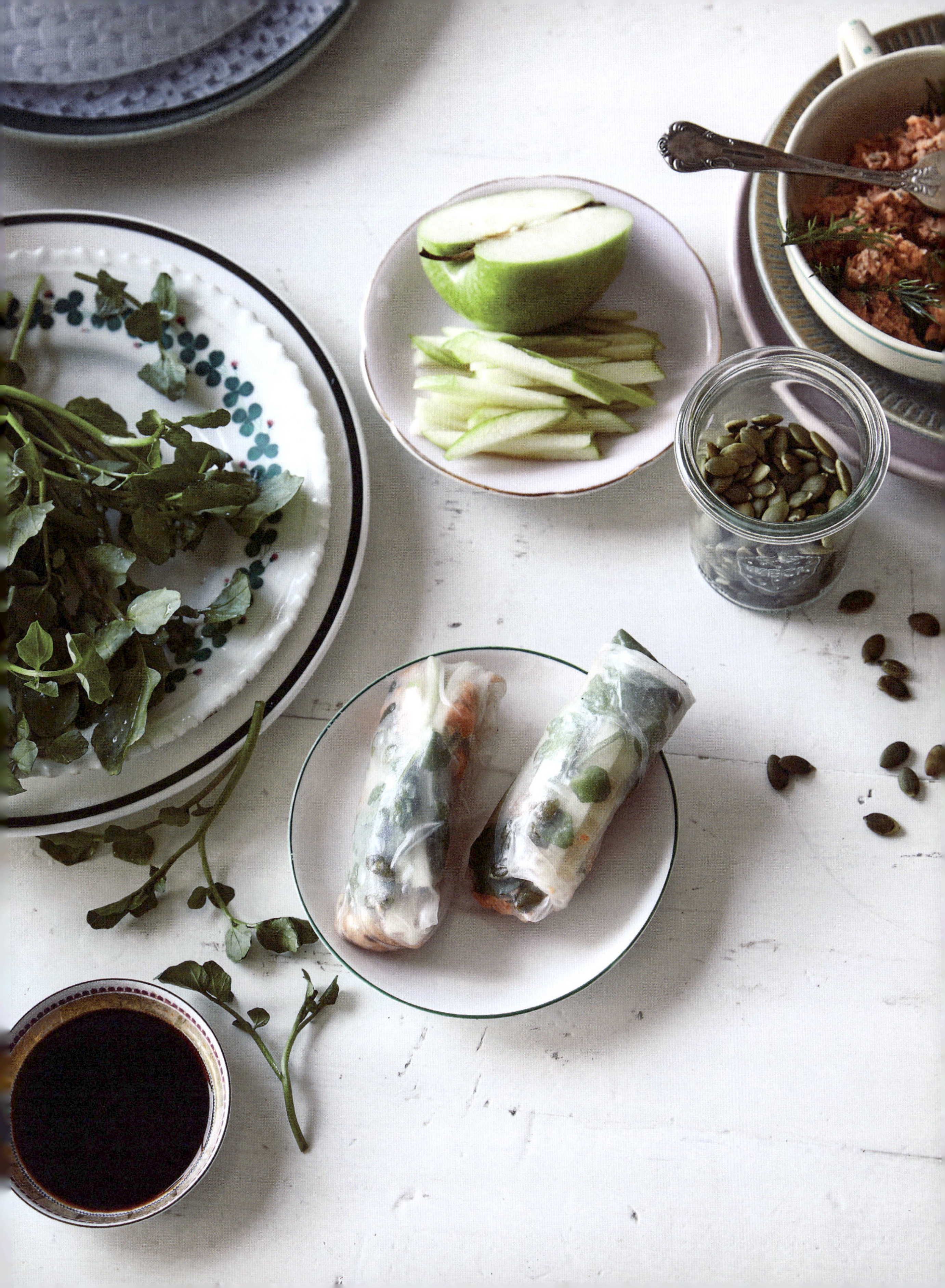

STORE-CUPBOARD FRITTATA

SERVES 6-8

This frittata takes no time at all and will feed six people with ease; eight if you have some good bread and the makings of a salad. Everything is lobbed into a bowl, briskly assembled then given the old one-two frittata technique of stovetop and grill. Important tip: check that your frying pan is ovenproof - or, if it has a plastic handle, make sure you can craftily position the pan so that the plastic bit is not under the heat. This seems obvious to mention, but you're busy, so. Consider it mentioned.

Content-wise, you can readily vary this frittata. If you don't have mint, use another herb, or some baby spinach (just chuck it in fresh). You could use sautéed mushrooms and kale instead of the peas. Or roasted sweet potato and red onion. Just make sure everything's cooked before it goes into the egg mix.

---

140 g (1 cup) frozen peas
12 eggs
250 g sour cream
finely grated zest of ½ lemon
1 teaspoon chilli flakes
125 ml (½ cup) olive oil
handful of finely chopped mint
200 g feta
25 g pecorino (or any other sharp cheese)

Take the peas out of the freezer. Crack the eggs into a large bowl, then whisk in the sour cream, lemon zest, chilli and all except 1 tablespoon of the oil. Season with salt and pepper, remembering that the feta will add some more salt.

Heat the grill to high.

Place a deep frying pan (mine is 24 cm in diameter, and 8 cm deep), ideally one with a heatproof handle, over medium-high heat and add the remaining tablespoon of oil. You want the pan to get very hot, to create a crust on the bottom of the frittata and ensure it doesn't stick. Add the egg mixture: you should notice it puffing up a bit when it hits the hot pan. Using a wooden spoon, drag the egg in from the sides to the centre a couple of times the way you would for an omelette. After a minute or so, leave it alone. Turn the heat down to medium, then add the peas and mint, pushing them down so they're submerged in the egg mixture. Crumble in the feta, partially submerging it so it resembles little feta icebergs. Grate the pecorino over the top and keep cooking for about 15 minutes - you should see the sides of the frittata getting brown and crusty, and the egg getting cooked, though it will still be very wobbly in the centre.

Slide the pan under the hot grill and cook until the eggs are just set and the top is nicely golden.

Allow the frittata to cool, then carefully run a knife or spatula around the edge. If all goes well, your frittata should slip smoothly onto a plate. On the off chance that it doesn't, just slice it in the pan.

FENNEL, WALNUT & SUN-DRIED TOMATO PAPPARDELLE

SERVES 6

Wendy first made this dish for me in London. And she's made it for me since in Melbourne and Sydney, and I've made it for people in LA and Adelaide, and I don't think she ever really gave me the exact proportions because she never really had them. It's a pasta sauce that uses fennel in a beautifully original way: so softened and caramelised that it's almost like a confit, but given a lovely depth with jammy sun-dried tomatoes, AND YES, I KNOW THEY ARE FROM THE NINETIES, BUT BACK OFF! (Do not, under any circumstances, use those awful semi-dried things. The tomatoes need to be sun-dried, soft and squishy, and deep, deep red. Or go home.) Plus walnuts. And lots of parsley. The net effect is rich and textured. What it's really like, I guess, is a vegetarian ragout.

---

1 large or 2 medium plump fennel bulbs
1 small brown onion
2 tablespoons olive oil (preferably from the tomatoes)
80 g (½ cup) walnuts
12 sun-dried tomatoes in olive oil
handful of chopped flat-leaf parsley
500 g dried pappardelle
200 g crème fraîche
finely grated parmesan, to serve

To begin, dice the fennel and the onion into about 5 mm dice. I never really enjoy dicing fennel – the only really satisfying game to be in with this vegetable is the mandoline, with its ever-attendant threat of finger loss – but the tedious dicing is worth it in this case.

In a frying pan set over low heat, sauté the fennel and onion in the olive oil until the fennel is soft, caramelised and golden. This will take about 20 minutes; it's the most time-consuming part of the dish, so have your guests stand next to you while you ruminatively stir and prod. Also, you will need to busy yourself with other prep, viz: put a large pan of water on to boil for the pasta. Chop the walnuts into pea-sized chunks. Chop the sun-dried tomatoes to comparable dimensions. And roughly chop the parsley while you're at it.

Add the sun-dried tomatoes and walnuts to the pan and cook for 5 minutes, stirring and squishing as you go. Salt your pasta water, and when it is at a rolling boil, add the pappardelle and cook according to the packet instructions. Drain, retaining a little of the cooking water in a teacup.

Stir most of the parsley into the contents of the frying pan, followed by the crème fraîche. It should now be a golden, silkily amalgamated yet chunky sauce that will fold gracefully through the pappardelle; if it seems too stiff, loosen with more crème fraîche or a dash of the reserved pasta-cooking water. Season to taste, then serve with the rest of the parsley and plenty of parmesan.

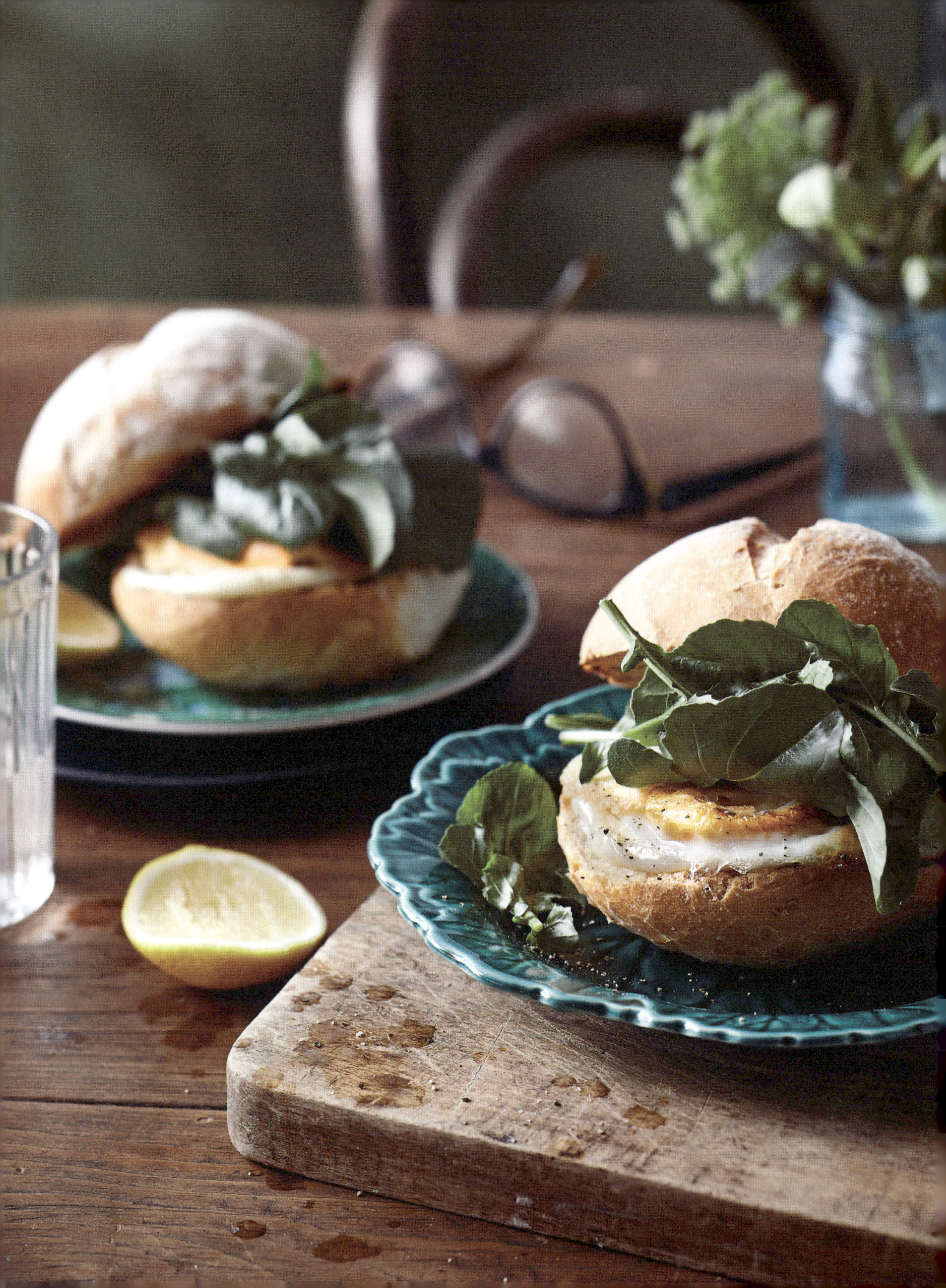

KEFALOGRAVIERA, FRIED EGG & ROCKET ROLLS

SERVES 6

In Borough Market in London, there are queues around the block for Brindisa's chorizo and rocket rolls: a salty, peppery pick-me-up for a late Saturday morning. Even if you don't eat meat, the appeal of the hand-held lunch is undeniable. This quick sandwich is a vegetarian salute to the concept. Essentially, it's a fried egg, done the normal way – except that, when you flip it, you incorporate a generous slice of the great Greek frying cheese, kefalograviera.

Kefalograviera is permanently on the menu at Adelaide's Estia restaurant: dredged in seasoned flour, pan-fried and then rushed to the table with a lemon wedge. (You do not want to let this cheese regain room temperature – it's like gnawing on a running shoe). Taste-wise, fried kefalograviera is like the crusty bit of cheese that escapes the jaffle, only all over. It is... fabulous. In Sydney, Potts Point eatery Apollo serves kefalograviera pan-fried with honey and dried oregano, which is just as great as you'd expect. But enough cheese digressions. In this dish, the cheese functions in the pan as a yolk insulator, so you can still have a runny yolk, even with a nicely tanned kefalograviera layer. Cook your eggs three to a pan, sandwiching them into the toasted rolls ready-prepared with rocket and mayonnaise.

---

1 tablespoon extra virgin olive oil
6 eggs – the fresher, the better
250 g kefalograviera, cut into 5 mm slices
6 crusty bread rolls, split in half
good-quality mayonnaise
2 generous handfuls of rocket leaves
juice of 1 lemon

EVEN EASIER

If you have no kefalograviera in your orbit, use halloumi. Good for most things. Or of course you could use chorizo, sliced thickly on the diagonal and browned in a hot pan. You won't need any oil for this task, as chorizo is plenty oily.

Heat a heavy-based frying pan over medium heat and add the oil. One by one, crack the eggs into a small bowl and slide them into the pan – ideally, you should be able to cook 3 eggs at a time. Fry them for about 2 minutes on the first side, or however long it takes for the white to reach a flippable consistency. Lay a slice of cheese over the egg, then flip it with a deft movement so the kefalograviera ends up under the egg. If this degree of hand-eye coordination eludes you, position the cheese in the pan and flip the egg onto it. Increase the heat slightly so as to give the cheese a good browning.

Meanwhile, toast the split rolls lightly and smear with mayonnaise. Toss the rocket leaves in the lemon juice, then stack a small handful on one half of each roll.

Slip each egg into a warm roll, then do the other 3 eggs. Serve the rolls on a decorative platter.

PEA RISONI WITH PARMESAN & PEPPER

SERVES 4

If there is a harder working store-cupboard saviour than risoni (AKA orzo) then I would like to meet it. One quite small bag (no wasted space in storage with this little grain-like pasta) can spring into action to feed, nay thrill, a group of last-minute guests. This combination redeploys ingredients that are pretty familiar in our recipes: frozen peas, mint, lemon and cheese. But if you have other things on hand - ham, prawns, left-over chicken, zucchini (courgettes), shallots - then chop them small, fry them up, and add them to the risoni with the mint, lemon juice and butter. In general, for each person, count on 75 g of risoni and just over the same weight in other ingredients.

---

300 g risoni (orzo)
40 g mint leaves (yes, it is a lot)
100 g parmesan
1 tablespoon green peppercorns in brine (although of course dried green or black peppercorns are also perfectly fine, as is black pepper)
a little olive oil
350 g frozen peas
juice of ½ lemon
40 g butter

Get the risoni in a big pan of boiling salted water and set a timer for the cooking time shown on the packet: usually about 7–9 minutes for al dente.

Use that time to finely chop the mint and grate the parmesan. Use a pestle and mortar to grind up the peppercorns with a bit of salt and a little olive oil, then transfer to a small serving bowl. There will still be time to sit back and happily contemplate the lopsided effort-to-deliciousness ratio of this dish.

When the timer goes, add the frozen peas to the pan. Wait until the water comes back to the boil (or until you are confident the peas are hot all the way through), then drain the risoni and peas and return to the pan. Stir through the mint, lemon juice and butter, and about half of the parmesan, then spoon onto plates.

I like to make the spicy fresh taste of green peppercorns a key component of this dish, but others might shy away from the heat, so let your guests help themselves to a spoonful to stir in. Or just let everyone take as many twists of the pepper grinder as they dare. Sprinkle with the remaining parmesan and get stuck in while it's hot.

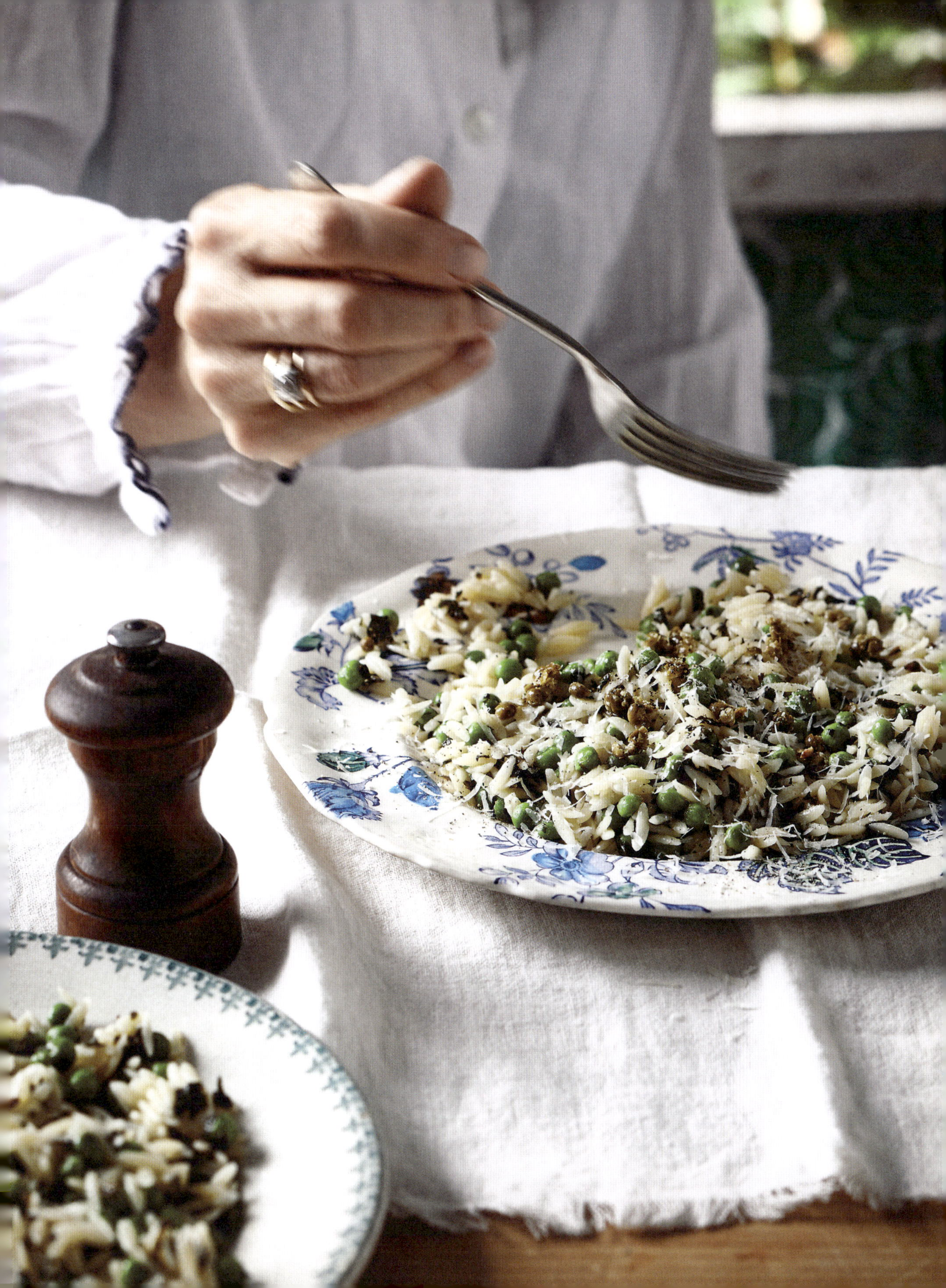

SPAGHETTI PANGRATTATO

SERVES 4

Stale bread is one of life's great fields of opportunity. And if you have half a loaf of sourdough that was at its best a day or two ago, please don't do anything so foolish as to throw it away. It takes no time at all to make breadcrumbs that will - down the track - be useful to a Hansel-and-Gretel degree. Some people will tell you to make crumbs by removing the crusts and pulsing in a food processor, and that is perfectly fine, but I prefer to use a serrated knife, cutting the bread into 5 mm thick slices, then into long strips, and thence into tiny dice. Put them into a snap-lock bag and into the freezer and then later - when you most need help - you will remember that you have the makings of pangrattato, and you will feel instantly buoyed.

Spaghetti pangrattato, with its double-carb thrill and its salty, crunchy heft, is a bullseye if you're rustling up lunch at short notice. Ask your guests to make a green salad while you work.

---

2 garlic cloves, finely chopped
80 ml (⅓ cup) olive oil
60 g (1 cup) stale sourdough breadcrumbs
500 g spaghetti
3 anchovy fillets
1 tablespoon salted baby capers, rinsed then drained well
2 tablespoons pine nuts
1 teaspoon chilli flakes
1 teaspoon finely grated lemon zest (and a squeeze of lemon juice, if you like)
large handful of coarsely chopped flat-leaf parsley

MAKE IT VEGAN
Omit the anchovies.

Preheat the oven to 180°C (160°C fan).

Mix the garlic with the olive oil, then pour half of the garlicky oil over the breadcrumbs and squish it through so they're all nicely coated. Spread out the crumbs on a baking tray and bake for about 10 minutes or until they're browned and crisp - we want to eliminate all chewiness.

Put a big pan of salted water on for the spaghetti. Add the pasta once it's at a rolling boil and cook for about a minute less than the cooking time suggested on the packet.

Meanwhile, add the rest of the garlicky oil to a heavy-based frying pan over medium heat and add the anchovies, capers, pine nuts and chilli flakes. Sauté until everything has softened, the anchovies have melted and the pine nuts are turning golden. Add the lemon zest now.

Okay, time to assemble. Drain the pasta well, then add it to the frying pan and toss to combine. Toss through the crispy crumbs, followed by the chopped parsley, and serve straightaway - with a squeeze of lemon, if you fancy.

FENNEL, GINGER & TOMATO BRAISE

SERVES 2–3

The roadsides around Two Wells, the town where we grew up, were absolutely lousy with wild fennel, the consumption of which would never have occurred to us. This is especially ironic considering the amount of the vegetable Wendy now buys from her local greengrocer in London. Maybe it's the whiff of the hot Adelaide Plains that keeps her so attached to fennel and all of its parts: its crunchy bulb, its feathery fronds, its fragrant seeds (delicious when dried, toasted and ground - and if you ever get hold of some fresh seeds, fill your pockets, because they are a liquorice-y pop of delight). In this braise, whipped together pronto, the fennel bulbs hold their shape and keep a decent crunch, and in their garlicky, gingery sauce, are pretty addictive. If you don't like ginger, leave it out and add a few more capers. Or some shiny black olives. Brown rice and a spoonful of goat's curd on top would make a complete meal for a late-home dinner. It would also partner up well with salmon, chicken or pork.

---

2 fennel bulbs
olive oil, for frying
1 heaped teaspoon fennel seeds
1 scant teaspoon sugar
10 cherry tomatoes, cut in half
3 garlic cloves, crushed
½ x 400 g tin of tomatoes
2 cm ginger, finely grated
1 tablespoon small capers in brine, drained well – optional
bread and chilli flakes, to serve

MAKE IT GLUTEN-FREE
Serve without bread.

Trim any tough parts from the fennel, reserving the best of the feathery fronds, then slice lengthways into quite thin pieces (this is a quick meal, so we want the fennel to cook fairly rapidly).

Take your largest frying pan and heat a tablespoon of olive oil. Add a layer of fennel, but don't stir it yet - we are trying to get some colour on the bottom of the fennel. When there are shades of delicious golden brown - only a minute or two - add another tablespoon of olive oil, flip the fennel over and let it brown on the other side. (If you are scaling up the recipe for more guests, or only have a small frying pan, you might have to do the fennel in batches.)

Towards the end of the browning process, stir in the fennel seeds and sugar. Next add the cherry tomatoes and garlic. Give everything a brief stir, then quickly get the tinned tomatoes in there with their juices: in the pursuit of speed we have a hot pan, but we want to avoid burning the garlic, and the tomato juices will prevent this. Stir, using a wooden spoon to break up the tomatoes, then add the ginger and capers.

Now clamp on a lid and let the braise simmer away for 3-4 minutes while you slice some bread, pour glasses of water and get the cutlery out. You're almost ready to go - just take the lid off for the final minute of cooking so the sauce reduces down to become slightly sticky and very delicious. Finish with an extra slick of olive oil, the reserved fennel fronds and a good seasoning of salt.

Serve straight from the pan at the table, with bread and a tiny bowl of chilli flakes on the side.

CLAFOUTIS, OR CHEAT'S QUICHE

SERVES 4 AS A LIGHT MEAL

This does need a bit of time in the oven for an impromptu lunch, but it is so quick to put together that most of the time between invitation and degustation will be spent in pleasant chat. This dish is also great at adapting to whatever you have in the fridge. Think of it as crustless, light quiche: any ingredients that work in a quiche format will work here too. I have written down some measured amounts before each ingredient, but to be honest, it seems like just about anything goes – the quantities and the ratio of eggs to dairy to flour can be stretched or skimped on, depending on what you have to hand. It also makes a very handy home-late-from-work scratch meal.

---

3 tablespoons self-raising flour
100 ml full-fat milk
4 large eggs (or 6 medium)
3 tablespoons sour cream or crème fraîche
pinch of salt
1 tablespoon chopped herbs (such as thyme or parsley) and/or 2 finely chopped spring onions
butter, for greasing
½ zucchini (courgette), cut into small chunks (or a handful of just about any other quick-to-cook vegetable, such as tiny florets of cauliflower, or a handful of chopped spinach or finely shaved asparagus)
50 g feta
8–10 cherry tomatoes, cut in half
35 g cheddar (or other hard cheese), grated
salad leaves, to serve

Get the oven preheating to 220°C (200°C fan) the second you initiate an invitation – even while your guests are still considering the offer.

Once they have accepted, lightly whisk the flour with a little milk to make a smooth paste, then whisk in the eggs, sour cream, the rest of the milk and the salt. Stir through whatever herbs or spring onions you are using.

Generously butter a high-sided baking dish (about 15 cm x 10 cm) or four 150–175 ml ramekins and pour in half the batter. Lay the vegetables on top, crumble over half the feta, then pour in the rest of the batter, followed by the rest of the feta. Finish with the tomatoes, arranging them cut-side up, and the grated cheese.

Get it straight into the oven and cook for about 20 minutes until puffy and lightly browned. Serve right away (it will lose a bit of its puff) with some salad leaves.

MAKE IT GLUTEN-FREE

Gluten-free flour works brilliantly in these sorts of recipes, where only a small amount is required to give a bit of body. Use either self-raising, or plain with a pinch of gluten-free baking powder.

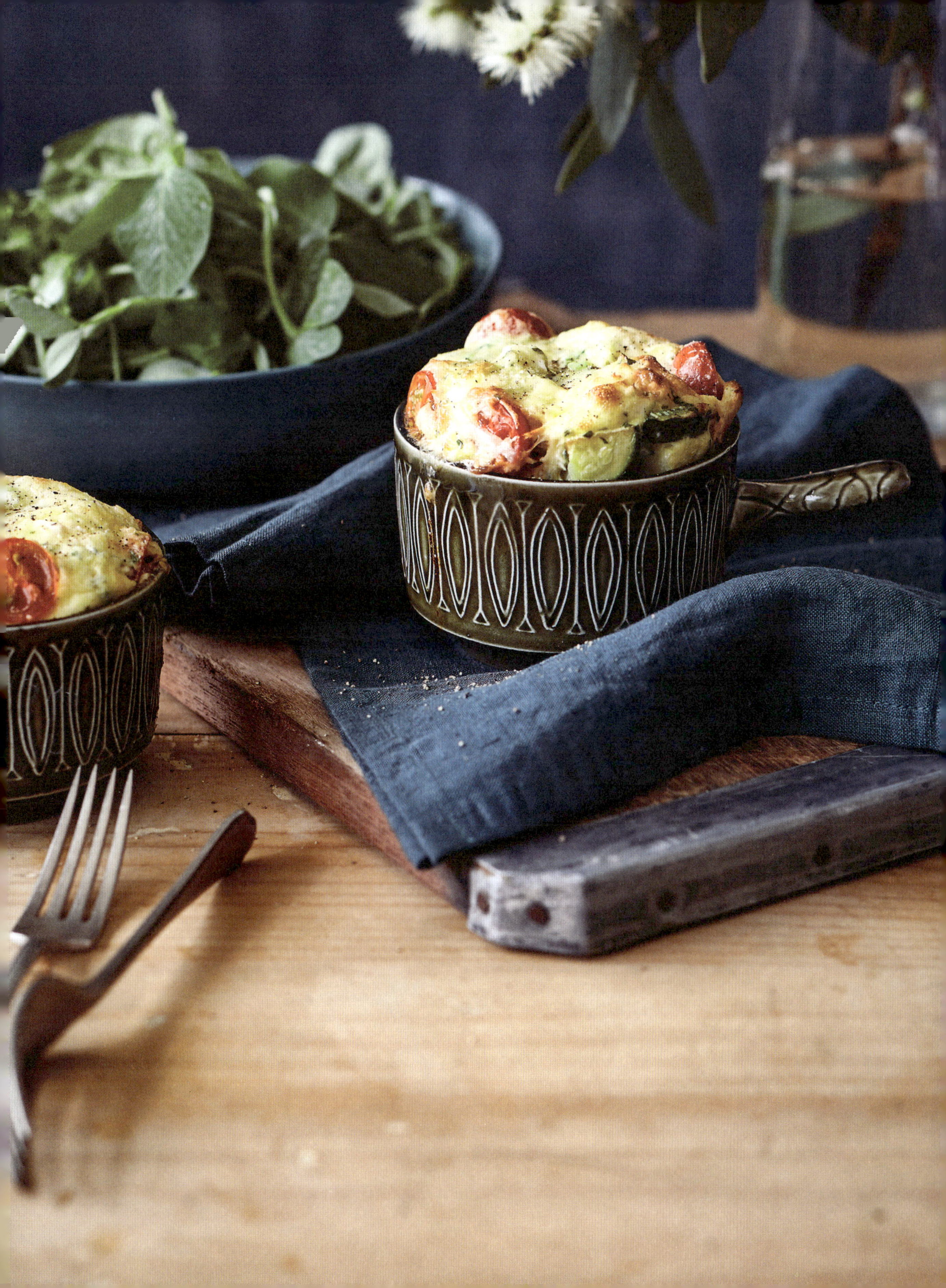

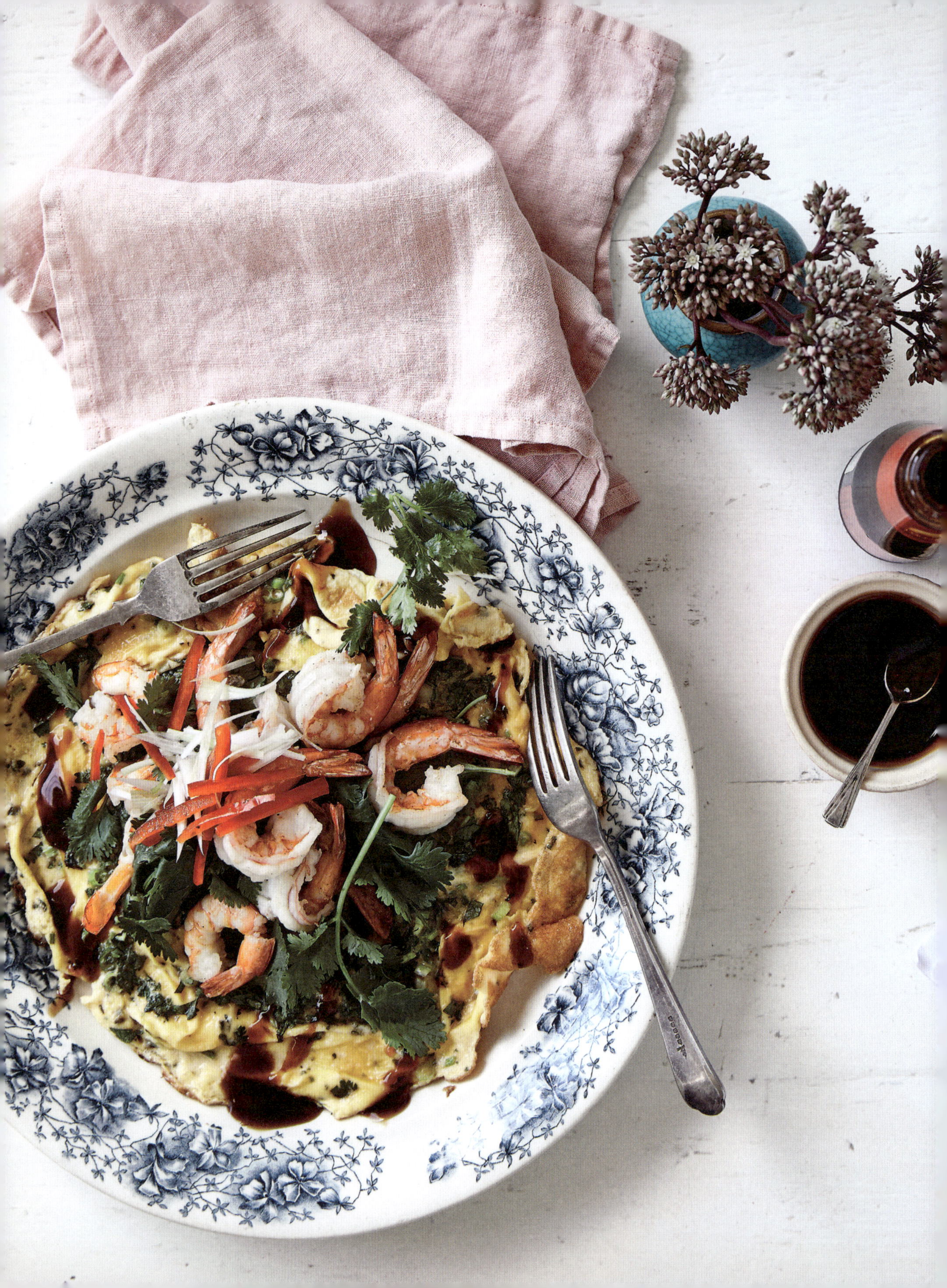

PRAWN OMELETTE WITH OYSTER SAUCE

SERVES 2 AS A GENEROUS LUNCH, OR 4 AS A SHARING PLATE

A bag of prawn cutlets in your freezer – the kind where they're frozen individually and clank about in the bag, rather than frozen altogether in a sort of brick – is an extremely valuable investment for the last-minute chef. Buy the Australian-caught ones. Admittedly, prawns aren't cheap, but if you can get four or five scratch meals out of a single bag, you're laughing. This omelette is a typical quick-fire dish in which a few prawns can be deployed to convert a lunchtime omelette into an Asian street food classic.

---

8 frozen raw prawns, peeled but with tails left on
3 spring onions
½ red pepper (capsicum)
6 eggs
6 sprigs of coriander, finely chopped (stalks and all), plus extra for garnish
3 tablespoons rice bran oil
½ teaspoon salt, mixed with ½ teaspoon white pepper
1 tablespoon oyster sauce

MAKE IT VEGETARIAN
Replace the prawns with 100 g firm tofu, dredged in the same salt and pepper mix, but with 1 teaspoon of cornflour, and use a mushroom-based vegetarian oyster sauce.

MAKE IT GLUTEN-FREE
Make sure your oyster sauce is gluten-free.

To speed-defrost your prawns, separate them out, zip them into a snap-lock bag and immerse the bag in a sink full of lukewarm water.

Meanwhile, thinly slice one of the spring onions into rounds, then cut the other two lengthways into long thin shreds. Remove any seeds and membrane from the pepper, then cut into matchsticks.

Whisk the eggs with a fork, adding 1 tablespoon of water. Whisk in the coriander and the spring onion rounds.

Place a well-seasoned or non-stick wok over high heat. Add a tablespoon of the oil and when it's smoking, add the prawns and stir-fry rapidly, sprinkling the salt and pepper over as you toss the prawns. When they are pink and firm, remove the prawns and – if necessary – wipe the wok with paper towel.

Add the rest of the oil to the wok and place over high heat. Swirl. When the wok is very hot, add the egg mixture: it will puff up at the sides. Drag the edges in repeatedly so that you get nice puffy folds, and give the wok a shake periodically so the omelette doesn't stick. Do not flip the omelette! Just encourage the uncooked bits to flow into the holes you're creating.

When it's all just about all cooked, take off the heat. Slide onto a plate or – if it has indeed stuck, despite your best efforts – simply serve it in the wok and assure your guest that you're all about the rusticity. Now stripe the omelette with oyster sauce and pile the prawns in the centre. Arrange the spring onion and red pepper strips on top, and a few extra coriander sprigs. Serve immediately as a shared plate.

SARDINE RESCUE

If you haven't opened a tin of sardines for a while, then do think about giving them a spot on your lunch menu soon. Much-loved standby of the home office worker, below (and over the page) are some ideas to take them from tasty to super-tasty in record time. At a pinch, one tin of sardines will feed two people, but for her workday lunches, Wendy will pile the fish up high and knock off the whole tin herself. There are recipes that call for sardines to be mashed up with various ingredients before being spread on toast. But that can feel a bit cat-foody. Try squishing the whole fillets gently onto the toast, with any extras added in a separate layer. Try to buy Australian tinned sardines whenever possible; if caught short, Portuguese sardines are reliably excellent. Companies these days seem to favour ring-pull technology on the tins, which has them open in a second. Wendy still yearns for the key-and-roll method fondly remembered from Saturday lunches of her childhood. In those days, boiling the unopened tins to warm the fish was also a thing. But room temperature is fine here.

THE LEVANTINE   SERVES 1–2

Once you've eaten this, you might wonder why a little bag of sumac doesn't come sticky-taped to every tin of sardines.

handful of herbs (any or all of coriander, rocket, parsley)
1 x 120 g tin of sardines in oil
1 scant teaspoon sumac
3–4 large green olives, pitted
pinch of coriander seeds
2–3 walnuts
good squeeze of lemon juice
2 slices of toast

Wash and dry the herbs, then put on a chopping board with the sumac, olives, coriander seeds and walnuts. Use a large knife to roughly chop everything, adding the lemon juice and a little of the oil from the sardines to help bring it all together. Add a pinch of salt if your olives don't have enough punch.

Pile the sardines onto the toast, top with the herb mixture and tuck in.

THE
LEVANTINE

THE VIRGIN
MARY >

THE VIRGIN MARY

SERVES 1–2

Choose the option of sardines in tomato sauce for this one. Or, if you don't have those, add a dash of tomato passata or some finely chopped cherry tomatoes to the horseradish mayonnaise. *Do not* be tempted to add tomato sauce (AKA ketchup), or the dish will immediately lapse into 1970s prawn cocktail gone wrong.

1 teaspoon grated horseradish (or whatever it takes to get a mild heat)
1 teaspoon mayonnaise
2 slices of toast
1 x 120 g tin of sardines in tomato sauce
good squeeze of lemon juice
worcestershire or tabasco sauce, to taste
½ celery stalk, very finely chopped, or 1 teaspoon finely chopped parsley

Mix together the horseradish and mayonnaise, then spread over the toast. Lay the sardines on top, pressing them down with the back of a fork so they stay flat. Dress with lemon juice and worcestershire or tabasco sauce, then sprinkle with the celery or parsley.

SARDINES WITH SPAGHETTI, CURRANTS & MINT

SERVES 2

A rush version of the Sicilian classic pasta con le sarde that exchanges fennel for mint, because it is quicker and because mint helps everyone feel better at lunchtime. Use dill if you prefer something more traditional.

200 g thin spaghetti
1 tablespoon tiny currants
1–2 saffron strands
1 tablespoon pine nuts
1 x 120 g tin of sardines in oil (or 2 if you are hungry)
1 tablespoon chopped mint
good pinch of chilli flakes
squeeze of lemon juice

Bring a large pan of salted water to a good rolling boil. Add the spaghetti and cook according to its packet instructions.

Put the currants and saffron in a teacup or small bowl and cover with 2 tablespoons of the boiling pasta-cooking water, then leave to steep. This will plump up the currants and draw out the saffron flavour. Briefly toast the pine nuts in a dry frying pan over medium heat until golden all over, then set aside.

Once the pasta is cooked, drain it and return it to the pan, then throw in the contents – fish and oil – of the tin of sardines, as well as the saffron and currants with their soaking liquid. Give everything a bit of a stir around the still-hot pan, then add the mint, chilli flakes and lemon juice. Sprinkle with the toasted pine nuts and serve.

THE SCANDI

SERVES 1–2

This remoulade-like sauce has as many recipes as there are people in Denmark, from where it hails. I am addicted to the stuff, leaning towards the completely unsubtle version that has just about every tasty ingredient from my refrigerator in it. Leave out anything you don't have or don't fancy, and it will likely still be jolly tasty. This is best if you can wait a while to let the flavours come together, so if you develop a taste for it too, it might be worth scaling up the recipe and having a pot pre-made in the fridge for a range of uses (by all accounts, the Danes have it on salmon, hotdogs and just about everything else).

⅛ red onion, as finely chopped as possible
1 teaspoon capers (drained well if in brine, rinsed then drained well if salted), finely chopped
1 good-sized pickled gherkin, finely chopped
1 tablespoon finely chopped herbs (dill, tarragon, parsley or chives), plus a little extra dill
1 tablespoon mayonnaise (or, if you don't shy away from the retro, some whipped cream)
½ teaspoon dijon mustard
scant pinch of curry powder
scant pinch of ground turmeric
good squeeze of lemon juice
2 slices of toast
1 x 120 g tin of sardines in oil

Stir the onion, capers, gherkin and herbs into the mayonnaise. Add the mustard, curry powder, turmeric and lemon juice and mix in well. Spread on the toast, top with the sardines and liberally sprinkle over some extra chopped dill.

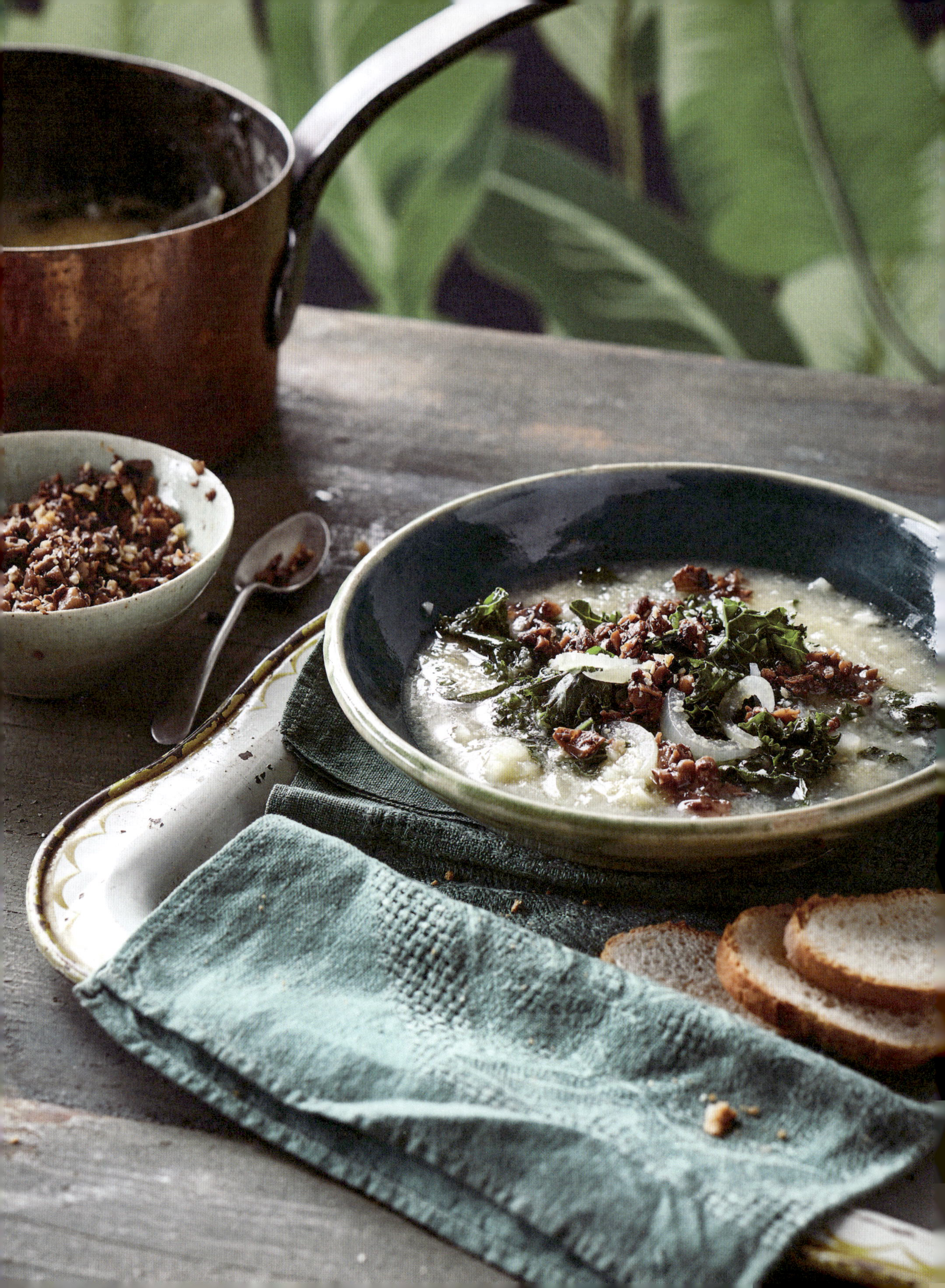

FRENCH MUSHROOM, KALE & POLENTA SOUP

SERVES 4

This super-hearty dish is based on tourain, a traditional soup from a tiny splinter of south-west France in the Périgord, which is usually passed around restaurants in one big communal tureen. The built-in entertainment at such times is watching the restaurateur's panic and flap when tourists, instead of ladling soup into their own bowls, begin eating directly from the tureen. In its original form, this soup is not much more than an unfeasible amount of garlic in molten goose fat – but here polenta recreates the silky texture and satiating properties of the goose fat, while the mushrooms offer an umami jolt and are a nod to the other passion of the region. Traditional eaters might not notice that this meal is gluten-free, nor that it is vegan.

---

1 brown onion
olive oil, for frying
10 large garlic cloves, roughly chopped
good handful of curly kale, well washed and any tough stalks removed
1.25 litres (5 cups) weak vegetable stock (or water)
75 g (scant ½ cup) fine polenta
250 g swiss brown (chestnut) mushrooms, finely chopped
few shakes of tamari sauce
125 ml (½ cup) red wine
25 g walnuts, finely chopped – optional
splash of white wine – optional
chopped tarragon or thyme, to serve

Cut the onion into quarters and then slice crossways into thin crescents. In a large heavy-based pan over medium heat, fry the onion in a good glug of olive oil until soft. Add all except ½ tablespoon of the garlic, swirling it around in the oil, but being careful not to let it brown. Tear up the kale and add that too. Now pour in 1 litre (4 cups) of the stock and bring to a slow simmer.

Meanwhile, in a heatproof jug or bowl, sprinkle the polenta into the remaining 250 ml (1 cup) of stock and whisk until it is lump-free. Add to the pan and cook for 10 minutes, stirring frequently, to make sure the thickening polenta doesn't catch and burn.

While the soup is simmering and thickening, fry the mushrooms and the reserved garlic in ½ tablespoon of olive oil (or butter, if you're not cooking for vegans) over medium heat. Once the mushrooms have released some of their liquor, season them with a few splashes of tamari sauce. Add the red wine, then return to a simmer and reduce for 3–4 minutes until you have a pesto-like consistency. Add the walnuts, if using – these make the soup thicker and slightly richer, but you can leave them out if you don't find any in your pantry.

Meanwhile, your soup should have thickened up nicely: you're after a creamy consistency, but not too thick – thin it down with a splash of white wine or water if necessary.

Serve in bowls with a good spoonful of mushrooms in the middle, plus a generous grind of black pepper and a light sprinkle of tarragon or thyme, if you like.

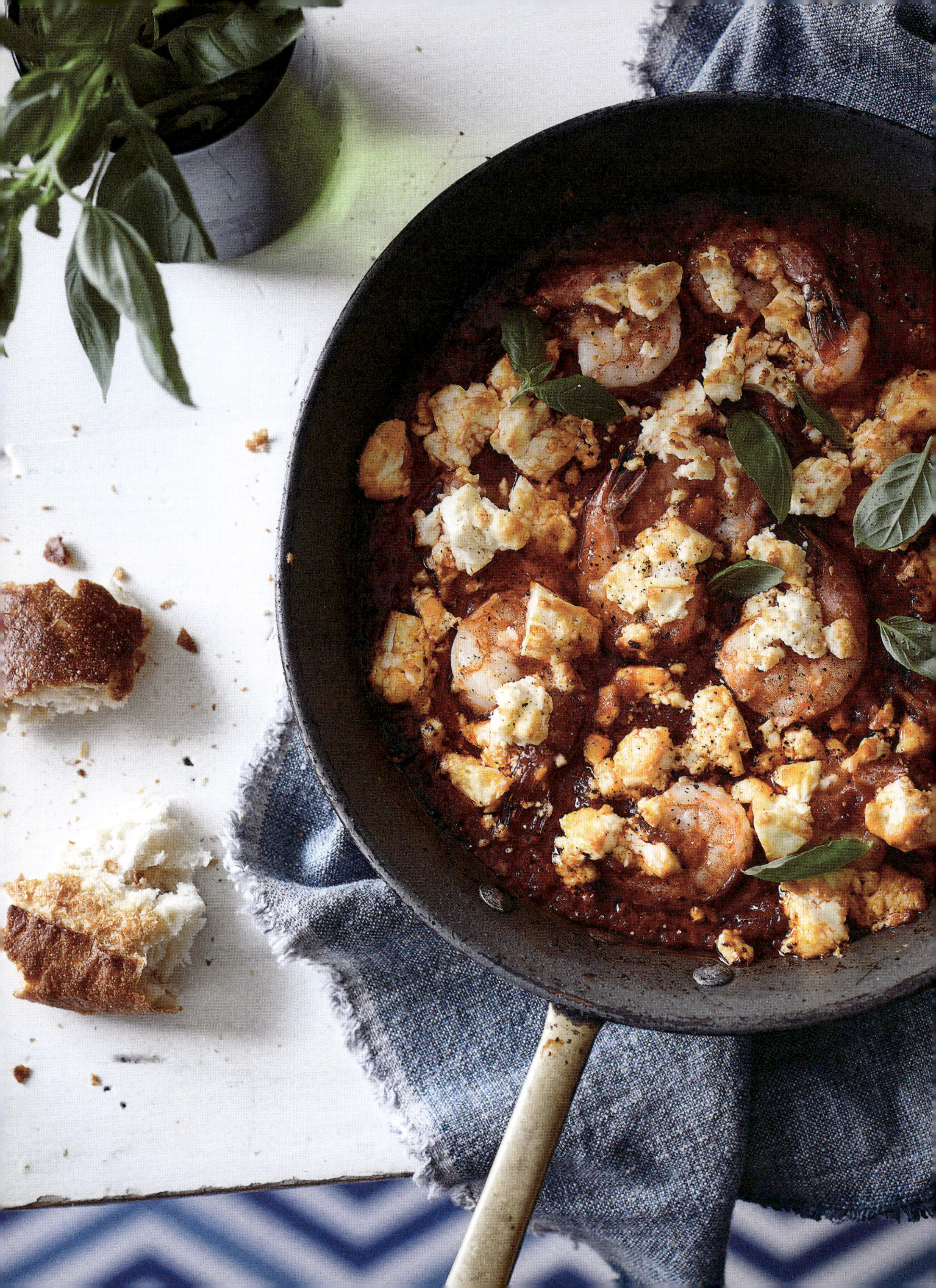

PRAWN SAGANAKI

SERVES 2

A quick, piquant seafood dish using the prawns you have strategically lodged in your freezer for exactly such an occasion. I know that seafood al forno doesn't exactly scream 'scratch lunch', but truly, this thing really can be assembled in ten minutes. The sauce gets its heat from garlic and chilli and its sharpness from lemon. The recipe will serve two generously for lunch – scale up if you have more guests, and don't overlook the fact that this dish provides a very sympathetic opportunity for crusty bread.

---

12 frozen raw prawns, peeled but with tails left on
1 tablespoon olive oil, plus extra for drizzling
1 garlic clove, finely chopped
1 anchovy fillet, roughly chopped
large pinch of chilli flakes
1 x 400 g tin of tomatoes
1 tablespoon tomato paste (concentrated purée)
juice of ½ lemon
75 g feta
basil leaves, to garnish
crusty bread, to serve

Preheat your grill to medium.

To speed-defrost your prawns, separate them out, zip them into a snap-lock bag and immerse the bag in a sink full of lukewarm water.

While that's happening, place a small, ovenproof frying pan over low-medium heat and add the oil. Sauté the garlic, anchovy and chilli flakes until the anchovy disintegrates. Add the tomatoes, squishing them with your wooden spoon. Add the tomato paste and lemon juice and cook down until the sauce has lost its wateriness. Season with pepper.

Okay – now it's time for the big finish. Poke your defrosted prawns into the sauce so they're mostly submerged. Crumble the feta over the top and drizzle with a little extra olive oil. Place under the grill and cook until everything's bubbling, the feta has browned and the prawns have gone pink in their tomato bath. This should take about 10 minutes.

Garnish with basil leaves and serve with crusty bread.

MAKE IT GLUTEN-FREE
Serve with gluten-free bread – or with none.

GINGER, RED LENTIL & TOMATO SOUP

SERVES 4-6

This soup relies on otherwise unremarkable ingredients until the last minute, when a huge amount of freshly grated ginger makes its way into the pot. (Fresh turmeric can be used instead, but be warned: your fingers will look like a pack-a-day smoker's for quite some time afterwards – and watch out for those marble benchtops, if you're lucky enough to have them.) You could use 2-3 large carrots instead of the butternut, but they won't melt into the soup quite as well so you'll end up with more texture.

The result is deliciously warming, even fiery, so you probably won't need any pepper or chilli. Scaled up, this soup could feed a large group of hungry but winter-weary guests, alongside a board full of cut bread and butter.

---

1 tablespoon olive oil
1 onion, finely chopped
1 tablespoon coriander seeds
2 x 400 g tins of tomatoes
500 g butternut pumpkin (squash), peeled and coarsely grated (or cut into small dice)
150 g red lentils, picked over
1 vegetable stock cube
50–75 g finely grated ginger
thick yoghurt (or cream cheese, if no one is looking) and a few herb leaves, to serve

MAKE IT VEGAN
Omit the yoghurt.

Heat the olive oil in a large heavy-based saucepan and fry the onion over low heat for about 10 minutes or until very soft, taking care not to let it brown too much. Add the coriander seeds and cook, stirring, for a few minutes, then tip in the tomatoes. Fill each empty tomato tin with water, swirling it around, and then slosh this tomato-y rinse into the pan. Now add the pumpkin and lentils and crumble in the stock cube. Bring to the boil, then reduce to a simmer and cook for 20 minutes.

When you are happy that the lentils and pumpkin are as soft as they need to be, add the ginger, not forgetting all the potent liquid that will have seeped out of the gratings. Use the back of a spoon to crush the tomatoes into smaller pieces and add a little extra water if it looks too much like stew. Now take to your soup with a stick blender and, depending on how you like your soup, either blitz it a little or a lot. I personally like to blend it about halfway to smooth, to gain some silkiness, but also keep some texture.

Serve with a dollop of yoghurt and a few leaves of your favourite green herb: mine is coriander for this soup, but parsley, dill, fennel fronds or rocket are all good choices.

PRESSURE-COOKER OPTION
Get the onion started with the olive oil in the pressure cooker, frying it briefly, then add the coriander seeds, tinned tomatoes (and two tins full of water), pumpkin, lentils and stock cube as per the method. Once all your ingredients are in, bring up to the boil, seal and cook at pressure for 7 minutes. Use the slow-release method to release the pressure, then add the ginger before blitzing and serving the soup as above.

TAGLIATELLE WITH LEMON CREAM, PINE NUTS & BROAD BEANS

SERVES 4

This blink-and-you've-made-it dish was inspired by a broad bean dip at a pub in Notting Hill, where they serve a mash of very lemony and cheesy broad beans on toast. Here, we sub out the toast for egg pasta and an emulsion that you can whip up in the time it takes the pasta to boil. Broad beans are a good thing to have in your freezer; once blanched and peeled, they add brightness to salads and can be mashed into dips or a fresh pesto. If you want to create a national scandal in America (harder and harder these days, given the competition) you could even mash some into your guacamole.

---

2 tablespoons pine nuts
400 g dried egg tagliatelle
200 g frozen broad beans
50 ml olive oil
juice and finely grated zest
    of 2 lemons
150 g finely grated parmesan

EVEN EASIER

Skip the broad beans and add torn rocket and basil when you are tossing the pasta in the emulsion – there should be just enough heat to slightly wilt the leaves. Most green veg would work well here too: try grated raw zucchini (courgette), blanched purple sprouting broccoli or just-wilted spinach. Of course mint would be superb with this dish, but then I say that about almost everything.

Set a dry frying pan over medium heat. When it's hot, add the pine nuts and toss for a minute or so, watching them carefully, until they have just taken on some colour. Remove immediately and set aside.

Bring a large pan of salted water to the boil. Add the tagliatelle once you have a good rolling boil going, and cook according to its packet instructions.

Run the frozen broad beans under some hot water from the tap to take them most of the way to thawed, then transfer to a bowl and cover generously with boiling water. Leave them until they are warmed through, then drain and rope in your guests to help you squeeze the beans out of their grey-ish outer skins. Set the lovely bright green beans aside.

Meanwhile, pour your oil into a large bowl, preferably metal, but otherwise heavy ceramic. Add the olive oil and half of the lemon juice, then whisk until smooth, adding about 3-4 tablespoons of the pasta-cooking water to bring it together.

Now whisk in the lemon zest, followed by the cheese in three lots, whisking in between each one, and adding the rest of the lemon juice as you go. You should end up with what looks like a slightly curdled, creamy sauce.

Once the pasta is cooked, drain it and then get it straight into your bowl with the lemon sauce and toss it as you would a salad. Sprinkle the broad beans and pine nuts on top, then serve right away, with a very good grinding of black pepper.

Stay for lunch

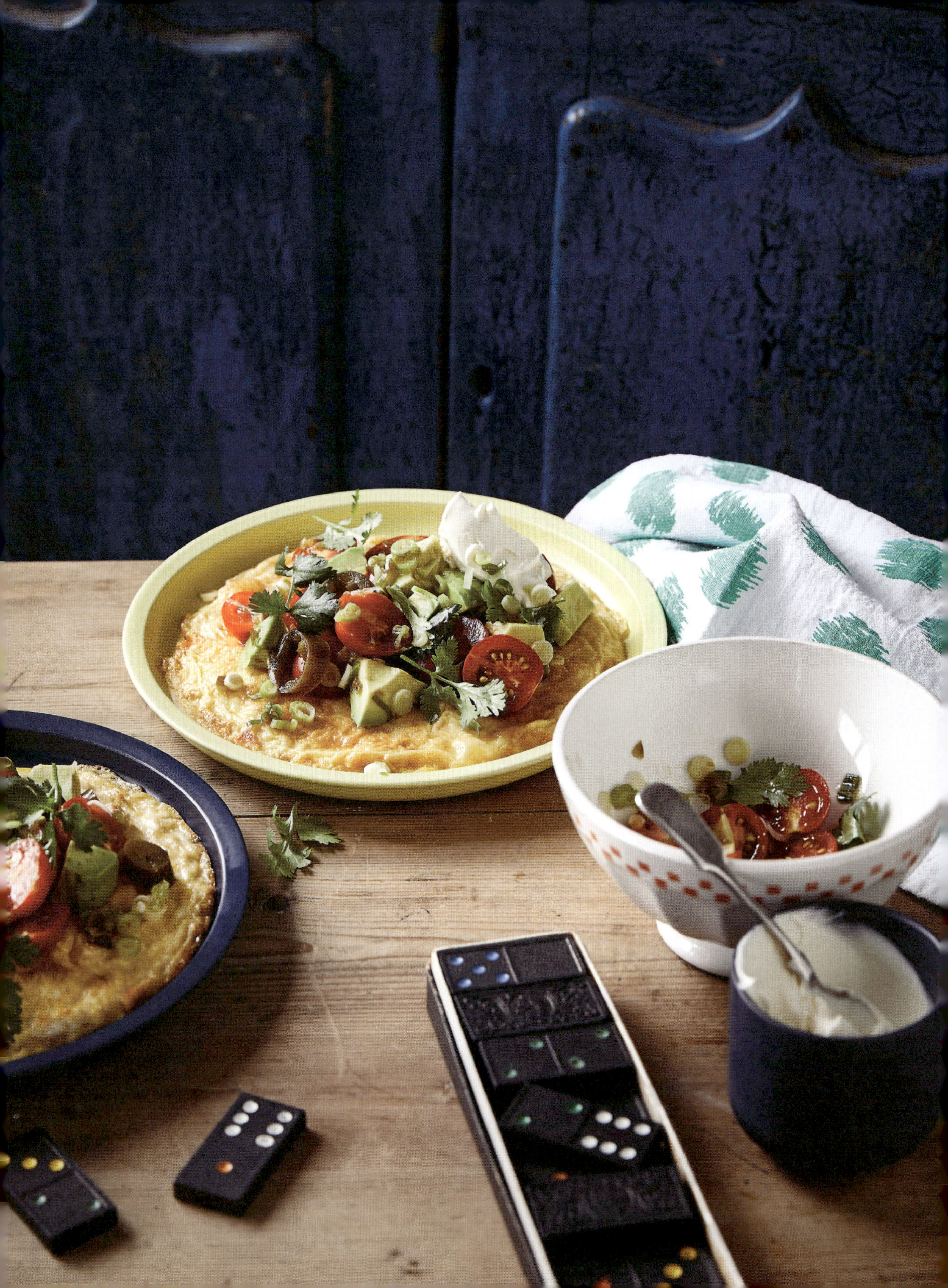

FLATBREAD OMELETTE WITH LIME & TOMATO SALSA

SERVES 2

When it comes to the supermarket tortilla wrap, there are two paths: exploit its convenience and have a packet in your cupboard at all times, or engage with the question of how or why a foodstuff can have such a long and unrefrigerated shelf life. We are in the first camp, heaven help us both. Here the flatbread lifts a few beaten eggs beyond omelette to crispy quick lunch snack (or a dinner, of which you might want to eat quite a lot). The only absolute requirement here is that you have a frying pan with roughly the same internal circumference as the round tortilla wrap. I remember Wendy making this dish – with a milder salsa – for her toddler daughter in London, and I'm not proud of how many bits I nicked from that kid's plate. Maybe because it looks slightly like pizza, most children just seem to gobble it down, no questions asked, so don't overlook this as a quick dinner for the kids.

---

2 tortilla wraps (or similar round flatbread)
4 eggs
butter, for greasing
60–100 g grated cheddar
sour cream, to serve

TOMATO SALSA
150 g cherry tomatoes, cut in half
1–2 spring onions, finely chopped
½ avocado, diced
3–6 pickled jalapeño slices from a jar, finely chopped
handful of coriander, roughly chopped
juice of ½ lime
dash of olive oil

EVEN EASIER
You don't have to make the salsa – you can just top your omelette with a few slices of tomato, a handful of rocket, a dab of tapenade or pesto, or even some thinly sliced ham with a little wholegrain mustard.

First of all, make the salsa by putting all the ingredients into a bowl and gently tossing together.

Have your tortilla wraps out and ready, as you'll need to work quite fast once you start cooking. Break the eggs into a bowl, season with a pinch of salt, and mix until just combined. Place a frying pan that is pretty close to the same size as the tortilla wraps over medium heat. Add a generous knob of butter and when it is sizzling, pour in half of the beaten egg and immediately sprinkle over the grated cheese. Then, while the egg is still runny, drop a tortilla wrap on top – the uncooked egg and melting cheese will glue the omelette to the wrap.

When you think the omelette is almost cooked through, take a large dinner plate and hold it firmly over the top of the frying pan while you deftly invert the pan (and plate), so that the omelette falls, tortilla-side down, onto the plate. Now carefully slide the construction back into the hot pan, tortilla-side down, so that the tortilla crisps up and the egg finishes cooking: use a spatula to lift the edges of the tortilla to see how well it is browning up underneath. When it's done to your liking, slide it out onto a plate. Repeat with the remaining beaten egg and tortilla wrap.

Serve the omelettes topped with the salsa and some sour cream.

MAKE IT GLUTEN-FREE
Use corn tortillas.

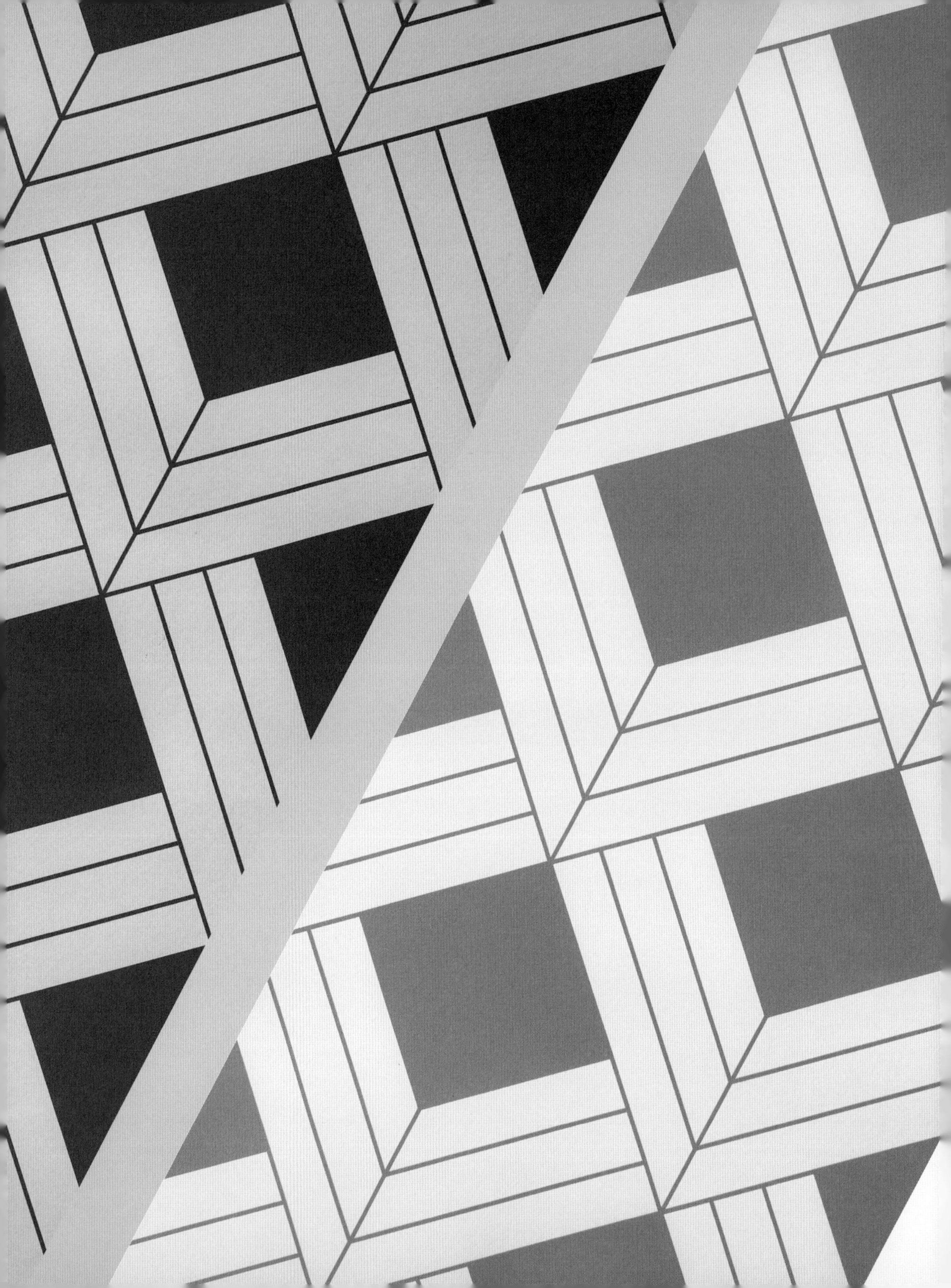

Here's one I prepared earlier

Think about what you want when you're invited for a meal at someone's home. Is it a flight of exquisite multi-element small plates? Or soufflé or steak tartare? No, probably not. Those dishes are for restaurants to provide. You want your host's company and chat, and to feel they're having as much fun as you are. So, give your guests what they really want: your unharried attention and time. Have the food prepared in advance, so there is - at most - only minutes of preparation needed when the guests arrive.

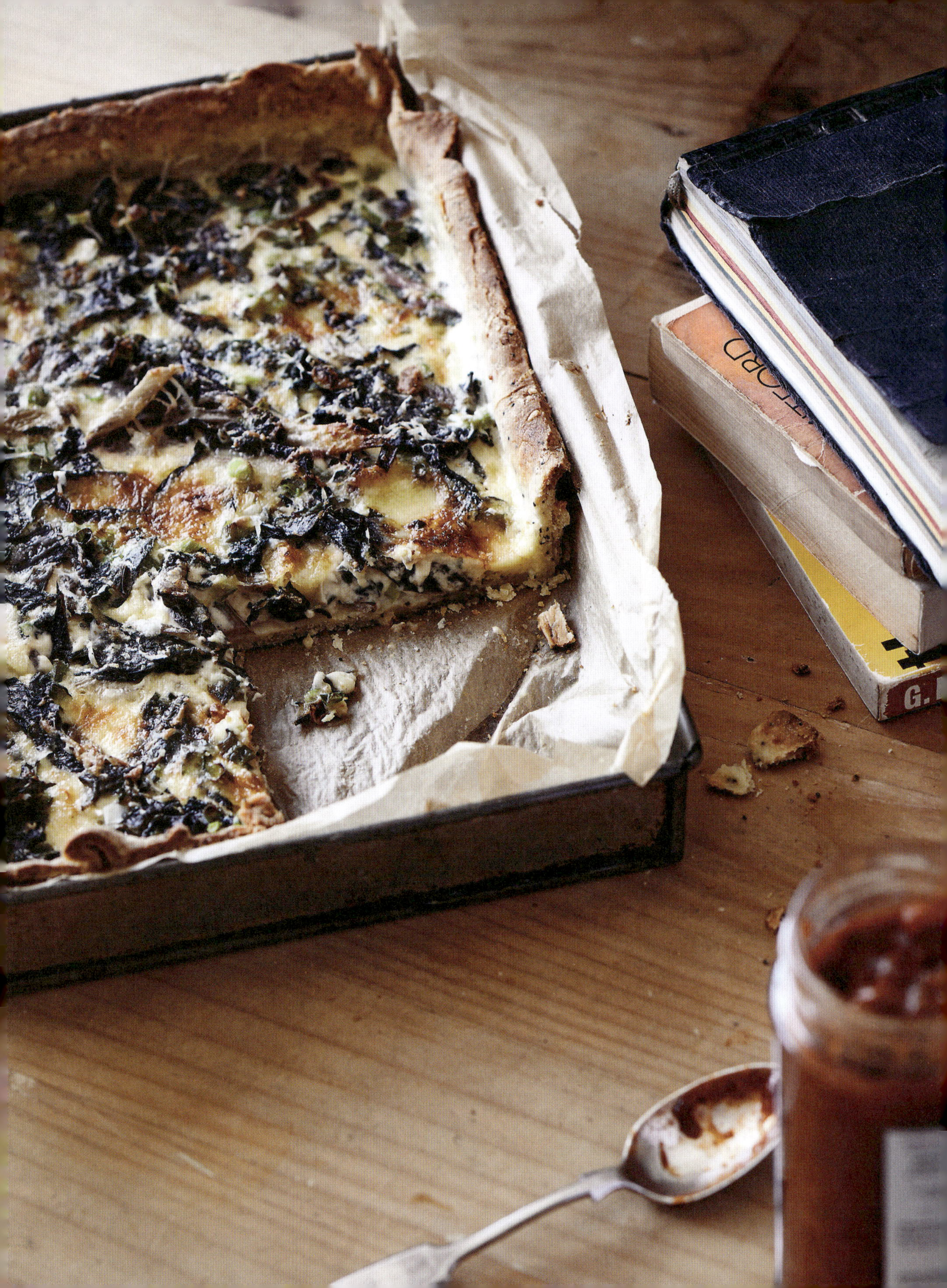

CHARD & CHEESE TART WITH POPPY-SEED PASTRY

SERVES 6

If you go to the effort of making pastry from scratch, you'll soon remember why you used to love tarts. And your guests will feel very, very loved, as the result differs so vastly from the stodgy throat-stickers in supermarkets. Scratch pastry is another country. And once you get the hang of it (if you haven't already), you can whistle up this tart in an hour, with nothing more to do when your guests arrive. The cheese in the pastry adds richness and the poppy seeds give it a crunchy edge. There's also vodka in it. This is not designed to maximise your chances of penning a gloomy play about ducks flying to Moscow. Vodka is included because alcohol - unlike water - does not aid in the formation of gluten, and is thus less likely to land you with tough pastry.

The tart filling is also great for using up those nubbly ends of cheese knocking around in the door of your fridge. Curd cheeses and hard cheeses give the best results: cheddar and parmesan are a good mix, and a bit of hard goat's cheese is excellent, but use white soft-rind cheeses (brie and friends) sparingly, as they can become oily when cooked.

---

250 g (1⅔ cups) plain flour
100 g cold butter, cubed
40 g cheddar, grated
½ tablespoon poppy seeds
1 egg, lightly beaten
1 tablespoon milk
1–2 tablespoons vodka, chilled
mild salad leaves and chutney, to serve

FILLING
200 g Swiss chard (silverbeet) - rainbow, if possible
4 spring onions, thinly sliced into rounds
300 ml cream
2 large eggs, beaten
100 g curd or hard cheese
2 tablespoons finely grated parmesan

To make the pastry, put the flour into a large bowl, then use your fingertips (or a food processor) to rub the butter into the flour until it resembles breadcrumbs. Stir in the cheddar and poppy seeds. Add the egg and milk and work the dough into a ball, using as much of the ice-cold vodka as needed to make it pliable. Roll out the pastry and use it to line a rectangular tin about 30 cm x 20 cm. Chill in the fridge for at least 20 minutes to allow the pastry to settle.

Preheat the oven to 200°C (180°C fan). Line your tart shell with baking paper and ceramic baking beans (or dried beans) and blind-bake for 15 minutes, then remove the beans and paper and give the tart shell another 5 minutes in the oven to crisp up. Set aside to cool.

Meanwhile, for the filling, wash the chard well - it is a tenacious hider of grit - then trim off any really dry bits, keeping as much of the stems as possible. Plunge the chard into a pan of boiling water for a few minutes, then refresh under cold water and wring it out like a sponge to get out as much water as possible. Roughly chop, give it another squeeze (any excess moisture will make your tart soggy) and put in a bowl. Add the spring onions, cream, eggs and whatever cheese you are employing - some grated and some cut into cubes.

Tip the filling into the cooled tart case, sprinkle with parmesan and bake for 20 minutes or until just set. Serve with salad and chutney.

STUFFED PEPPERS WITH FETA & BEANS

SERVES 4 AS A MAIN, OR 8 AS A SIDE

This is such a cheery, colourful and dead-easy dish: peppers stuffed with salty feta, then baked with creamy white beans. You can make it using ordinary peppers but hands-down the best result is with the long kind, which come in red, green and sometimes a pale greeny-yellow. This is now on high rotation in my kitchen - it can be prepped ahead of time, looks nice on the table, and works perfectly as a stand-alone meal, served with couscous or bread, or as a foil to a huge leg of roast lamb.

---

2 leeks, pale parts only, thinly sliced
1 garlic clove, crushed
olive oil, for cooking
½ teaspoon coriander seeds
2 x 400 g tins of cannellini or other white beans, rinsed and drained
150 g green olives (optional)
handful of flat-leaf parsley leaves, chopped
splash of white wine, stock or water
8 long peppers (capsicums), red or yellow, or a mix
2 x 200 g blocks of feta
250 g cherry tomatoes, cut in half, or 3 vine-ripened tomatoes, roughly diced
3 tablespoons pistachios, flaked almonds or pumpkin seeds, toasted
handful of chopped dill

HERB SAUCE - OPTIONAL

4 tablespoons Greek-style yoghurt
juice of ½ lemon
2 tablespoons finely chopped mint, dill and/or coriander (or ½ teaspoon dried mint)

In a sturdy roasting tin or large ovenproof frying pan set over medium heat, fry the leek and garlic in a generous amount of olive oil for 2-3 minutes until the leeks have softened. Stir in the coriander seeds and fry for another minute or so, then add the beans, olives and parsley and mix everything together.

If you've got some white wine on the go, you can sacrifice a splash of it to the pan at this point; otherwise, add a dash of stock or water. Spread out the bean mixture evenly in your roasting tin, or transfer from the frying pan to an ovenproof dish.

To prepare the peppers, cut off the tops - just a centimetre or so below the stem - and use your fingers to clear out as many seeds as you can. Cut each block of feta into five strips. And here is where the advantage of using long peppers instead of the more bulbous sort becomes apparent: push a strip of feta inside each pepper and it should fit perfectly. Very satisfying for neat freaks. Lay the peppers on top of the beans and crumble the last two strips of feta over the top, then scatter over the tomatoes. Set aside until you're ready to bake - if that's more than a couple of hours away, pop it in the fridge.

If you want to serve the herb sauce with your stuffed peppers, simply mix together all the ingredients and refrigerate until needed.

About an hour before serving time, preheat the oven to 180°C (160°C fan). Drizzle the peppers and tomatoes with olive oil, season with a pinch of salt, and bake for 40-50 minutes. The peppers should look defeated and collapsed - but appetising! They'll be fine kept warm in a 160°C (140°C fan) oven for a bit longer, but you may need to add a small splash more wine, stock or water to stop them from drying out.

To serve, remove from the oven and leave to sit for 5 minutes. If using the herb sauce, flick it in frantic zigzags across the top, then sprinkle with the toasted nuts or pumpkin seeds and finish with a scattering of dill and a good grinding of pepper.

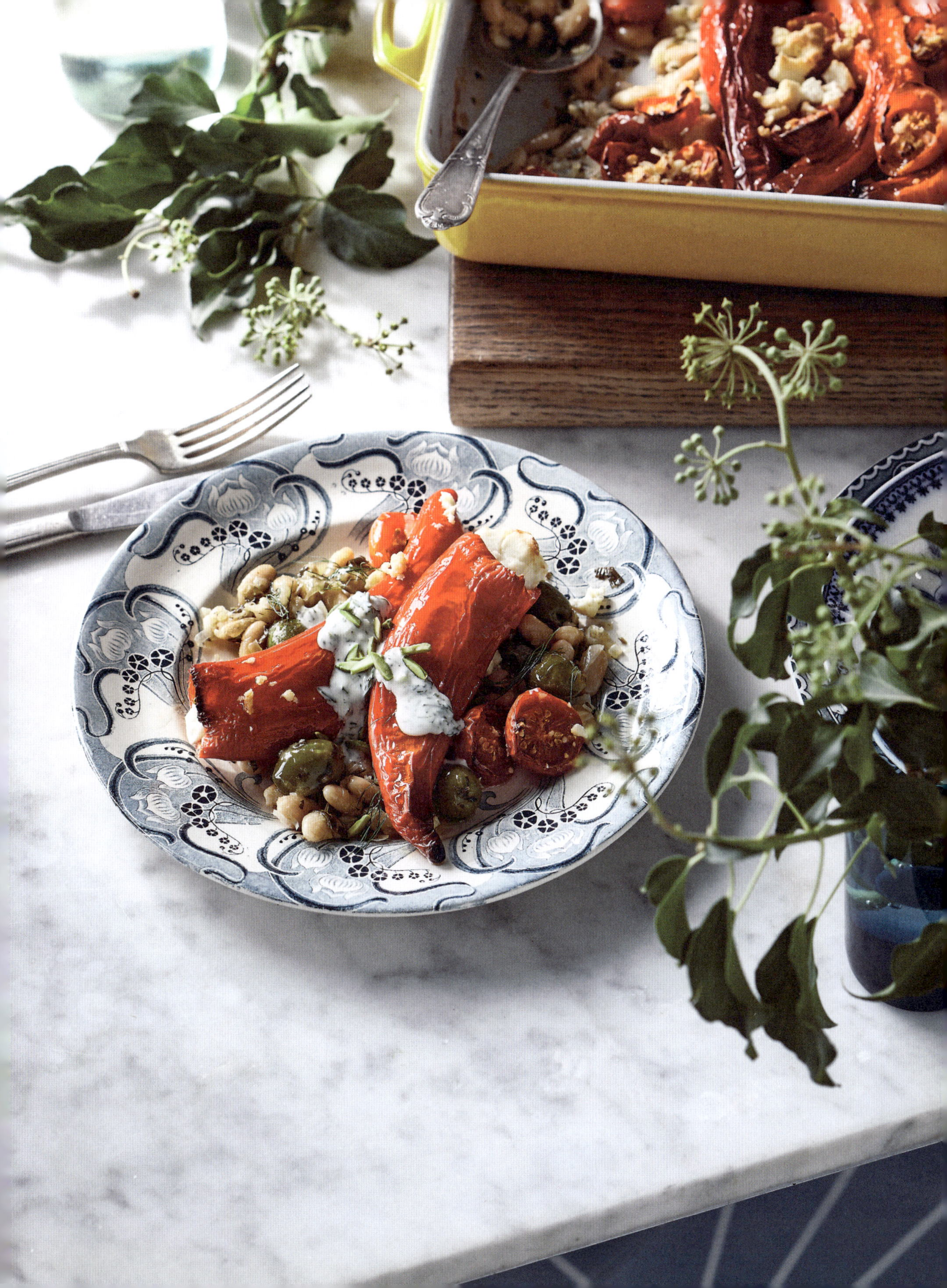

FUSS-FREE SALMON BURGERS

SERVES 4

The homemade burger for guests – it sounds so easy, right? But, catering-wise, it can be a real banana skin. You start out with a vision of simplicity and then, before you know it, you're frantically chopping various fillings and shaking squeezy bottles of sauce with increasing urgency, while half-assembled burgers cool as you try to remember who wanted cheese, and who's freaked out by pickles. Well, all that's in the past now. This is your burger future: a streamlined salmon version that wants for nothing in the taste department and collapses all the contents and condiments into one seamless pan-to-bun action.

A cross between some Jamie Oliver fishcakes that somehow never quite stay together like they do on the telly and a Peter Gordon dish of scallops with chilli jam and crème fraîche, these salmon patties can be pre-cooked and reheated, for easy assembly.

If you are scaling up for a larger crowd, do the chopping of your salmon in batches. Trying to mush up more than half a kilo of fish on one chopping board is a bit icky.

---

1 stalk lemongrass (tender white part only)
1 kaffir lime leaf
1 garlic clove
1.5 cm ginger
zest of ½ lime
2 tablespoons chopped coriander stalks (keep the leaves to garnish)
500 g salmon fillet, skin off
pinch of salt
neutral-flavoured oil, for frying
4 burger buns
4 iceberg lettuce leaves
4 teaspoons sweet chilli sauce
4 heaped teaspoons sour cream

Take your biggest chopping board and chop the lemongrass and lime leaf as finely as you can. Finely grate the garlic, ginger and lime zest over the lemongrass and scatter with the coriander stalks, then scrape it all up into a small pile to one side of the chopping board. Now cut the salmon into 1 cm cubes and set about half of it aside. Work the lemongrass mixture into the rest of the salmon, along with the salt, chopping everything together as you go, so that you arrive at a chunky, flavoursome paste. Mix in the reserved salmon cubes until just combined. Use your (clean!) hands to bring the mix together into four equal-sized round patties, then set aside on a plate lined with baking paper and chill until you want to cook them.

When you're ready to make your fish burgers, preheat the oven to 160°C (140°C fan). Cut the burger buns in half, sit them on a baking tray and pop in the oven to warm gently for about 5 minutes. Arrange the whole lettuce leaves on a serving plate.

The secret to cooking the salmon patties is a non-stick frying pan, and leaving them alone until they have formed a crust. Get your pan quite hot and add just a dash of oil, then wipe off most of it with paper towel (the oil from the fish, and the non-stick surface, should be enough to keep the patties from sticking). Carefully add your salmon patties, but don't be tempted to move them around the pan or fiddle with them for at least the first minute of cooking.

When the underside has developed a good, crisp crust, gently flip them over. And here is where you will realise that, in the fish-burger game, some days you win, and some days you lose. And that is exactly why we are going to hide the results of this endeavour in a burger bun. So if there are fissures and cracks in your patties, or they fall apart, don't worry. Cook for another few minutes, until crisp and golden on the other side.

If you're serving these right away, drizzle some sweet chilli sauce over the salmon patties in the pan and let it drip down the sides and sizzle away. Dollop a spoonful of sour cream on top of each one, then sprinkle with the coriander leaves.

(If you're preparing ahead, transfer the just-cooked salmon patties to a lined baking tray and refrigerate for up to a few hours until you are ready to eat. Slide them into a preheated 240°C (220°fan) oven for 5 minutes, then drizzle with chilli sauce and give them another couple of minutes. Slip the burger buns onto the bottom shelf to warm at the same time. Remove everything from the oven and add the sour cream and coriander leaves to the patties.)

To serve, bring the frying pan or baking tray of salmon patties to the table, along with the plate of lettuce leaves and the warm burger buns. Let people grab a roll and a lettuce leaf, then you just need to make the rounds popping an ooey-gooey patty into each roll and your work is done. Have a pile of paper towels to hand, because these things are messy.

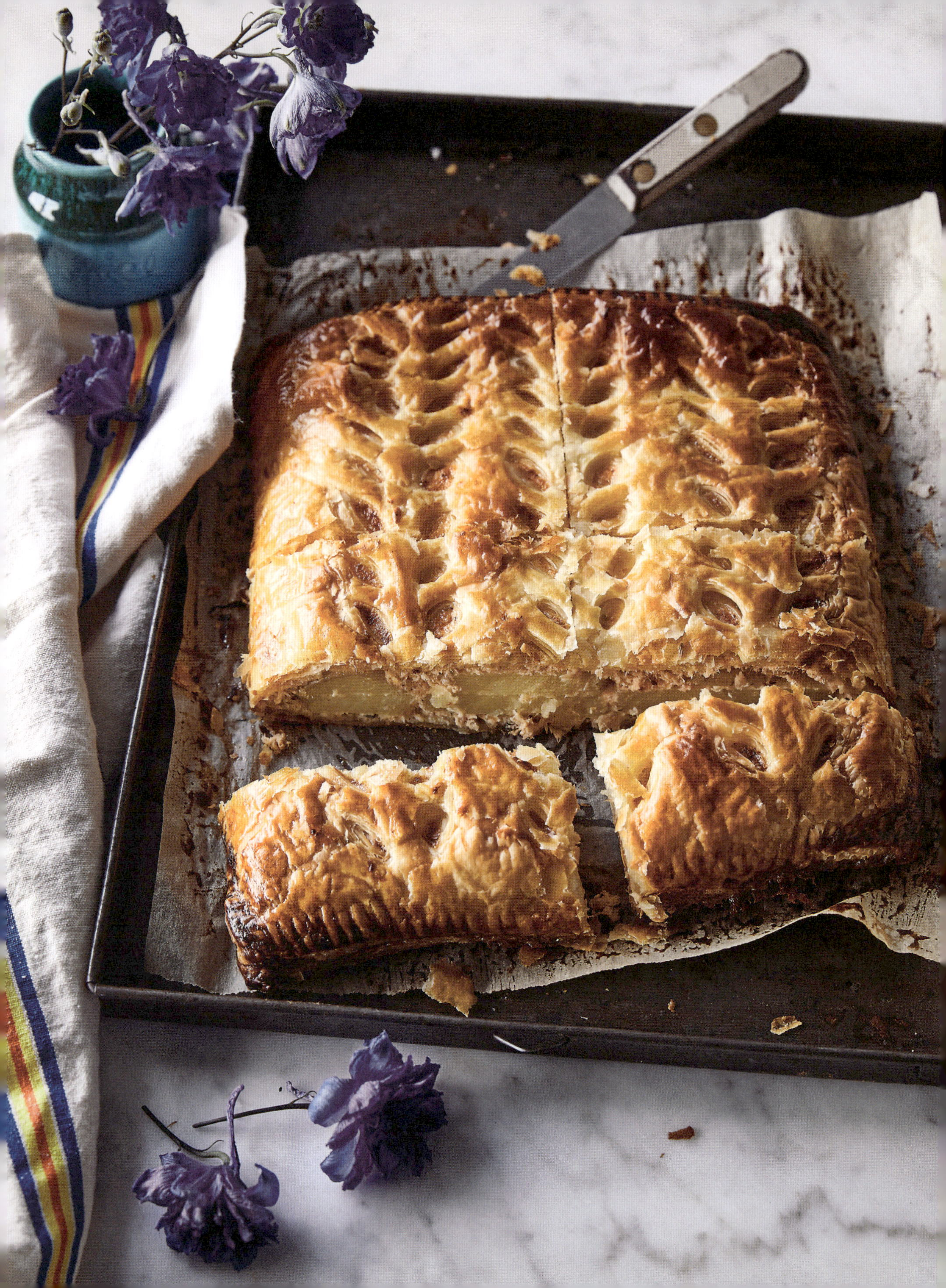

SALMON & FENNEL PIE

SERVES 4 GENEROUSLY

Hot-smoked salmon - available from most supermarkets these days - is an extremely convenient thing to have in the fridge. It can be flaked into a simple salad or pasta, or mashed into rillettes. Here, tarted up with fennel seeds, it provides the backbone for a tremendously easy pie, which can be prepared in advance, kept in the fridge for up to 24 hours and then slid into the oven half an hour before you're planning to eat. Cut it up at the table and augment with green beans and a salad of baby spinach or rocket.

---

500 g (about 6 medium) potatoes, dutch cream or similar
300 g hot-smoked salmon (if you want to try making your own, there's a recipe on page 184)
200 g crème fraîche or sour cream
2 eggs
1 teaspoon horseradish cream sauce
1 teaspoon fennel seeds, toasted in a dry pan then crushed
finely grated zest of ½ lemon
2 sheets all-butter puff pastry
1 spring onion, thinly sliced into rounds
large handful of dill fronds, finely chopped
1 egg yolk, whisked with 1 teaspoon water

Boil the whole, unpeeled potatoes until they're cooked, about 25 minutes. Drain and set aside until cool enough to handle.

Meanwhile, in a food processor or blender, whizz the salmon, crème fraîche, eggs, horseradish, fennel seeds and lemon zest to a thick paste.

On a baking tray lined with baking paper, lay out a sheet of puff pastry and spread half of the salmon mixture over it, leaving a 1.5 cm border all round the edges. Season with salt and pepper, then sprinkle over the spring onion and dill. Slice the potatoes into 1 cm thick rounds and lay them on top, overlapping like fish scales. Spread the rest of the salmon mix over the potatoes. Brush the pastry border with egg wash and lay the second sheet of pastry over the top, tucking it around the filling and pressing down on the edges to seal.

Now, if you're the sort that loves a fancy decorated lid to your pie (pastry fish, leaves, cherubim or whatever), then go for it. For this pie, I tend to just use the tip of a knife to make small diagonal slits in a pleasing pattern. Whatever you decide, don't forget to brush the whole thing with egg wash before baking.

When you're ready to cook the pie, preheat the oven to 200°C (180°C fan). Bake for about 25 minutes or until puffed up and deep golden. Check that the bottom is crisp too - if it's soggy, use the baking paper to help you slide the pie off the baking tray and sit the pie (still on its baking paper) directly on the oven rack to crisp for a few minutes.

Here's one I prepared earlier

TURMERIC FRIED FISH WITH NOODLES

SERVES 6

Do you ever seriously address the question of which cuisine you would spend the rest of your life eating, if you had to confine yourself to a single one? I think about it a lot, and I reckon in the end – after substantial culinary dithering – I would plump for Vietnamese food. I love the freshness of it, and the way the Vietnamese sometimes just king-hit you with a totally left-field combination of ingredients. Dill and turmeric, for example. Where the hell did that come from? And yet it's the dill and turmeric that make this fried fish dish so wonderful – complemented by the salty, sweet, sour, spiky and eminently quaffable national sauce that is nuoc cham. Like many travellers to Hanoi, Jeremy and I went to Cha Ca La Vong, a famous restaurant in the old town where only one dish is served. This one. The sizzling pan of golden crunchy fried fish, the deep green of the spring onions and dill, the deep thrill of not having to choose anything; now there's a great restaurant. Later I found out that Penny Wong came back from a trip to Vietnam similarly obsessed, and we've had a number of happy conversations about it since.

You can prepare all the constituent elements of this dish (pictured over the page) before your guests arrive. Cook the noodles, oil them lightly with a flavourless oil like vegetable or rice bran, then leave them in a colander under a clean tea towel. Cut the fish into chunks. Make your turmeric and rice flour blend. Chop the spring onions and herbs. Toast the peanuts and make your dressing. Now you're ready to cook and go.

---

100 g (⅔ cup) salted peanuts
200 g dried rice vermicelli noodles
10 spring onions
large bunch of dill
600 g firm white fish fillets
   (I usually use ling)
80 g (½ cup) rice flour
1 tablespoon ground turmeric
200 ml rice bran oil

NUOC CHAM SAUCE
2 tablespoons grated palm sugar
4 tablespoons fish sauce
3 tablespoons rice vinegar
3 tablespoons lime juice
1 chilli, thinly sliced

First, make the nuoc cham. Warm 125 ml (½ cup) water in a small saucepan and dissolve the palm sugar in it. Take off the heat and transfer to a small serving bowl. When it has cooled a little, stir in the fish sauce, rice vinegar, lime juice and chilli. Taste: it should be deep and salty, but also sweet and acidic.

Toast the peanuts in a dry frying pan, stirring regularly, until brown. Tip into a small bowl and set aside. Next, cook the vermicelli noodles according to the packet instructions: usually, all they need is a quick dunk in boiling water.

Cut the green parts of the spring onions, and the dill, into 2 cm lengths, then place in a bowl. Slice the white parts of the onions more finely, into 3 mm rounds, and add them to the bowl.

Have your nuoc cham, peanuts, noodles and greens all set out in their bowls on the table.

Now for the fish. Cut it into chunks – maybe 5 cm by 2 cm. Dredge with the combined rice flour and turmeric: the easiest way to do this is to put the flour and spice into a snap-lock bag and heave the fish chunks into it, then shake until they're evenly coated.

Pour the oil into a skillet or heavy-based frying pan. Heat until an experimental piece of spring onion sizzles vigorously when dropped in. If you are thinking at this stage that this is a lot of oil to be using: yes it is, and that's just the way things are. This is not a slender dish but, by god, you won't mind when you eat it.

Put the fish into the pan. Let it crisp up a bit before turning, and don't turn it too often; you want the fish to get good and golden and crunchy. The oil will turn a vibrant yellow from the turmeric. Once you've got a fine crunch going, you're ready to serve.

Take the sizzling skillet to the table. Dump in the spring onions and dill and toss them through the hot oil. They will wilt and combine with the fish and the golden oil.

Now all your guests have to do is help themselves to a pile of noodles and a spoonful of golden fish and greens, then augment with a sprinkling of peanuts and nuoc cham, which will combine with the oil from the fish to make a delicious, beautifully coloured dressing.

The original Hanoi restaurant aggressively maximises the crunchy bits by setting the hot skillet over a table-top burner, so that the flakes of fish left behind continue to cook in the oil. I think this is eminently sensible, but if your kitchen infrastructure doesn't run to portable burners, just keep it simple.

EVEN EASIER

For this dish – with its volumes of chopped spring onions and dill – slide a sheet of newspaper under the board first. Scrape off any waste from your chopping board as you work (spring onion top and tails, dill stalks), straight on to the paper. Once you are finished, wrap the whole lot up in the paper for the compost heap, or tip the sheet of paper's contents into your food-waste bin.

< TURMERIC
FRIED FISH
WITH NOODLES

PIEROGI
RUSSKI >

PIEROGI RUSSKI

MAKES ABOUT 24

My friend Dan and I travelled around Poland for a good stint in the mid-nineties and quickly learned all the Polish words for 'vegetarian': there aren't many, and in Poland at that time you needed every one of them. The potato was our dear friend; the Poles really know how to handle themselves around a tuber. They also - like many of their geographical neighbours - are devoted to the fresh curd and farm-style cheeses that power their dumplings and cakes. I'd always assumed that pierogi russki, a satisfying dish of potato and cheese dumplings served with sour cream and fried onions, had something to do with Russia. Not so, apparently. But for a comforting dish that can be made in advance, it's a winner. And, as you'll see from the photo on the previous page, it's also very suitable for children going through that weird 'white food' stage. Leave out the dill and fried onions, and this dish is whiter than *The Australian*'s opinion page.

---

1 kg floury potatoes, washed, skins on
150 g ricotta, drained
100 g feta
good pinch of white pepper
40 g butter
2 brown onions, finely diced
100 g sour cream
chopped dill, to serve

PIEROGI DOUGH
300 g (2 cups) plain flour
1 teaspoon salt
1 egg
about 250 ml (1 cup) lukewarm water
1 tablespoon olive oil

Preheat the oven to 220°C (200°C fan). Put your potatoes in a dry roasting tin (no oil, no nothing) and bake for about an hour or until cooked through - test them with a skewer from time to time. When they're done, let them cool until you can comfortably pick them up.

Meanwhile, make your pierogi dough. Put the flour, salt and egg in the bowl of a stand mixer and use the dough hook to combine, gradually adding the water and ending with the oil. If you don't have a mixer, use a spoon for this and come to terms with the fact that you're going to have to get your hands in there to knead it and get messy! When you have a smooth dough, cover and leave to rest for 20 minutes.

Now turn back to your warm potatoes. Slice each one in half lengthways, and use a sharp-edged teaspoon to scoop out the insides into a bowl. (If you have time on your side, do this extra-carefully to leave a couple of millimetres of potato flesh attached to the skins, for exciting reasons outlined opposite. But let's not get distracted.) Add the ricotta, feta and pepper and mash with the potato flesh until everything is incorporated.

Set a frying pan over low heat and add the butter. When it is sizzling, add the onions and sauté, stirring regularly, until soft and golden. Remove half and stir into the bowl with the potato and cheese - this is your completed pierogi filling. Keep cooking the remaining onions over low heat, stirring every now and again to prevent catching. Once nicely caramelised, they will be the garnish for your dumplings.

Okay: pierogi time! Put a large pan of salted water on to boil.

Cut the dough in half. Roll out half on a floured board to about 2 mm thick. Use a round cutter (mine is about 8 cm in diameter) to cut out circles. Take a teaspoonful of the filling and lay it on one side of the circle, then fold the other side over to make a semicircle and press the edges together firmly to seal, moistening with water if necessary. Repeat until you've used up all the dough and filling: you should get around two dozen pierogi.

Working in batches, drop the pierogi into the boiling water – they're done when they float to the surface. Lift them out one by one with a slotted spoon.

If you're feeding a crowd, toss the pierogi in sour cream (they just need a light coating) and pile onto a platter, then top with the caramelised onions and some chopped dill.

If you're prepping ahead, just cook the pierogi and arrange them in a single layer on a lined baking tray in the fridge, where they'll keep well for a day or two. Or freeze them for a few months! When you want to deploy them, simply defrost and then plunge into boiling water for a minute or two to heat through.

CRISPY POTATO SKINS

Don't throw out the potato skins. They will make a crispy treat that will enhance your household standing enormously. Just slice the skins into wedges and toss them with a little olive oil, lemon zest, black pepper and salt. Or one of the flavoured butters from page 40! Crisp them up on a baking-paper-lined tray in a 220°C (200°C fan) oven. If you can't be bothered making these crispy potato skins right away, stash them in the freezer until the moment arises. As it surely will.

Here's one I prepared earlier

SLOW-ROASTED TOMATO PAPPARDELLE WITH OLIVE TAPENADE

SERVES 4

It is a perfectly respectable thing to have a favourite restaurant where a person, despite being an adventurous and curious eater, orders the same dish every single time simply because it is So. Damn. Good. Focaccia #2 at the Amalfi Pizzeria Ristorante in Adelaide is that over-and-over dish for both of us – and thank you to them for keeping it on the menu for more than twenty years. It has a super-generous slathering of olive tapenade (tastes a bit kalamata-ish to me) with basil and fresh tomato. And here it is celebrated via a modest recreation of the tapenade on top of what may well be the easiest dish in the book.

30–50 ml olive oil
4 tasty large tomatoes
10 cherry tomatoes
8 large garlic cloves, unpeeled
400 g fresh pappardelle
75 ml cream
plenty of shaved parmesan

OLIVE TAPENADE
50 g kalamata olives
25 g rocket
handful of basil leaves
1 anchovy fillet

MAKE IT GLUTEN-FREE
If you can get your hands on a really good wheat-free potato gnocchi, swap it with the pasta for a delicious, and coincidentally gluten-free, alternative.

Preheat the oven to 170°C (150°C fan). Take a large deep baking tray or roasting tin and pour in a very generous amount of olive oil – you want a visible layer in the bottom. Cut the large tomatoes into wedges and lay them, skin-side down, in the oil, then throw in the cherry tomatoes. Rub some olive oil over the skin of the garlic cloves, add them to the tomatoes and give everything a good sprinkling of salt. Tuck the tray away in the oven for about 40 minutes. If you are making this ahead, let the slow-roasted tomatoes and garlic cool and then refrigerate them – they'll be fine for 2 or 3 days.

When you are ready to serve, put the tomato tray into a preheated 180°C (160°C fan) oven for about 5–7 minutes to warm up, and bring a large pot of salted water to boil for the pappardelle.

Take the tray of warm tomatoes out of the oven and use the back of a fork to squish out all the gooey garlic goodness from the skins (discard the skins and any green shoots), then mash the garlic into the tomatoes, which will release a whole lot of very tasty juices. Prick the cherry tomatoes a few times before you squash them – the cheeky blighters will squirt everywhere given half a chance.

For the tapenade, pit the olives, then roughly chop the flesh with the rocket, basil and anchovy on a big board until you have a coarse paste – this should only take a few minutes.

Once the pappardelle is cooked, drain off most of the cooking water (a little of this starchy water will help the sauce to cling to the pasta), then tip into the tray of squished tomatoes. Splash the cream on top and use two wooden spoons to gently toss the pappardelle with the cream, tomatoes and garlic. Distribute the tapenade over the pasta and serve with a self-service pepper grinder and lots of parmesan.

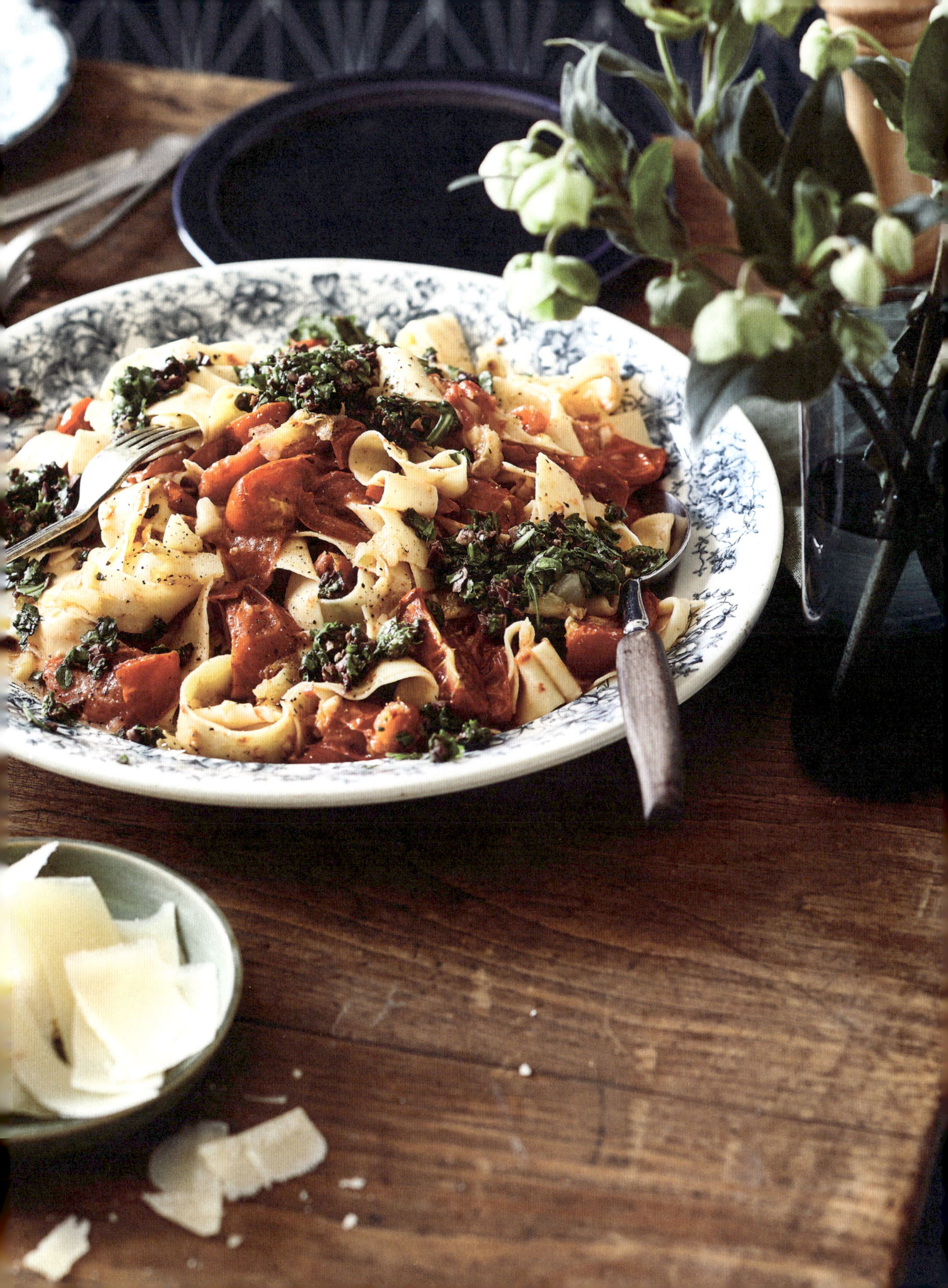

MARINATED TOFU WITH SOY BEANS & PICKLED CABBAGE

SERVES 4

Adelaideans may know this dish as 'BBC', from the much-loved and iconic restaurant Ying Chow, and will completely understand our need to recreate it while living outside the festival state. BBC stands for Broad bean, Bean curd and Chinese chutney. No one seems to quibble with this name, even though the dish doesn't contain any broad beans at all; the Ying Chow original is a bright mix of spicy soy beans, thin slivers of marinated tofu, and some very tasty greens. This version (pictured over the page) isn't quite as it appears in its Gouger Street home, but it still has the two key elements of marinated tofu and a topping of hot and tangy soy beans and pickles. Both are jolly quick to make and - if you can get into the habit of keeping some pickled Chinese cabbage close to hand - easy to muster at a moment's notice. The preparation can be done in advance, leaving little more than ten minutes of baking/reheating between you and getting dinner on the table.

---

1 x 280–300 g block of firm tofu
250 g frozen podded soy beans (edamame)
2 tablespoons neutral-flavoured oil
5 garlic cloves, finely chopped
4 spring onions, thinly sliced into rounds (including quite a bit of the green parts)
2 red chillies, finely chopped (and deseeded, if you like)
100 g (½ tin) pickled Chinese cabbage or mustard greens (from Asian grocers)
handful of chopped coriander, stalks and leaves kept separate
steamed rice and lime wedges, to serve

TOFU MARINADE
1 teaspoon finely grated ginger
juice of 1 lime
1 tablespoon tamari sauce
1 tablespoon neutral-flavoured oil

Cut the block of tofu horizontally into four sheets, place on a double thickness of paper towel (or a clean tea towel) and cover with the same. Sit something weighty on top - like a chopping board - and leave for 10-20 minutes to press out any excess water.

Meanwhile, make up the marinade by mixing together all the ingredients in a small bowl.

Transfer the drained tofu sheets to a dish that will hold them in a single layer. Pour the marinade over the top, lifting up the tofu so that the marinade might sneak underneath. Cover and leave to marinate in the fridge for a few hours, or overnight.

Tip your frozen soy beans into a large heatproof bowl and pour over enough boiling water from the kettle to cover them and start the defrosting. They will have already been cooked, so you need only to warm them up. Meanwhile, set a wok or frying pan over medium heat. Add the oil, and when it's hot, stir-fry the garlic, spring onions and chillies: slightly browned garlic is fine here, but you need to keep everything moving to stop the garlic becoming burnt and bitter. Once you have a tinge of colour to the garlic and the pan is smelling very good, add the well-drained soy beans and give them a few minutes, stirring every now and then, until they are hot.

Drain the pickled cabbage, squeezing out as much liquid as you can, then chop it into small pieces and stir it through. (Since the little dark green pickle-y parts are the bits I end up chasing around the plate at Ying Chow, I usually use an entire tin. I realise that quite so much pickled cabbage is not to everyone's taste, but stay open to the idea of adding some more...)

All the elements of the dish are now ready and will wait happily for a few hours. When you are good to go, lift the tofu sheets out of their marinade onto a lined baking tray and cook in a preheated 200°C (180°C fan) oven for 10 minutes.

Gently reheat the soy beans and pickles, throwing the excess marinade into the pan (who would waste that ginger and lime?!) and then stirring in the chopped coriander stems.

To serve, place the tofu on plates, spoon over the soy beans and pickles, and top with the coriander leaves. Serve with some plain rice and lime wedges.

EVEN EASIER
Buy pre-marinated tofu or replace the tofu with a gooey-yolk fried egg and some rice – less elegant, maybe, but highly recommended if you are making this for yourself for a weeknight dinner. Or, if you prefer, spoon the soy bean and pickle topping over a pan-fried fillet of salmon or chicken.

< MARINATED TOFU
WITH SOY BEANS &
PICKLED CABBAGE

CRISPY-SKIN FISH
WITH ROSEMARY &
ANCHOVY CREAM >

CRISPY-SKIN FISH WITH ROSEMARY & ANCHOVY CREAM

SERVES 6

What is the best thing about fish in a restaurant? Crispy skin. Many's the home chef who has wondered why their own private attempts at fish-frying yield skin that is slimy and unappetising, rather than gloriously crunchy like it is on the thirty-bucks-a-serve fish. Moreover, if you're in plan-ahead mode, you might instinctively avoid fish because you have understandable concerns about the feasibility of turning out six perfectly cooked portions all at once. But – with a few tips and some careful planning – it *is* possible.

A quick word about fish. The best candidate here is kingfish, which crisps up beautifully in the pan, as do snapper and barramundi. The finished dish (pictured on the previous page) is best paired with baby potatoes dressed with olive oil and lemon juice.

---

6 x 150 g fillets of white fish, skin on
olive oil, for frying
8 garlic cloves, finely chopped
8 anchovy fillets
2 tablespoons chopped rosemary leaves
150 ml cream
750 g green beans, topped and tailed
250 g cherry tomatoes, cut in half

The key to achieving a crispy skin on your fish is to make sure it is as dry as possible before cooking. Use a knife like a kind of squeegee to press out as much water from the skin of the fish as possible, then pat dry with paper towel. (If you have time, leave the fish uncovered, skin-side up, in the fridge for an hour to dry it out further.)

Right, time for some prep. You don't want to put too much space between cooking fish and serving fish, so plan to do this no longer than just a couple of hours before serving – you'll still have time to wash your dishes, open the windows to get rid of any fish-cooking smells and have a shower before your guests arrive.

Season the fish well with salt and rub on some oil. Add a little oil to a large frying pan, then wipe most of it off with paper towel. When your pan is scalding-hot, even starting to smoke a little, carefully lay in the fish, skin-side down. Don't overcrowd the pan: two fillets at once is probably best.

The most important thing now is not to move the fish – you need to let the skin get crispy first. Use a spatula to gently press the fillets down if they arch up too much when they hit the heat. You will soon see the flesh next to the skin starting to cook through. After about 90 seconds, gently lift out the fillets and lay them, skin-side *up*, on a clean plate. Once all the fish is cooked, refrigerate until needed.

Give the pan a light wipe with paper towel, then add a tiny splash more oil and gently fry the garlic, anchovies and rosemary until fragrant and the anchovies have melted into a paste. Stir in the cream, then decant into a small jug and chill until ready to serve.

About an hour before you want to serve, preheat the oven to 220°C (200°C fan).

Blanch the green beans for 3 minutes in boiling water and refresh in cold water. Spread them out in a higgledy-piggledy manner in a large roasting tin, then scatter over the cherry tomatoes.

Gently reheat the cream sauce and keep warm. Pour half the cream sauce over the beans and tomatoes, along with a splash of boiling water, then give them 5 minutes in the oven. Remove and add the fish, skin-side up, to the hot tangle of steaming beans. Pour in a little more cream sauce, then give it another 5 minutes in the oven, depending on the thickness of your fish: when it's done, the flesh should be opaque all the way through.

Lift out each fillet with a good serving of the green beans and tomatoes underneath (use a spoon for extra sauce), then pass around a jug of the remaining cream sauce.

MORE ANCHOVY IDEAS

A tube of anchovy paste kept in the fridge is an umami shot in the arm for any dips, flavoured butters and sauces. Add a couple of anchovy fillets to a tomato sauce for pasta, pound to a paste and fold through mayonnaise for a punchy salad dressing, or put them right up front and centre in a Provençal pissaladière.

PALERMO PEPPERS ON TOAST

SERVES 4

A riff on the excellent Piedmontese peppers, but with the unmistakable flavours of Sicily, this is the easiest-peasiest standby meal ever. Once prepared and cooked, the peppers will keep in the fridge for a couple of days. In fact, they may be all the better for the sojourn. To serve, all you have to do is reheat gently before sitting them on toast. They're delicious with scrambled or poached eggs, or they can be served over some short pasta, such as penne or rigatoni, with an extra glug of olive oil. What's more, one of these peppers paired with a slice of grilled halloumi in a roll makes an excellent vegetarian burger. All in all, a great standby to have in your repertoire.

---

4 red peppers (capsicums)
8 anchovy fillets
2 garlic cloves, very thinly sliced
1 tablespoon capers (drained well if in brine, rinsed then drained well if salted)
1 tablespoon currants (or sultanas)
16 cherry tomatoes
1 teaspoon chilli flakes – optional
olive oil, for drizzling
1 tablespoon good-quality red wine vinegar (or balsamic vinegar or lemon juice)
toast, mint or rocket leaves and toasted pine nuts, to serve

MAKE IT VEGAN
Replace the anchovies with halved and pitted kalamata olives.

Preheat the oven to 170°C (150°C fan).

Cut each pepper in half lengthways and remove the seeds and membranes. Be careful to leave the outer walls and stem intact, since you want all the delicious juices to stay inside the peppers as they cook.

Lay the peppers, skin-side down, in a lightly oiled baking tray or ovenproof dish. Into each pepper half, put 1 anchovy fillet (ripped into a few pieces), a few slivers of garlic, ½ teaspoon capers, a few currants and some chilli flakes, if using. Cut the cherry tomatoes in half and add 4 to each pepper, squashing them in where you need to. Drizzle a little olive oil over each pepper, then cook in the oven for about an hour or until the peppers have collapsed and each one is harbouring a tasty slick of flavoursome juices.

Remove the roast peppers from the oven and sprinkle a drop or two of red wine vinegar into each one. (The red wine vinegar should be delicious enough to have a small sip on its own without you puckering up your face too much; otherwise, sub in a few drops of nice balsamic or a squeeze of lemon juice). Keep the peppers refrigerated until about an hour before you want to eat. They are best eaten at room temperature or just slightly warmed.

When you are ready to serve, make some toast and place a pepper on top of each slice, being careful not to spill any of the juices - collect and restore with a spoon if you do. Strew with some thinly sliced fresh mint or rocket, and sprinkle with toasted pine nuts. If you are with close friends, encourage them to flip their peppers over so the juices sink into the toast.

ROAST MUSHROOM CANNELLONI

SERVES 4 GENEROUSLY

When he pioneered his famous dish 'The Crunchy Part of the Lasagne', Italian chef Massimo Bottura articulated a deep-seated truth about what we're all really looking for in a baked pasta dish: cheesy, crusty bits.

This mushroom cannelloni has all the attributes that make an al forno dish ideal for low-stress entertaining: it's substantial, can be made a day in advance and needs no accompaniment other than a quick green salad. I love the idea of cannelloni, but always find the dried pasta cannelloni tubes totally perplexing. Unless you are seriously prepared to use a piping bag, how does one elegantly get the filling into the tube? Mine always end up smeary and sub-optimal. So now I just use fresh lasagne sheets (or dried ones, cooked until they're pliable) to make cannelloni, spreading the filling on like peanut butter on a sandwich, then rolling, slicing and packing snugly into place. Stand the pasta tubes upright: having them stand to attention in this way maximises the potential for crunchy bits.

---

800 g mushrooms (swiss brown or portobello are best)
80 ml (⅓ cup) olive oil
3 garlic cloves, finely chopped
6 sprigs of thyme, leaves picked
1 teaspoon finely grated lemon zest
1 x 680 g bottle of tomato passata
500 g ricotta
1 egg, lightly beaten
50 g pecorino, finely grated
6 fresh lasagne sheets (approximately 30 cm x 18 cm)
large handful of grated mozzarella

Preheat the oven to 220°C (200°C fan).

Clean the mushrooms and cut into 2 cm chunks. Toss with the oil, garlic, thyme and lemon zest, then tip them into a roasting tin lined with baking paper. Roast the mushrooms for 15-20 minutes or until they are deeply golden and their liquid has sizzled away. Once they're done, let them cool, then whizz to a chunky paste in a food processor (or set about them with a big knife and a chopping board). Season with salt and pepper to taste.

Take a straight-sided baking dish or tin (I use a 20 cm cake tin, but a soufflé-type dish would work nicely too) and tip the bottle of passata into it.

Mash the ricotta with the egg and pecorino. Lay out your lasagne sheets, then spread a layer of the ricotta mix on each lasagne sheet, followed by a layer of the mushroom paste. Now roll up each pasta sheet and slice into thirds. Pack the little rolls into the tin or dish, side by side and with a cut-end facing up. Make sure the passata coats the sides of each roll so they're all standing in a pleasant tomatoey bath. Finally, sprinkle the mozzarella on top. The oven-ready cannelloni will keep in the fridge for up to 24 hours – just cover with plastic wrap or foil to keep it from drying out.

When you're ready, bake the cannelloni, uncovered, at 210°C (190°C fan) for about 30 minutes, until heated through and golden on top.

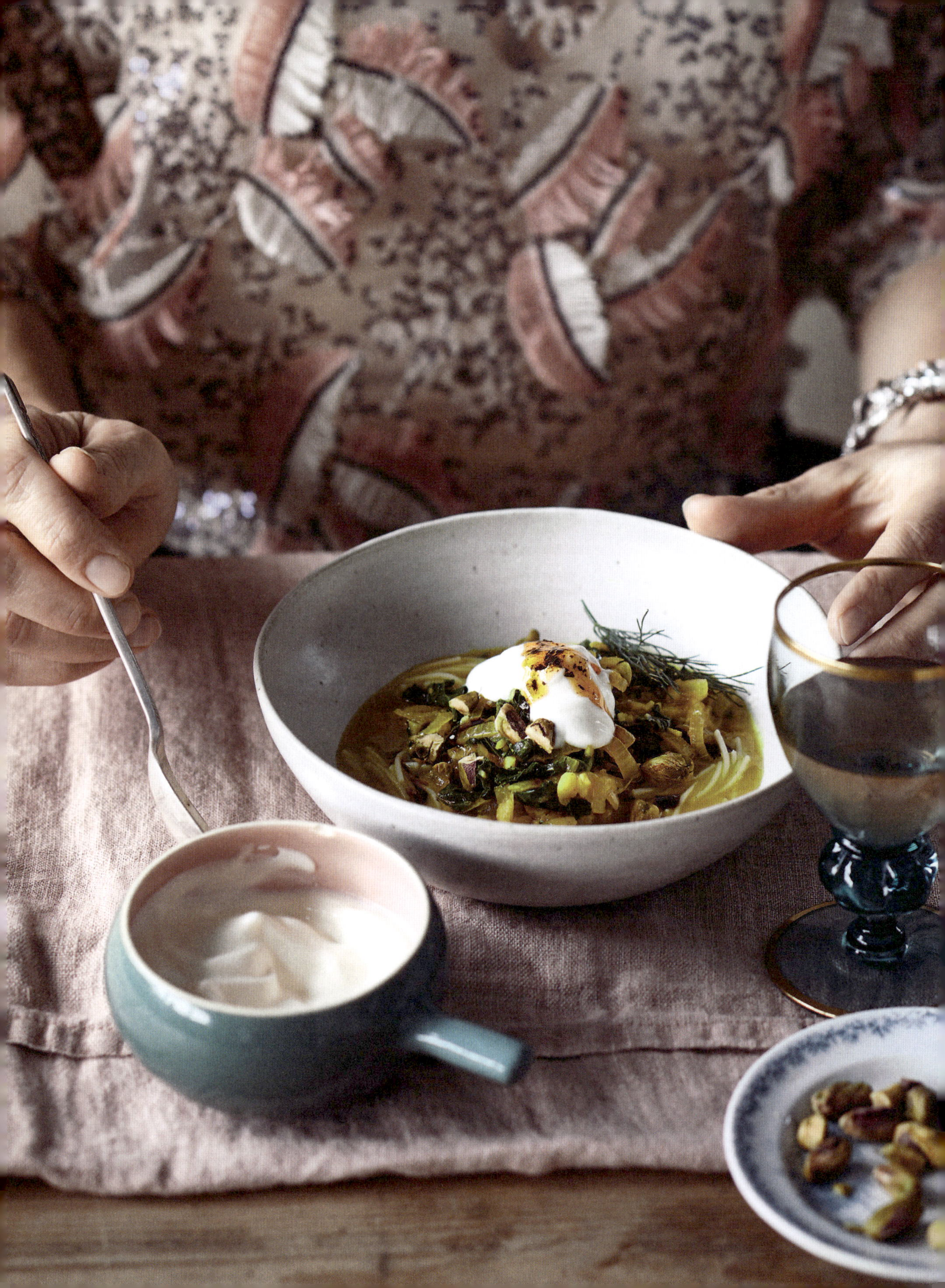

PERSIAN NEW YEAR SOUP

SERVES 6

Ash-reshteh is a Persian soup traditionally eaten to celebrate the Zoroastrian new year, which falls around mid-March, while it is still quite cool in Iran. For Australian Zoroastrians, or other observers of Persian new year, here is a lighter version, since March can still serve up some very hot days. You don't have to be flipping open a new calendar of any persuasion to enjoy this soup, which offers vibrant colour and flavour, thanks to turmeric and ginger. We've used thin egg noodles here, to keep it a shade lighter, but normally this would be made with wide, flat egg noodles like fettucine. Having said that, you won't need much for dessert; all those noodles and beans can fill a person up. No Zoroastrian ceremony is complete without a sacred fire, so perhaps incinerate something to keep it authentic. Check for fire bans, though.

---

25 g butter
2 brown onions, thinly sliced into half-moon shapes
8 garlic cloves, finely chopped
2 teaspoons ground turmeric
125 g yellow split peas (or chana dal)
500 ml (2 cups) weak vegetable stock or water
½ x 400 g tin of red kidney beans
2 teaspoons finely grated ginger
good handful of kale or spinach, well washed and any tough stalks removed
4 tablespoons pistachios
50 g dried egg vermicelli noodles, broken into short lengths
thick yoghurt, pomegranate molasses (or lemon juice) and chopped dill or coriander, to serve

MINT BUTTER
50 g butter
½ teaspoon smoked paprika
2 teaspoons dried mint

Melt the butter in a heavy-based saucepan over low heat and fry the onions for about 15 minutes until they are meltingly soft – a little bit of browning is fine, but take care to not let them burn. When the onions have been on the go for 10 minutes, add the garlic, keeping it on the move to avoid burning. After 5 minutes, sprinkle in the turmeric and stir for 30 seconds or so, just to take away its rawness.

Meanwhile, pick over the split peas, then tip into a small saucepan. Cover with water and bring to the boil, then reduce to a simmer and cook for about 20 minutes or until soft. Drain, rinse and then add to the pan with the onions. Now pour in the stock or water, bring back to a simmer and add the kidney beans and ginger. Plunge the kale or spinach into a pan of boiling water and blanch for a minute, until just wilted. Drain, then chop roughly and add to the soup. (At this stage, the soup can be cooled then refrigerated for up to 48 hours, until you're ready to make the mint butter and serve.)

For the mint butter, melt the butter in a small saucepan until it starts foaming, then remove from the heat and let it cool for 30 seconds. Sprinkle in the paprika, mint and a pinch of salt, and stir to combine.

When you're almost ready to serve, gently reheat the soup. Toast the pistachios for a minute or two in a dry frying pan, stirring and shaking the pan so they don't burn, then chop roughly. Cook the vermicelli according to the packet instructions, then rinse and divide between six bowls. Ladle in the soup, finishing each bowlful with a generous spoonful of thick yoghurt, a few drops of pomegranate molasses, a drizzle of the mint butter, some chopped dill or coriander and toasted pistachios.

SHIITAKE & BOK CHOY NOODLE SOUP WITH PICKLED EGGS

SERVES 4

What do you do when you can't quite decide which noodle soup mast to nail your colours to? Do I love pho best? Or ramen? Do I really have to choose? To be honest, both versions are quite difficult to find in a good vegetarian format, so when a proper meatless and tasty clear noodle soup becomes available to me, the love runs deep. After much deliberation, I decided to split the difference and make a soup that combines the best elements of pho and the best elements of ramen. And, in the process, offend every pho and ramen purist around. But, my argument would be that it is a beautiful marriage of two beautiful soups: the broth has the earthy depth of cloves and star anise, but the vegetables and egg are punchier and align themselves more with Japanese flavours. This soup looks more complicated than it is – yes, there are a few different elements, but most of them can be done well in advance – days even.

---

200 g fresh shiitake mushrooms
1 tablespoon neutral-flavoured oil
few shakes of tamari sauce
4 heads of bok choy
1 tablespoon rice wine vinegar
squeeze of lime juice
200 g instant noodles
chilli oil and stalks of coriander, mint and/or dill, to serve

PICKLED EGGS
4 eggs
2 teaspoons sugar
1–2 tablespoons hot water
2 tablespoons rice wine vinegar
125 ml (½ cup) light soy sauce

STOCK
1 brown or white onion
7 cloves
2 celery stalks
2–3 fennel stalks with fronds – optional
75 g fresh ginger
3 star anise
7 black peppercorns

Start with the eggs, to give them time to pickle. Boil the eggs: I like to start them in cold water, bring them to the boil and then immediately reduce the heat to barely a simmer and cook for 7 minutes, before dunking them straight into a sink full of cold water.

In a bowl big enough to hold the eggs, dissolve the sugar in a tablespoon or two of hot water, then add the vinegar and soy sauce.

Peel the eggs, then slip them into the pickling liquid and sit a small plate on top of them to keep them submerged. Leave to pickle for 2–5 hours. Once they are done, you can keep them in a well-sealed container, refrigerated, for a few days.

For the stock, peel the onion, and make a few slashes here and there to increase its surface area, but leave it whole. Use it as a pin-cushion for the cloves. Put this spiky onion into a stockpot or large saucepan, pour in 1.5 litres (6 cups) water and bring to the boil. Meanwhile, give the celery and fennel stalks (if using) a bit of a bash with the back of a knife and put those in too. Peel the ginger, then cut it into about four pieces, bruise it a bit and add it to the pot, along with the star anise and peppercorns. Keep the pot covered and simmering for about 20 minutes. Leave the stock to cool, then strain and set aside until you need it (if this is more than a couple of hours away, keep it in the fridge).

You are on the home straight now!

When you are almost ready to eat, gently reheat the stock. Thinly slice the mushrooms and throw them into a wok or frying pan with the oil. After a few minutes, turn the heat down and season with a few shakes of tamari sauce. Now add the bok choy and stir-fry for just a few minutes, then add the rice wine vinegar, clamp on a lid and let the vegetables steam for a minute. Finish with a squeeze of lime juice and you are done.

Cook the noodles according to the packet instructions. Drain and drop them straight into bowls, then top with some mushrooms and bok choy. Lift the eggs out of the pickling liquid and cut in half, then add two halves to each bowl. Pour the hot stock into a jug and pour over the top. Put any extra stock on the table, along with the chilli oil and herbs, for guests to help themselves.

MAKE IT GLUTEN-FREE

Use rice (not wheat) noodles, and substitute tamari sauce for the light soy sauce in the pickled eggs.

VEGETABLE & GREEN OLIVE TAGINE

SERVES 4

Easy as you like: just pile the vegetables and chickpeas in layers, with no frying or fuss. Pour on the chermoula and slow-cook so the tomatoes melt down into the chermoula to make a light and tasty sauce. I tend to use whole unpitted olives here, for better flavour, but do warn your guests! For the cook, the lovely thing about this dish is that it puts a lot of distance between the preparation and the eating. There's no tasting along the way, so by the time you eat it, the flavours are new – almost as though someone else has made it. Those who cook a lot will know just what a treat this can be.

---

olive oil, for drizzling
1 large fennel bulb, very thinly sliced
1 green pepper (capsicum), cut into long strips
1 red onion, cut into wedges
1 x 400 g tin of chickpeas, rinsed and drained
3 large carrots, cut on the diagonal into 3 cm slices
12 large green olives
5 large tomatoes, diced
6 cherry tomatoes, cut in half
couscous, coriander leaves and harissa (see page 14), to serve

CHERMOULA
4 tablespoons olive oil
1½ tablespoons ground cumin
1 teaspoon ground coriander
2 tablespoons chopped coriander leaves
handful of chopped parsley stalks
6 garlic cloves, finely chopped
2 good pinches of salt
1 good pinch of chilli flakes
5–6 saffron strands
2 strips of lemon zest from an unwaxed lemon
1 thumb-sized knob of ginger, finely chopped

Preheat the oven to 180°C (160°C fan).

First of all, make the chermoula by mixing all the ingredients together in a bowl with 4 tablespoons of water. Have a sniff – it should smell terrific. (If you have time on your hands, you can grind your own cumin and coriander by dry-frying the seeds until aromatic and then grinding them using an electric grinder or a pestle and mortar. The result will be fresher and less 'dusty' – but do not feel bad in the least if you can't be bothered.)

Take a heavy casserole (ideally a cast-iron one) that measures about 23 cm across its base. Add a splash of olive oil, then lay in the fennel, followed by the green pepper, onion, chickpeas, carrots and olives, poking them down into the gaps so that you aren't wasting too much space.

Spread the chermoula evenly over the top, making sure to use every last bit. Top with the diced tomatoes and halved cherry tomatoes, spreading them out evenly. Give your tagine a final drizzle of olive oil and a good sprinkling of salt, then clamp the lid on top and cook in the oven for about an hour. When it's done, the fennel and carrots should be lovely and soft but still holding together.

Serve with couscous, a generous scattering of coriander leaves, and some harissa on the side. Don't forget a small bowl for the olive pits…

FOR THE MEAT-EATERS
This tagine goes beautifully with chicken.

MAKE IT GLUTEN-FREE
Serve with brown rice or quinoa.

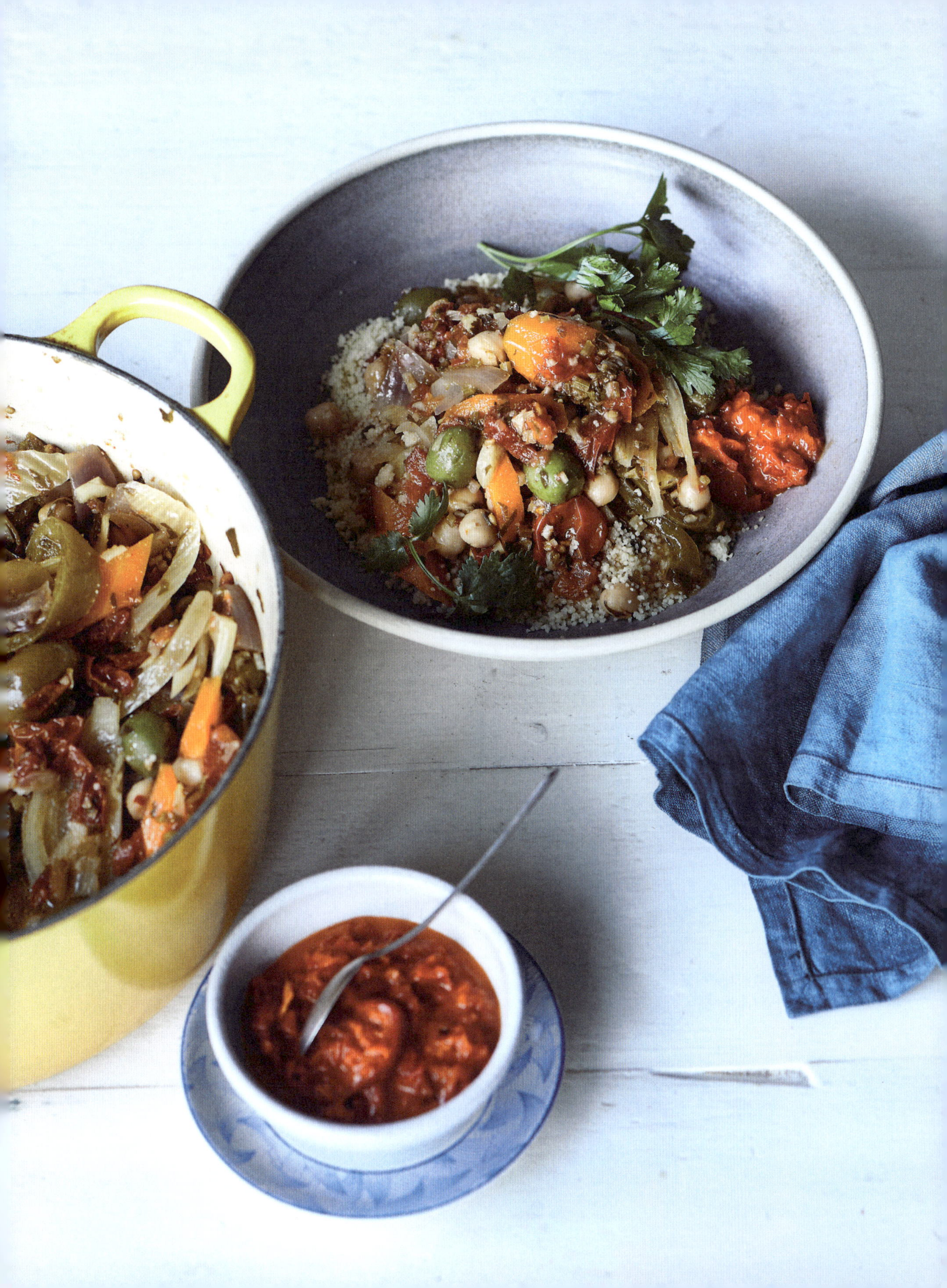

SMOKY EGGPLANT PARMIGIANA

SERVES 8

This dish may look tricky and long-winded, but once you have your head around each step, it actually doesn't take too long. You could make it in the morning and then slip it into the oven about 1½ hours before your guests are due. The smoked cheese and paprika give the dish a happy retro air - cheap and cheerful local Italian restaurant, circa 1983 - and we don't apologise for that (but feel free to substitute ricotta for the smoked mozzarella, if you prefer). Eggplants are notorious oil-sponges, and when fried will hoover up whatever you pour on them, so any dish like this runs the risk of epic oleaginousness. But you can mitigate this risk by giving them a quick dunk in some oil and baking them instead.

---

3 eggplants (aubergines)
3 pinches of salt
2 tablespoons olive oil
200 g mozzarella, cut into 1 cm slices
200 g smoked mozzarella (scamorza), cut into 8 mm slices
handful of breadcrumbs
25 g grated cheddar or parmesan
1 tablespoon finely chopped parsley (or a pinch of dried oregano)
crisp green salad, to serve

TOMATO SAUCE
3 garlic cloves
3 good handfuls of basil leaves, torn
1 x 400 g tin of tomatoes
400 ml tomato passata

WHITE SAUCE
50 g butter
50 g plain flour
500 ml (2 cups) milk
1 teaspoon dijon mustard
pinch of smoked paprika
50 g grated cheese (cheddar or parmesan, or a mix)

First, preheat the oven to 180°C (160°C fan) and get your eggplants on the go. Cut each one in half lengthways, then cut into half-moon shapes about 1 cm thick. Place in a big bowl, add the salt and olive oil, and then, working with great haste, toss to coat. If you aren't quick about this, the first and nearest piece of eggplant will suck up all your oil like a greedy sponge. Spread out the eggplants on a large baking tray in something near enough to a single layer and bake for about 15-20 minutes, until they have browned slightly and shrivelled into oily, tasty crescents. (Sadly, three eggplants bake down to not that much, but it is perfectly okay to eat a couple of pieces straight out of the oven - cook's privilege and all. With a squeeze of lemon juice and a few chilli flakes, there is almost nothing better.) You can do this step the day before and refrigerate the eggplants overnight.

For the tomato sauce, crush the garlic into a large jug, add the basil, then tip in the tomatoes and passata. Use a knife to cut through the tomatoes until each one has been hacked to thirds or quarters.

For the white sauce, melt the butter in a saucepan over medium heat, stir in the plain flour and cook for a minute. Take the saucepan off the heat and add the milk. It will look lumpy, but nothing a stern whisking won't quickly fix. I know there are more elegant ways to make white sauce, but this is what works for me every time. Keep it over low heat, stirring constantly with a wooden spoon, tracing figures of 8 around the pan. When the sauce is starting to show signs of thickening, add the mustard, paprika and cheese and keep stirring (if the paprika clumps stubbornly, you may need to briefly revert to the whisk) until the sauce simmers and thickens - it will still be fairly thin, so don't worry about it not being thick enough.

Right, we're now ready for assembly. Pour a thin layer of tomato sauce in the bottom of a large lasagne dish, followed by a quarter of the eggplant, a quarter of both mozzarellas, and a ladle of the white sauce in a stripe right down the middle. Repeat these layers until everything is used up, finishing with white sauce.

Mix together the breadcrumbs with the grated cheddar or parmesan and parsley, sprinkle over the top of the parmigiana, then put aside in the fridge until you are ready to cook.

About 1½ hours before you want to eat, preheat the oven to 200°C (180°C fan). Bake your eggplant parmigiana at this temperature for 30 minutes or until things are looking a bit brown, then turn the oven down to 180°C (160°C fan) and cook for another 40 minutes, until hot right through and the cheese is bubbling. This is definitely better on the side of well done, and will be fine kept warm in a 160°C (140°C fan) oven for a bit longer. When you're ready to serve, bring it to the table and serve with a crisp green salad.

MAKE IT GLUTEN-FREE

Omit the breadcrumbs or make them from gluten-free bread, and use gluten-free flour in the sauce.

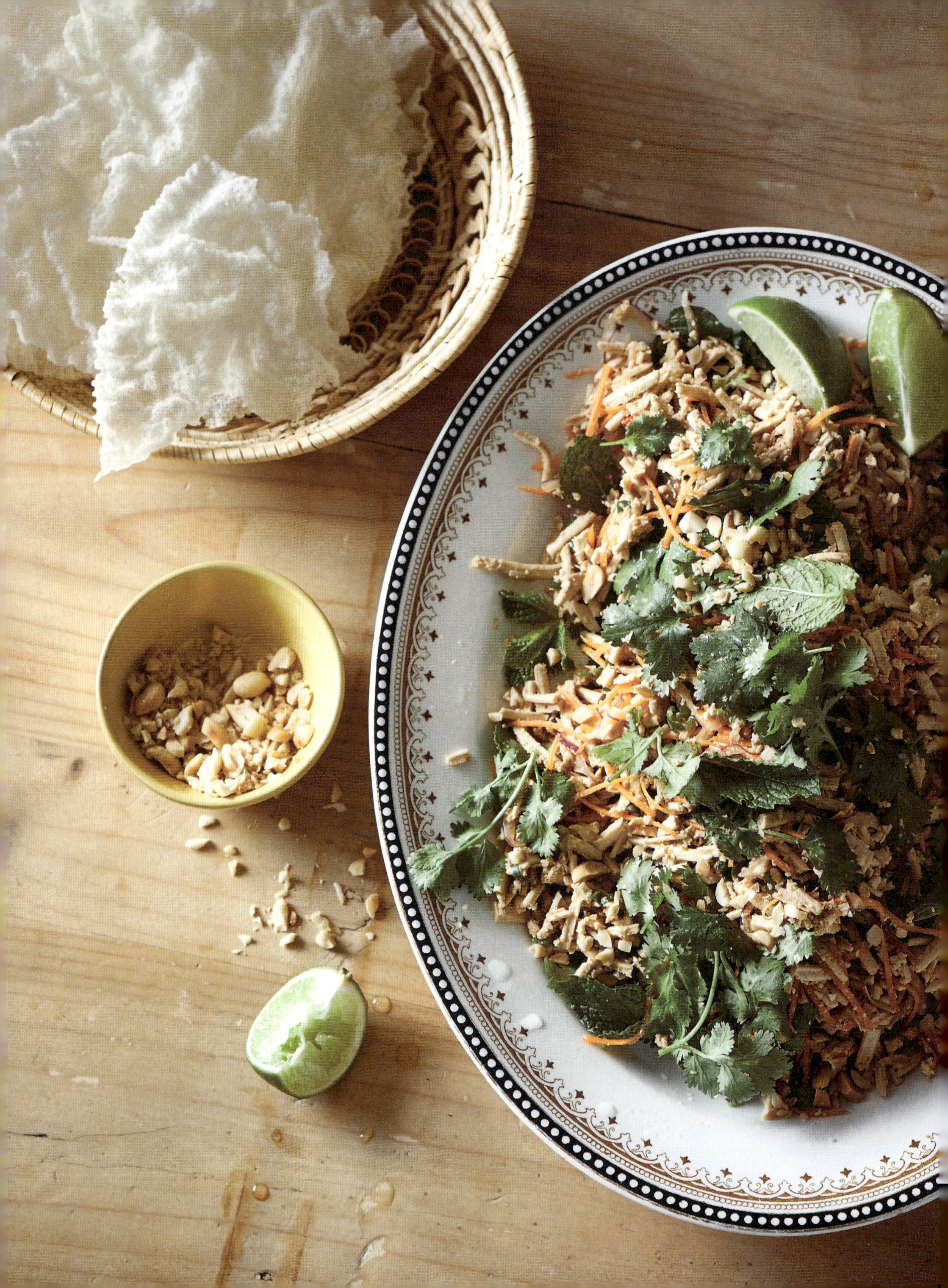

TOFU LARB

SERVES 6 AS A STARTER OR SIDE

The idea of the Thai larb salad (minced pork, chicken or prawns cooked with spices and served in a lettuce leaf) is a super-attractive one. But it's never been much fun for the herbivores. This no-cook tofu larb, though, is popular even with meat-eaters. I first met tofu larb when my friend Kate brought some around to my place; it's a staple at hers, and even her husband – a dirty great chop gobbler and general carnivore – loves it.

Larb is a perfect dish to make ahead, as sitting around in its juices only enhances its character. I like to serve this on frazzled rice paper, with some fresh herbs and toasted peanuts added at the last minute for extra zing and crunch. But it would be equally at home in an old-school lettuce leaf. I would happily eat this as a main dish, though it's especially good as a substantial salad in a buffet-style lunch.

---

2 tablespoons white rice
500 g firm tofu, coarsely grated
1 carrot, finely grated
1 small red onion, thinly sliced
3 spring onions, thinly sliced
1 stalk lemongrass (tender white part only), finely chopped
1 garlic clove, finely chopped
2 small red chillies, thinly sliced
3 juicy limes
2 tablespoons tamari sauce
1 tablespoon caster sugar
large handful of coriander leaves
large handful of mint leaves
70 g (½ cup) peanuts, toasted in a dry frying pan until golden then chopped

RICE PAPER CRISPS
250 ml (1 cup) rice bran oil
8 small rice paper wrappers

Preheat the oven to 180°C (160°C fan). Place the rice on a piece of foil, turning up the edges to hold it in place, then roast in the oven for about 10 minutes or until lightly browned. Transfer to a mortar and pestle and grind to a powder.

Put the ground rice into a large, shallow serving bowl, add the tofu, carrot, red onion, spring onions, lemongrass, garlic and chillies and combine well. Add the zest of one of the limes.

In another bowl, whisk the juice of all the limes with the tamari sauce and caster sugar. Pour over the larb and toss everything together. The larb can now be refrigerated until you want to serve it; indeed, it will improve if left for at least an hour. But it's not the end of the world if you eat it straightaway.

Right before you serve the larb, coarsely chop the herbs and gently toss them through, then scatter with the peanuts.

For the rice paper crisps, heat the oil in a wok until a test fragment of rice paper dropped into the oil frazzles instantly. Fry each wrapper individually: they should puff up within seconds. Just use a metal implement to keep it immersed in the oil so it puffs up evenly. Drain on paper towel and serve immediately, in a stack next to the larb.

CAULIFLOWER RAREBIT

SERVES 2 AS A MAIN, OR 4-6 AS A SIDE

Yet another chapter in that glorious and expanding book: *Terrific Things You Can Do With Cauliflower*. Today, it's being a rarebit! Rarebit is that ancient UK dish that is essentially tarted-up cheese on toast with crazed local variations like soaking the bread in beer or browning the cheese with an iron. Welsh rarebit is the only dish I have ever heard Julia Gillard lay claim to making: she offered a recipe for it to a Parliament House cookbook in the early 2000s, but it did not enlist any cruciferous vegetables.

On one level, of course, this is a gluten-free rarebit. But don't make the mistake of considering it a second-class dish. Cauliflower, it turns out, can hold its head high in any rarebit company. With the flavours of dill and caraway, and served with a pickle on the side, it has a whiff of New York deli to it. My cauliflower slices always seem to end up varying wildly in size, so I like to serve smaller pieces next to steak, while offering larger pieces to non-meat-eating guests.

---

1 cauliflower
oil or butter, for frying
4 large eggs
2 tablespoons sour cream
2 teaspoons wholegrain mustard
120 g grated cheese (I use a mix of cheddar and gruyère)
20 g dill, finely chopped
pinch of caraway seeds
dill pickles, worcestershire and tabasco sauce, to serve

Preheat the oven to 200°C (180°C fan).

Cut the cauliflower into thick slices. I have never managed to cut more than two clear and coherent cross-sectional slices from a cauliflower, so I usually end up with two nice neat-ish slices and two round-ended, slightly falling-apart slices. Heat a little oil or butter in a large frying pan and when it's hot, lay the large slices in the pan first, then fit in the rest around them. Give each side 3-4 minutes: there should be a little browning and also the cauliflower will have softened a bit. Now transfer the cauliflower to a greased roasting tin or deep baking tray, fitting the cauliflower slices in a single layer and as close to each other as possible.

In a large bowl, mix the eggs, sour cream and mustard with a pinch of salt, then fold in the cheese, dill and caraway seeds.

If you want to go ahead and finish the dish right away, spoon the egg mixture over the cauliflower, placing it on top of the slices as best you can, although you'll inevitably get a bit of spillage down the side. Now bake for about 8-10 minutes, or until the rarebit is bubbling and speckled with brown but still has bit of wobble.

If you are making this in advance, keep the fried cauliflower and the uncooked egg mix in the fridge. When you are ready, warm the cauliflower in a preheated 200°C (180°C fan) oven for 5-10 minutes before spooning the egg mix on top and baking as above.

Serve with dill pickles, or assorted bottles of worcestershire and tabasco sauce, for guests to help themselves.

SUMMER EGGPLANT CURRY

SERVES 4

This is, I think, the first dish that Jeremy ever cooked for me. I was pretty much in the bag after that. It's an astoundingly simple curry of just six ingredients, and so is guaranteed a podium presence at the Minimalist Curry Olympics, yet it really does taste amazing – fresh, light and perfect for a quick summer feast. One thing: this is a celebration of that great workhorse of a spice blend, garam masala, so do yourself a favour and use a fresh blend, not one that has been sulking in the cupboard since the Rudd years.

Because it's served at room temperature, this curry can be made ahead with ease. The final step is pretty much just stirring and garnishing – the work of moments. You can serve it with naan to chunk it up a bit, if you like, or with poppadums to make the whole deal gluten-free.

---

2 large eggplants (aubergines)
1 brown onion, diced
1 tablespoon rice bran oil
1 tablespoon garam masala
3 large or 4 small tasty tomatoes
300 g Greek-style yoghurt
large handful of coriander leaves

Preheat your oven to 200°C (180°C fan). Plonk the eggplants on a baking tray and stab each one a couple of times with a paring knife (this is to avert the slim chance of egg-splosion) and consign to the furnace. Bake for 20–25 minutes or until the eggplants are nicely collapsed and their skins are browned. Set aside to cool.

Meanwhile, set a heavy-based frying pan over low–medium heat and sauté the onion in the oil. You want the onion to be softened, but *not* browned, so be vigilant. Add the garam masala and stir for another minute or so… It will start to smell very good.

Strip the skin from the eggplants and cut the flesh into large cube-style chunks – about 4 cm is the size you're after. Discard any juices, then add the eggplant cubes to the frying pan.

And that's it for the cooking! You can do all of these steps in advance, because this is served at room temperature and so just needs to be assembled.

When the time comes, cut up the tomatoes, scrape out the seeds and pulp, and dice the flesh chunkily (I don't bother skinning them).

Stir the yoghurt and tomatoes through the eggplant mix. Once everything is nicely amalgamated, all you need to do is tip it into a bowl, top with coriander and serve.

MUSHROOMS, WHITE BEANS & RADICCHIO WITH SOFT POLENTA

SERVES 4-6

Before you flick on... I do understand the impulse to reject polenta. Anyone who has tried to dine out as a vegetarian for any length of time will recognise the kind of polenta that is more a form of punishment than a foodstuff: tasteless, tough, deep-fried. What purpose does it serve, other than to fill up space on the plate? Soft polenta is in a different category altogether - a starchy scaffold for a lot of tasty molten cheese. Gluten-free, it can be prepared ahead of time and isn't nearly as fiddly or temperamental as you might think. If you have a whisk, there is not a lump that can't be sorted out. Received wisdom has it that soft polenta needs to be cooked to order. But frankly, this method turns out a very acceptable result. And if there is anyone who'd refuse something hot and with this much cheese in it, then I want a word with them.

---

12 flat field mushrooms
80 g butter
2 garlic cloves, finely chopped
1 x 400 g tin of cannellini beans, rinsed and drained
olive oil, for drizzling
180 g (1 cup) polenta
1 head of radicchio (substitute with rocket if this is unavailable or you find it too bitter), leaves separated
125 ml (½ cup) red wine
about 100 ml milk - optional
100 g grated parmesan (or a mix of grated parmesan and taleggio cut into small pieces)

Preheat the oven to 180°C (160°C fan). Flip the stalks out of your mushrooms, give them a brush down, and lay them, cap-side up, in your largest roasting tin or deep baking tray.

Now put 30 g of the butter in a small saucepan over low heat, and as it melts, add the garlic. Let it sizzle for a couple of minutes until it starts to foam at the edges and smells like essence of garlic bread.

Spoon the garlic butter into the mushroom caps (don't wash the pan yet - you'll need it again), then roast the mushrooms for 15 minutes. By this time they should have released some of their umami juices; carefully drain these into the little saucepan you used for the garlic. I like to give the mushrooms a gentle squeeze with my tongs to get some more of the garlicky juices into the pan.

Return the mushrooms to the oven and cook for another 20 minutes. They will look quite dark and inviting by this time. Remove from the oven and tip in the cannellini beans, spreading them out between the mushrooms, then give them a quick drizzle of olive oil, season with salt and set aside until just before you want to serve; if this is more than an hour or two away, cover and refrigerate.

For the polenta, bring 1 litre (4 cups) of lightly salted water to the boil in a heavy-based saucepan. Transfer the polenta to a jug and, holding the whisk in your dominant hand and the jug in your other hand, slowly, slowly pour the polenta into the gently boiling water, all the while whisking without cease. Don't worry if there are a few lumps - just keep whisking as the mixture thickens before your eyes.

Now turn the heat down as low as it will go and cook the polenta for about 20 minutes, giving it a vigorous stir with a wooden spoon every 5 minutes or so. Polenta varies a lot, and different brands have different levels of coarseness, so do be guided here by any cooking instructions given on the packet. When the polenta is done, you can forge ahead if you are going to serve it right away. Or, if you are making in advance, set the polenta aside until you are ready (it will keep for a few hours at room temperature, or for at least a day in the fridge). Note that it will set into a block as it cools.

Close to serving time, put the mushrooms and beans into a preheated 200°C (180°C fan) oven for 10 minutes, adding the radicchio when there's just 2 minutes to go.

Meanwhile, set your pan of garlicky mushroom juices over medium heat and add the red wine. Cook for just long enough to burn off the alcohol, and to let the sauce reduce slightly.

To revive set polenta, place the pan over low heat, add a splash of milk or water and gently start whisking until it starts to loosen into a thick purée, adding more milk or water bit by bit, so you don't accidentally add too much and end up with cornmeal soup.

Now for the best bit: sprinkle the parmesan (and taleggio, if using) into your warm, creamy polenta, along with the remaining 50 g of butter, and stir while it melts.

In some parts of Italy, the polenta is poured out onto a wooden board in the middle of the table to be shared. It is a very festive and communal experience if you have the space and equipment to go that way: spread out your polenta to about 5 cm thick on a large board. Make a shallow depression in the centre and fill it with the mushrooms, beans and radicchio, then pour over the sauce.

Otherwise, fill the bottom of each bowl with a scoop or two of polenta, arrange a few mushrooms on top and spoon over some beans and radicchio. Pour over a little of the garlicky wine sauce and rush to the table.

All you need with this lovely winter dish is lots of black pepper, and a glass or two of red wine.

Salads for all

Sometimes the best option for a table with as many dietary differences are there are people, is to choose one robust salad as the centre, around which all requirements can orbit. With some additions and subtractions here and there, everyone will be catered for. What might stand alone as a vegetarian meal could also partner nicely with roast chicken. Or roast lamb. Swap out prawns for tofu or boiled egg and everyone is catered for, no one is left out or feels different. All that is left is to find a spot in your cupboard big enough to house all those giant platters you'll now need.

ROASTED & RAW VEGETABLE SALAD WITH ZHUG

SERVES 4-6

Is this a salad or a plate of roasted vegetables? Well, it's both. This will sit happily alongside a plate of roast meat, but equally it runs its own game perfectly well. Mix up whatever vegetables you favour, or have to hand, adding the roasted vegetables according to the time they'll need in the oven: aim for about 400 g veg per person. The mix-and-match of raw and cooked provides a full palette of textures, but the legwork is really done by the zingy, aromatic Yemeni hot sauce known as zhug.

ROASTED VEGETABLES
olive oil, for drizzling
potatoes, left whole if small, cut into chunks if larger
carrots, peeled and trimmed
beetroot, peeled and sliced into rounds
cauliflower or broccoli, broken into florets
zucchini (courgettes), cut into chunks
unpeeled garlic cloves
green beans, topped and tailed
squeeze of lime juice – optional

RAW VEGETABLES
red cabbage, thinly sliced
avocado, cut into quarters
little gem lettuce, cut into wedges or chunks

ZHUG
60 g coriander, leaves and stalks, roughly chopped
2 garlic cloves, roughly chopped
2 tablespoons olive oil, plus 1–2 tablespoons extra, if needed
1 tablespoon lemon juice
½ teaspoon ground cumin
¼ teaspoon coriander seeds
¼ teaspoon cardamom seeds (scrape them from the pods)
3 pickled jalapeño slices
4 good grindings of pepper

Preheat the oven to 220°C (200°C fan). Set up your largest roasting tin with a bit of olive oil in the bottom and heat in the oven for a few minutes. Carefully add the potatoes, carrots and beetroot to the hot oil, toss to coat and season with salt, then roast for about 20 minutes. Add the cauliflower or broccoli, zucchini and garlic cloves and roast for another 10 minutes. Meanwhile, blanch the green beans in boiling water for a few minutes and drain well before adding them to the roasting tin for the last few minutes.

While all this is going on, make the zhug. For hundreds of years, people have been making this sauce with a mortar and pestle, but with this much fresh coriander to pulverise, my vote goes to putting all the ingredients (apart from the extra olive oil) in a small food processor or blender and blitzing for about 20 seconds. Add the extra olive oil at the end to adjust the texture as required – you want something quite runny, like a sauce rather than a stiff pesto. Taste and season accordingly.

Once your roasted vegetables are done, transfer to the hugest serving platter you have and let them cool for a few minutes before adding the red cabbage, avocado and lettuce. If you know that all your guests are up for a spicy green sauce, put dabs of zhug over the top. If there are spice-avoiders at the table, drizzle the salad with olive oil and a squeeze of lime juice and pass the zhug separately.

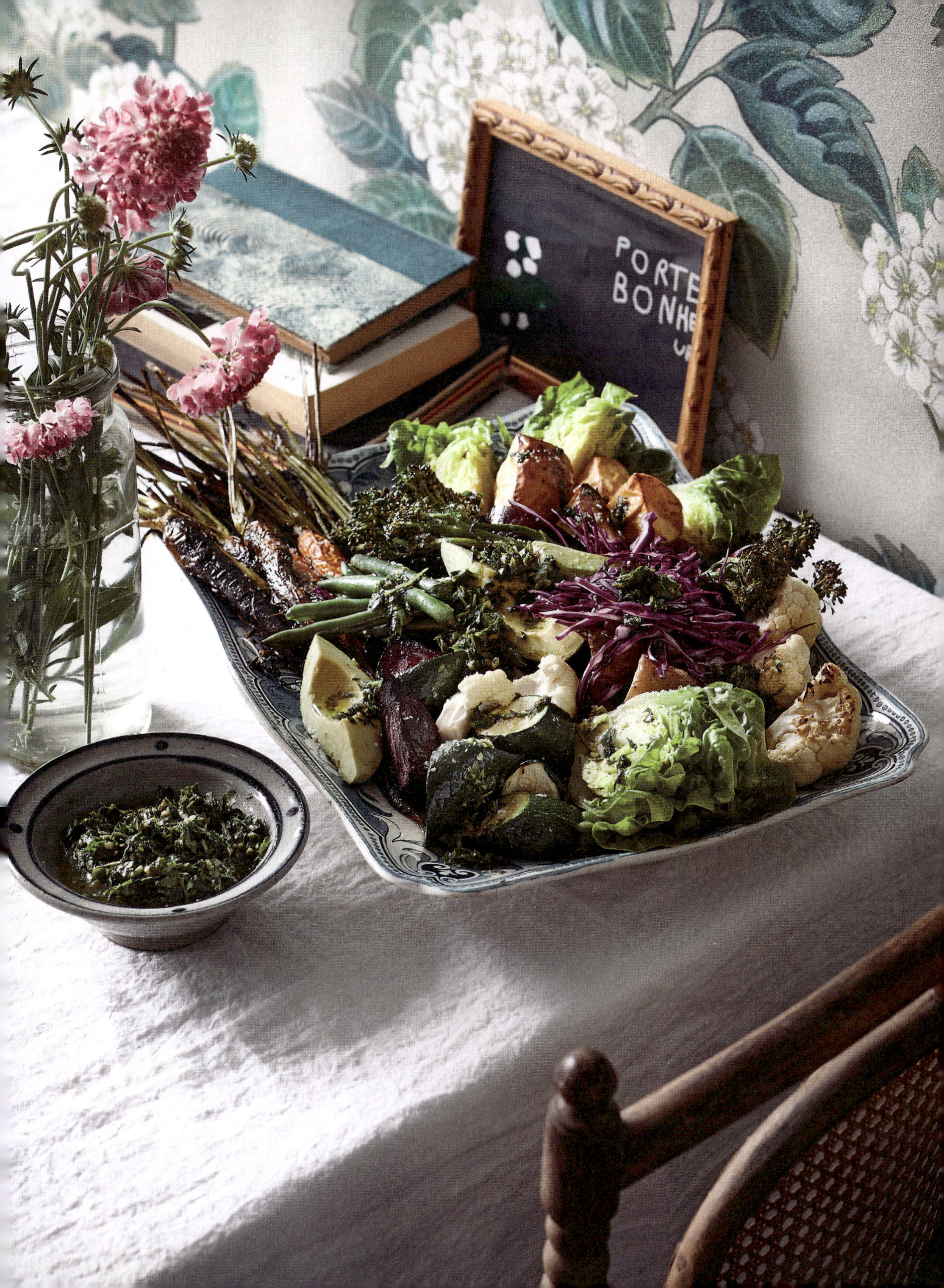
PORTE
BONHE

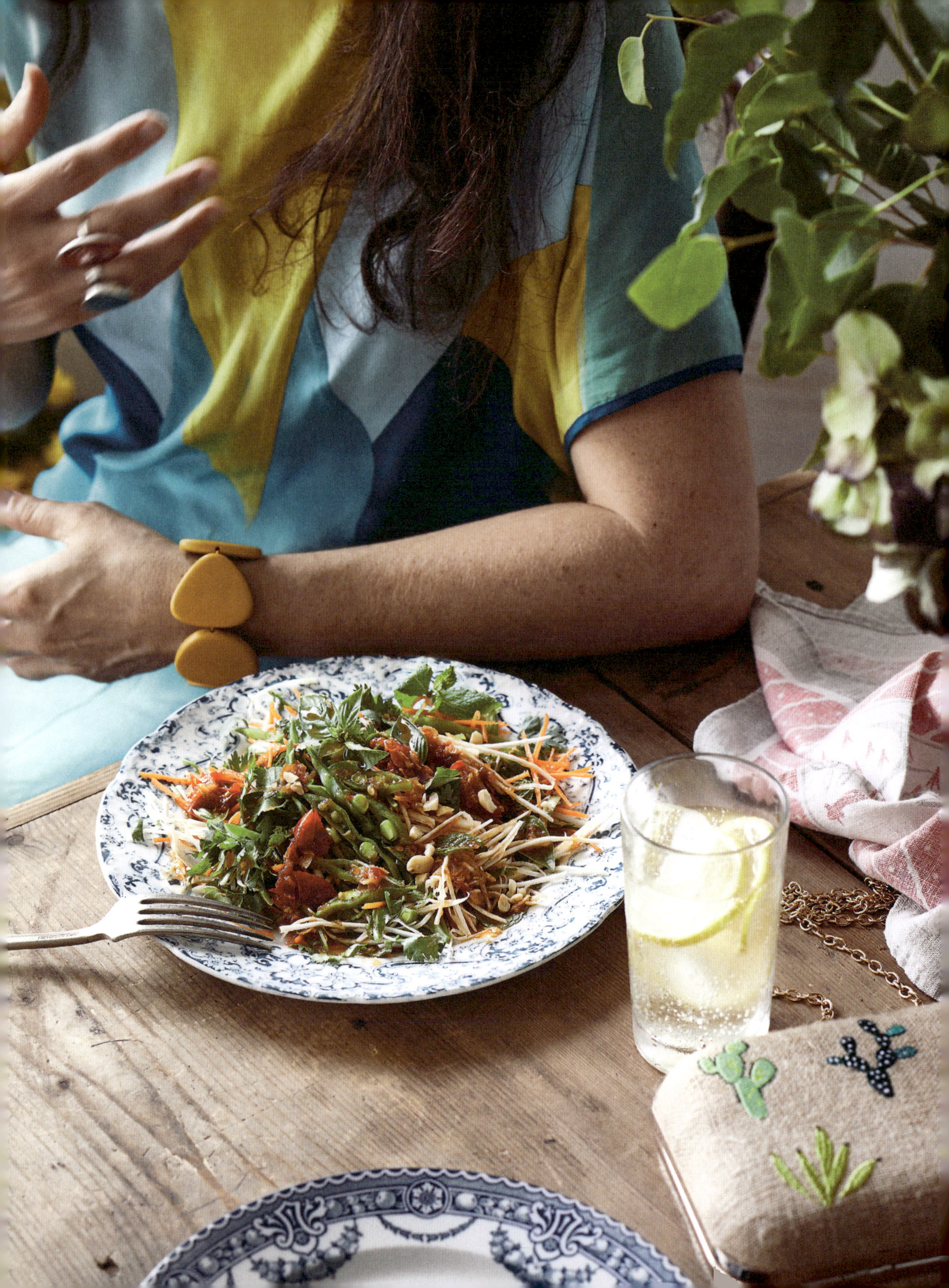

THAI CELERIAC SALAD WITH PEANUTS & DRIED SHRIMP

SERVES 4-6

I love celeriac and I love green papaya salad (som tam), but green papaya isn't always easy to find. If you have the patience to julienne some celeriac very finely, or have a food processor to do the job for you, then celeriac seems absolutely born to this salad. As with actual green papaya, a box grater doesn't work so well – you need terrifically long, tangly strands of vegetable, so use one of those julienne vegetable peelers, a mandoline with a julienne cutter, or a very sharp knife.

Serve this with pan-fried prawns, or shredded chicken or duck. Our old standby, hot-smoked salmon, is also a good match here. And don't forget to fire up the rice cooker for some steamed jasmine rice, for a delicious contrast between hot rice and cool salad.

---

3 garlic cloves
1 red chilli (take out a few seeds if you don't like it hot)
1 tablespoon dried shrimp – optional
pinch of salt
2 tablespoons grated palm sugar or dark brown sugar
10 cherry tomatoes, cut in half
3 spring onions, thinly sliced into rounds
juice of 2 limes
2 tablespoons fish sauce
50 g peanuts (or cashews)
½ large celeriac
1 large carrot
100 g snow peas (mangetout), thinly sliced
20 g coriander, leaves and stems, finely chopped
a few mint leaves, shredded
handful of basil leaves, torn

Use a large mortar and pestle to crush the garlic, chilli and dried shrimp (don't worry if you don't have any – you can compensate with fish sauce) with a pinch of salt for abrasion. Add the sugar and, one by one, the cherry tomatoes, followed by the spring onions. Now add half the suggested quantities of lime juice and fish sauce, mix well, then taste and add more until you're happy with the balance of flavours. (You can make this dressing in advance and shred the vegetables within half an hour of serving time so the celeriac doesn't brown and sag too much.)

Toast the peanuts (or cashews if there are specific peanut allergies) in a hot pan for 4-5 minutes, or give them 15 minutes in a 180°C (160°C fan) oven, until brown. Allow to cool, then chop roughly.

Now shred your celeriac into long strands, using a very sharp knife, a mandoline with a julienne cutter, or a food processor, and then do the same with the carrot. Transfer to a large serving bowl and add the snow peas, coriander and mint. Pour over the dressing and toss everything together, then sprinkle over the peanuts and basil leaves.

MAKE IT VEGAN
Omit the dried shrimp, and use tamari sauce in place of the fish sauce.

CARROT, FETA, OLIVE & LENTIL SALAD

SERVES 6-8

The carrot is so often an accompaniment that it feels somehow fair and reasonable to have a dish in which it plays the principal role. Wendy has an extreme fondness for carrots; I recall her eating so many during her first pregnancy that she turned a bit orange, and she can still put away half a kilo in a day, easy.

The dressing will be tastier if you toast the spices, but don't bother if you're in a hurry; what is more important is to use ground cumin that is reasonably fresh. The sachet that has been with you for two house moves? That stuff won't do, and it is time to start again.

---

500 g carrots, peeled and cut into roughly 7 cm batons
250 g creamy feta, rather than the very firm sort, cut into small (about 1 cm) cubes
50 g cooked Puy-style lentils (from a tin is fine)
12 kalamata olives, pitted and cut into slivers
handful of mint leaves
1 teaspoon sumac
lemon wedges, to serve – optional

DRESSING
1 teaspoon ground cumin
pinch of coriander seeds
2 tablespoons olive oil
squeeze of lemon juice

For the dressing, mix together the ground cumin and coriander seeds, using the back of the spoon or your fingers to crush the seeds slightly. Add the olive oil and a squeeze of lemon.

Bring a large pan of salted water to the boil, then plunge in your carrots. When the water returns to the boil, give them 1-2 minutes - you want them to lose their raw crunch, but still be firm. Drain and pat dry, then transfer to a serving bowl. Immediately pour over the dressing and scatter with the feta. Toss everything together, so the feta melts slightly to coat the carrots.

Let the salad cool for a few minutes, adding the lentils, olives and mint at the last moment. Give the salad a generous sprinkle of sumac and serve at room temperature, with some more lemon juice if you like.

EVEN EASIER

Use pitted green olives from a jar. The colour may not be as eye-catching, but they'll work just as well. I personally don't think the same of pitted black olives in a jar, which I've never found to be much chop.

MORE OPTIONS

For vegetarians, you could increase the amount of lentils and serve this with bulgur wheat or couscous as a complete meal. For meat-eaters, a few slices of roast lamb, or warm kibbeh meatballs, would be just the ticket.

CAULIFLOWER SALAD WITH SHERRIED CURRANTS, CAPERS & MINT

SERVES 2 AS A GENEROUS MAIN, OR 6 AS A SIDE

This is - finally - the decade of the cauliflower. Once known for little more than its habit of sheltering tastelessly under a calorific blanket of white sauce (and having its name traduced by association with the deformed ears of professional rugby players), this noble brassica is now being roundly fêted for the delight that it is.

Roasting cauliflower is, because of its natural sugars, a transformative experience. You can roast one whole, like a modestly sized vegetarian ox, but for this salad (pictured over the page) it's roasted in pieces, then enlivened with chilli, capers and lemon, and some currants plumped with Pedro Ximenez sherry.

1.5 litres (6 cups) vegetable stock (from powder or a cube is fine) or water
1 cauliflower, broken into florets
3 tablespoons extra virgin olive oil
1 teaspoon chilli flakes
1 large lemon
2 tablespoons currants
1 tablespoon Pedro Ximenez sherry
2 tablespoons pine nuts
2 tablespoons slivered almonds
2 tablespoons tiny salted capers, rinsed then drained well
generous handful of coarsely chopped flat-leaf parsley
generous handful of coarsely chopped mint

Preheat the oven to 220°C (200°C fan).

Bring the stock or water to the boil in a saucepan, add the cauliflower and blanch for 5 minutes, then drain.

Tip the cauliflower into a roasting tin and toss with 2 tablespoons of the olive oil, sprinkling in the chilli flakes as you go. Add the finely grated zest of the lemon and season with salt and pepper, but go easy on the salt as you've already cooked the cauli in stock and there are capers still to come. Roast the cauliflower until it's deep gold in colour and the edges have started to char, about 20 minutes. Remove from the oven and leave to cool slightly.

Meanwhile, combine the currants and the sherry in a teacup or small bowl and leave to soak, giving them a stir every now and then.

In a small dry frying pan, toast the pine nuts and almonds over low-medium heat until golden brown, keeping a close eye on them.

Tip the nuts out into a dish. Add a glug of olive oil to the frying pan and fry the capers until crisp, squishing them with a wooden spoon.

To assemble the salad, toss the cauliflower with the sherried currants, parsley and mint. Squeeze in the juice of the lemon, then apply a final drizzle of olive oil for shine and sprinkle with the pine nuts, almonds and crisp capers.

Salads for all

< CAULIFLOWER SALAD WITH SHERRIED CURRANTS, CAPERS & MINT

GLASS NOODLE SALAD WITH PRAWNS & PINK GRAPEFRUIT >

GLASS NOODLE SALAD WITH PRAWNS & PINK GRAPEFRUIT

SERVES 4

A Vietnamese-style salad can be everything to everyone: changeable according to preference, perfectly sufficient as a main course, but brilliant as an accompaniment too. I think it's what I would eat for the rest of my life if I had to narrow it down to one dish. You can use rice vermicelli here, no problems, but I love the transparent bean thread 'glass' noodles for their beauty, and because they don't break down in the dressing so much, making them a hardier leftover. The Vietnamese-style dressing is jazzed up with a little grapefruit juice, and the whole thing is given crunch by the ubiquitous crispy fried shallots that are never far from any dish in that part of the world; available in packets or jars from Asian grocers, these will keep virtually for ever in an airtight container.

Making this salad (pictured on the previous page) is much quicker if you have an implement that makes short work of julienning papaya or apple. For years, I wandered the globe unable to find exactly the right thing, but recently I found one at an anonymous stall in my local shopping centre. I take it on holidays, it's so good; like a mandoline but with square raised grating parts that produce matchstick-sized julienne. If you have not had this brush with grateness (see what I did there?), use a mandoline to achieve thin slices, then a sharp knife to cut them into matchsticks. Use a plain box grater if you absolutely must, but the sliced version will be neater and bruise the fruit less.

---

20 raw prawns, peeled, butterflied and deveined
200 g dried glass noodles (bean thread vermicelli)
2 ruby grapefruit
2 spring onions, cut into fine matchsticks
2 large red chillies, thinly sliced
1 green papaya (or green apple), cut into fine matchsticks
large handful of coarsely chopped mint
large handful of coarsely chopped coriander
crispy shallots, to garnish

First, cook the prawns. The simplest way is to boil them very briefly in salted water, until they're pink and just firm. It will take about a minute – *do not* let them overcook, or it will be like dealing with long-abandoned beach thongs. Drain and set aside to cool.

Put the noodles into a heatproof bowl and cover with boiling water. Give them a stir and monitor them as they soften. When they're tender and ready to eat, drain, then rinse under cold running water. By all means be guided by the packet instructions (if there are any), but in my experience glass noodles can be awfully fickle, so keeping tabs on them as they soften in the hot water is the best way.

Take the grapefruit and – with a sharp knife – cut off the peel and pith. This will involve a small sacrifice of flesh (the grapefruit's, not yours) as you want all the pith to be gone, leaving you with a beautiful pink globe marked only with the divots where the membranes run between the fruit's segments. With your knife, cut along these membranes so as to extract perfect wedge-shaped segments. Do this over a bowl to catch the juice.

DRESSING

- 3 tablespoons ruby grapefruit juice (from segmenting the fruit above – see method)
- 3 tablespoons lime juice
- 1 tablespoon fish sauce
- 2 teaspoons tamari sauce
- 2 tablespoons grated palm sugar
- 2 cm ginger, finely grated

Once you've cut all the segments out, you will be left with a sadly deflated handful of membrane. Squeeze this over the bowl. When you've done this to both the grapefruit, you will have the juice for your dressing.

Speaking of which: whisk all the dressing ingredients together until the palm sugar has dissolved.

Now assemble the salad. I like to do this in a big bowl, adding most of the dressing to the slippery noodles and making sure they're all covered before adding the prawns, grapefruit, spring onions, chillies and papaya, and most of the coriander and mint. Once everything's in, add more dressing if you think it needs it, then decant the finished salad into a large shallow serving dish. Finish with the rest of the coriander and mint, and a scattering of crispy shallots.

EVEN EASIER
Use pre-cooked prawns.

MAKE IT VEGAN
Toss some slices of firm tofu in cornflour seasoned with salt and white pepper. Fry until crisp, then slice into the salad, in place of the prawns. Leave out the fish sauce in the dressing and add more tamari to taste.

DIY CRISPY FRIED SHALLOTS
If you're super-keen, you can make these yourself by thinly slicing shallots (the bulbous, brown-skinned kind) and crisping them in hot oil. Drain well, then store in an airtight container and use within a couple of days.

MOGRABIEH SALAD WITH TOASTED NUTS

SERVES 6

Mograbieh - also known as giant couscous, Israeli couscous or pearl couscous - is quite widely available in Australia now, but I first came across this semolina-based delight in London. Having bought a packet on impulse and read somewhere about the importance of toasting it before boiling, I embarked on a ramshackle series of test cooks and arrived at a method (and set of companion ingredients) that might well invoke indignation across the Levant. So: apologies. In this dish, the little toasty pasta balls are swathed in a zingy, herby, chermoula-like dressing. You could elevate it to main-course status by adding some fried halloumi - or, if you're that way inclined, a lamb chop.

---

400 g (2 cups) mograbieh (giant couscous)
2 tablespoons olive oil
1 litre (4 cups) vegetable or chicken stock
65 g (½ cup) slivered almonds
50 g (⅓ cup) pine nuts
1 tablespoon butter
1 x 400 g tin of chickpeas, rinsed and drained
40 g (¼ cup) barberries or currants

HERB DRESSING
100 ml olive oil
juice of 2 lemons
1 garlic clove, roughly chopped
large handful of roughly chopped coriander
large handful of roughly chopped flat-leaf parsley
handful of mint leaves, roughly chopped
½ preserved lemon, finely chopped
6 saffron strands, soaked in 1 teaspoon hot water for about 5 minutes
2 teaspoons cumin seeds, toasted in a dry pan then ground
1 teaspoon coriander seeds, toasted in a dry pan then ground
1 teaspoon smoked paprika

First, prepare the mograbieh. Pour the olive oil into a large heavy-based saucepan over medium heat and add the mograbieh. Fry, stirring, for about 10 minutes until it's a lovely deep toasty colour. Once you're happy with the colour, add the stock. Lower the heat and cook, covered, until the liquid is nearly all absorbed. Uncover and stir until the liquid has completely gone, then spread out the couscous on a lined baking tray or large plate to dry out.

Now fry the almonds and pine nuts gently in the butter until they're burnished with gold - keep an eye on them, as they can quickly burn.

For the dressing, just whizz all the ingredients in a small food processor or blender, adding salt and pepper to taste.

When you're ready to serve, tip the mograbieh into a large bowl, prodding and poking to separate the grains. Add the chickpeas and barberries. Pour over the dressing and stir well to coat all the ingredients. Sprinkle with the toasted nuts.

MAKE IT VEGAN

Dry-fry the nuts, or use a dash of olive oil and a pinch of salt instead of the butter.

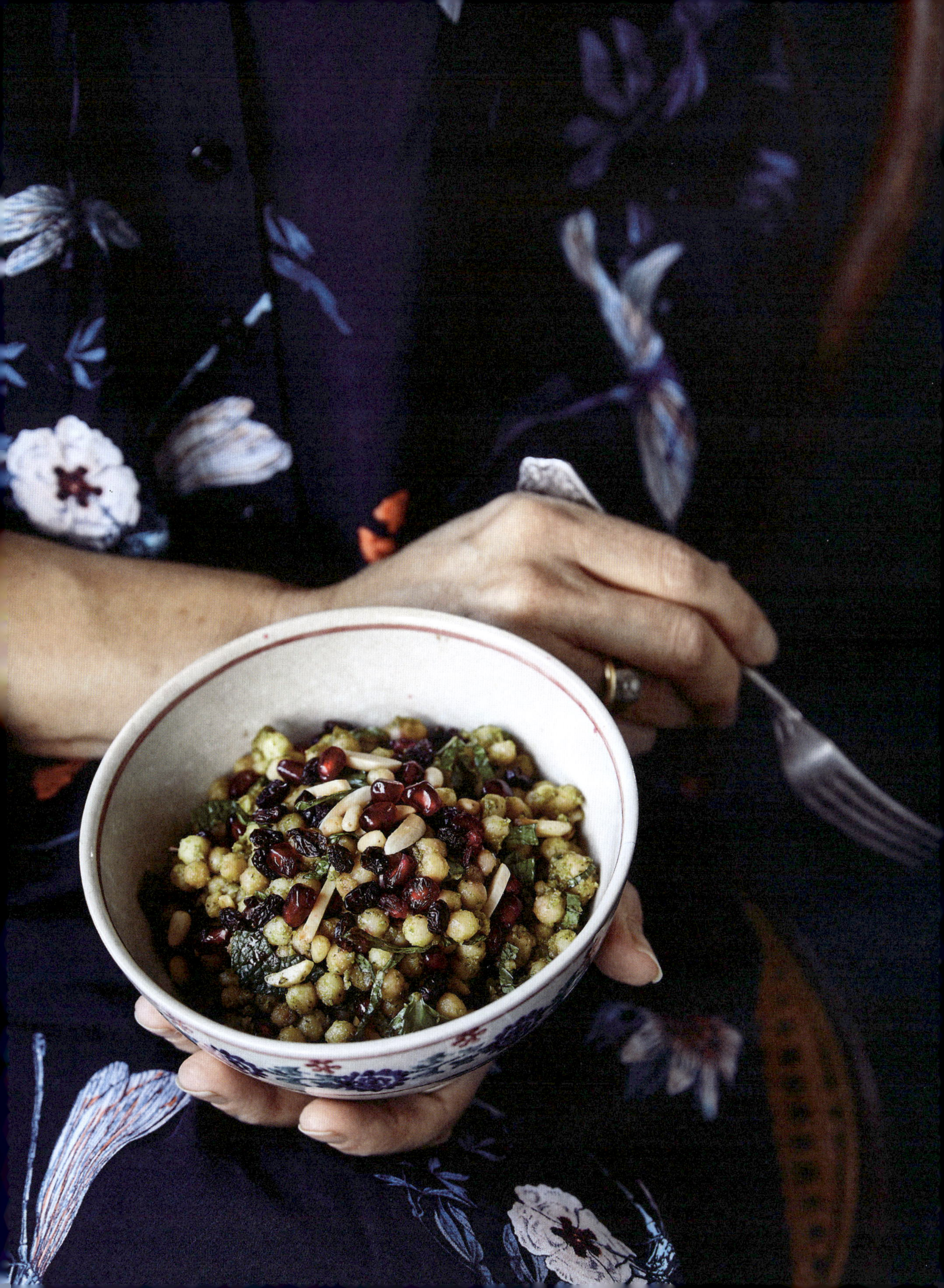

MOZZARELLA SALAD WITH SPRING VEG & LEMON-INFUSED OIL

SERVES 6

When that short window of good local asparagus availability is open, there is almost no excuse for eating anything other than that. The same goes for the first of the season's peas, when they are almost too sweet to be considered a vegetable, especially if you can get them from your own garden or a farmers' market. This salad is a celebration of all those deliciously sweet and tender spring vegetables that herald the end of winter.

I had long believed flavoured oils and vinegars to be a gimmick, or at the very least too expensive for what they were. But a gift of lemon-infused oil found its way into almost everything I made over the next month: bowls of spaghetti, steamed vegetables and vinaigrettes. Somehow, lemon-infused oil captures the true flavour of a lemon, without the acidity, which is especially nice on this salad where the sweet, delicate flavours of young spring vegetables can shine through.

---

600 g green spring vegetables: asparagus and peas, plus as many of the following as you like – podded and skinned broad beans, snow peas (mangetout), thinly sliced baby zucchini (courgettes), pea shoots, radishes, torn nasturtiums or rocket leaves
50 ml lemon-infused oil (see page 15)
3 x 125 g balls of buffalo mozzarella, thickly sliced or torn
1 teaspoon white balsamic vinegar
toast, to serve

Have a big pot of boiling water on the go, and blanch each vegetable separately, since they will need different cooking times. As each one cooks to bright green and tender, refresh under cold running water. Combine all the blanched vegetables in a big bowl and set aside until you're ready to serve. (Don't do this too far in advance, or you'll start to lose some of the freshness you're after – a few hours is fine.)

When it's time to serve, dress the vegetables with some of the infused oil, some generous pinches of salt and a lot of ground pepper. Lay the mozzarella on a big platter, dress with a little oil, then scatter the green vegetables over the top so that the pristine white cheese peeks through. Sprinkle a few drops of vinegar on the greens, then serve with toast.

EVEN EASIER

Put some asparagus spears in a hot pan with a tiny splash of olive oil and half an unwaxed lemon, cut-side down. Once the lemon has seared and caramelised, take it out. Add a splash of water and quickly, quickly, clamp the lid on tight to steam the asparagus. Remove from the heat and squeeze over the juice of the other (uncooked) half of the lemon. Serve the mozzarella on a raft of asparagus spears, with the charred lemon on the side, a good pinch of salt and lots and lots of pepper.

POTATO SALAD WITH SAMPHIRE & LEMON

SERVES 6

Samphire is a tremendous vegetable. A succulent that grows in salty marshland close to the seashore, it's sometimes called 'the asparagus of the sea'. It even makes a brief appearance in *King Lear*, when Edgar describes an imaginary samphire picker ('dreadful trade') to his blinded father. And it turns out that the hinterland at Lower Light, north of Adelaide, is carpeted with the stuff. In the dry months, it's stalky and tough. But after rain, the fresh green shoots pop out and can be harvested and scoffed. We have both, at various times, packed parcels of samphire to airlift to Sydney. I took some to Amanda Vanstone once, and she was so enthusiastic that I ended up putting her on to my dad, who obligingly delivered a ute-load of plants to her city home. I've seen samphire at the greengrocers a few times, but the best way to find this sea vegetable is still to forage for it - check out foraging websites in your nearest coastal area for tips. You'd be surprised where this stuff shows up; I'm told you can even find samphire growing around Sydney Harbour.

And it's surprisingly versatile. Pickled, it tastes like fish and chips at the beach. You can use the tips in a prawn-and-cream kind of pasta dish or, if you are out for a picnic, pick the very tender ends and add them to your sandwich, as I heard Hugh Fearnley-Whittingstall propose once. Here, we've put it into a potato salad. I think this is perfectly satisfying as is, but it would be really good alongside a whole baked fish, or with some slender fillets simply floured and pan-fried in butter. If you wanted to make this a more substantial vegetarian dish, you could add a soft-boiled egg.

---

1 kg small potatoes
100 g samphire, any tough bits picked out
4-5 spring onions, thinly sliced into rounds
3 tablespoons olive oil
juice of 1 lemon

PRESSURE-COOKER OPTION

Pour in a little vegetable oil and briefly fry the potatoes. Add 50 ml water and 1 tablespoon lemon juice and cook at pressure for 6 minutes. Release the pressure, tumble the potatoes into a large bowl and dress with the olive oil, spring onions, a pinch of salt and a dash more lemon juice. Because these potatoes cook in such a small amount of water, they are deliciously creamy.

Boil the potatoes in plenty of salted water until very tender and starting to fall apart just a little bit.

Meanwhile, plunge the samphire into a pan of boiling water and blanch for 2-3 minutes, then drain and dunk it straight into a bowl or sink full of very cold water so it keeps its nice bright green colour. Now pinch the samphire into little pieces.

Drain the potatoes thoroughly and tip into a serving bowl. While they're still hot, add the rest of the ingredients except the samphire, and mix well. Just before serving, toss in the blanched samphire.

CHICKPEA SALAD WITH CUBAN MOJO

SERVES 4

Wendy discovered mojo sauce (unfortunately, it is pronounced mo-ho) via 'The Splendid Table', a really useful podcast for those of us who like to fill our heads with thoughts of food and cooking anywhere and everywhere, even while on the bus or jogging in the park. Handy. This particular podcast covered the Spanish version of the sauce, from Gran Canaria, but Wendy found that she preferred the Cuban sort, and then tinkered with it further until she was satisfied. You should do the same: try less coriander, or more chilli, or skip the mandarin and use unadulterated lime juice. Whatever sauce you end up with, this salad is fast to prepare and goes beautifully with roast pork or baked chicken. The smoky chickpeas and halloumi add enough protein and taste for any vegetarians in the group not to be left wanting; serve with cooked bulgur wheat or quinoa for more heft.

---

1 x 400 g tin of chickpeas, rinsed and drained
1 tablespoon olive oil, plus extra for dressing
250 g halloumi
3 good handfuls of baby spinach leaves
2 good handfuls of rocket leaves
1 ripe mango, thinly sliced
1 avocado, thinly sliced
squeeze of mandarin or lime juice
good pinch of smoked paprika

MOJO SAUCE
1 garlic clove
2–3 slices of onion
½ teaspoon ground cumin
generous pinch of salt
pinch of dried oregano
pinch of chilli flakes
50 g chopped coriander, leaves and stalks
a few mint leaves
8–9 basil leaves
juice of ½ mandarin (or orange)
juice of ½ lime
4 tablespoons olive oil

Preheat the oven to 200°C (180°C fan). Use paper towels to pat the chickpeas dry. Hold back a tablespoon of chickpeas for later, then tip the rest into a bowl with the olive oil and a pinch of salt. Toss to coat, then scatter over a baking tray and roast for 10 minutes.

Meanwhile, cut your halloumi into cubes about the size of board-game dice and leave to drain on paper towels. Arrange the spinach and rocket leaves on a serving platter, then top with the mango and avocado. Dress with olive oil and mandarin or lime juice.

To make the mojo sauce, put the reserved tablespoon of chickpeas into a large mortar and add all the other ingredients except the citrus juices and olive oil. Use the pestle to bang away, rather than grinding, until a rough paste starts to form. (I have also used a blender for this, with some success, but find that the mortar and pestle gives better results and is hardly any slower.) Now add the citrus juices and the olive oil. Leave for a few minutes to let the flavours blend before you taste it, then adjust the balance of citrus, salt and chilli until you get it just right.

Take the roast chickpeas out of the oven, scrape to one side of the baking tray and then set aside until you are about 10 minutes away from serving time. Add the halloumi to the vacant half of the baking tray and return to the oven for 10 minutes: the chickpeas should be a bit crispy on the outside but still creamy on the inside; the halloumi should be tinged golden-brown, and that much more delicious because it is warm. Sprinkle the smoked paprika over the chickpeas, then spread them out over the salad, rapidly followed by the halloumi. Drizzle generous amounts of the mojo over the salad and serve right away.

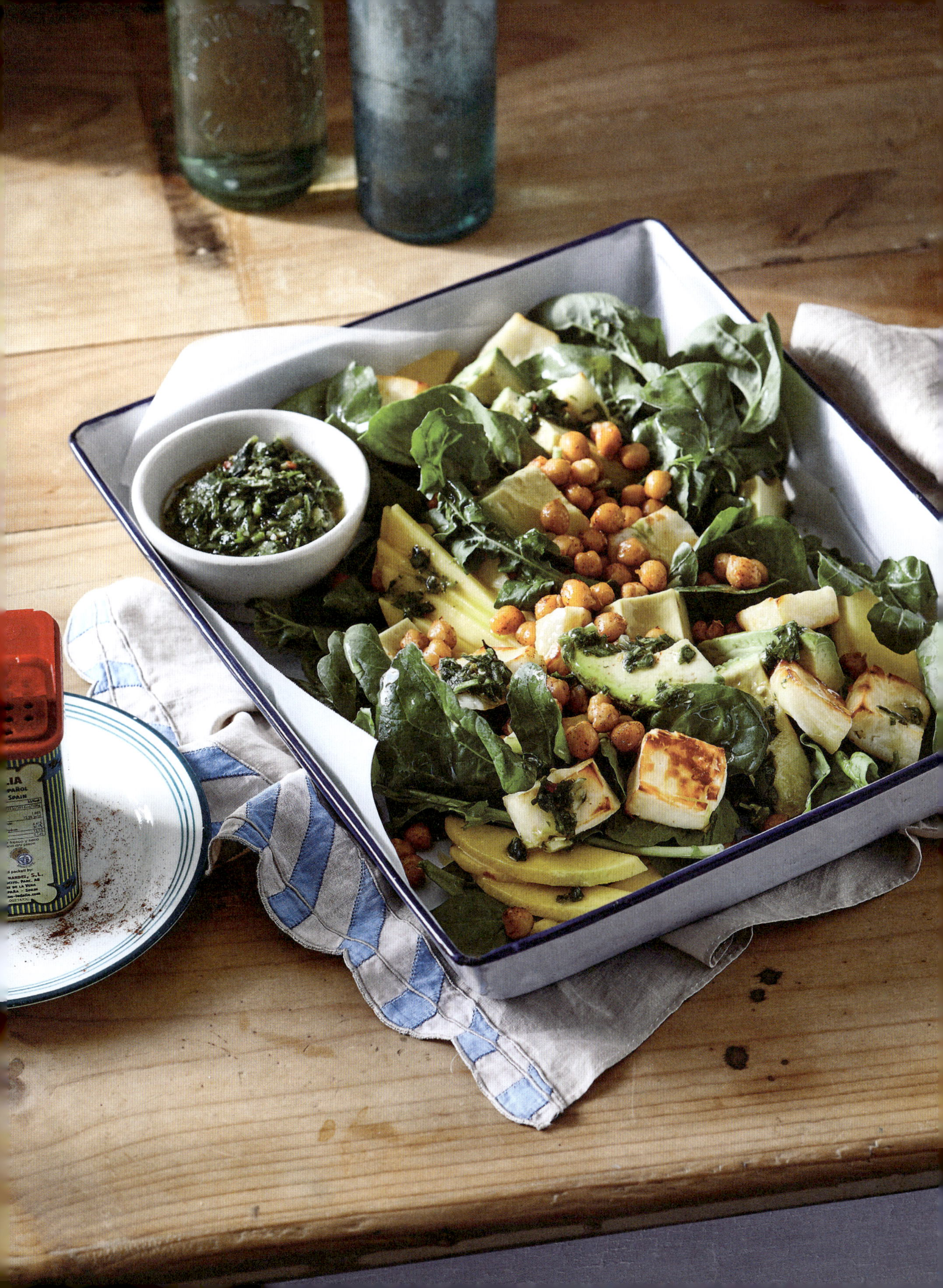

CORN-COB SALAD WITH MASALA BUTTER & COCONUT SAMBOL

SERVES 4–8

Much butter was harmed in the making of this book. So many iterations of flavoured butters were tried and tested, and this was a firm favourite. The only one to be cooked, indeed slow-cooked, it is worth making a fairly large quantity, then you can freeze the left-over masala butter in small batches. Lavished on the corn, it has a lovely mellow flavour that works in perfect harmony with the zesty coconut and coriander sambol.

Messily gnawing the corn straight from the cob, butter dripping down your chin, is a nice way to eat this salad, which is pictured over the page. However, there is also something to be said for slicing the kernels from the cob with a knife and fork, corralling all the condiments and scraping up as much butter as you can with the liberated kernels before tucking in. This way you won't waste any of the tasty extras. Since the main dressing for this salad is butter, it needs to be served warm. This makes a great side salad with roast fish, chicken or pork, or some marinated tofu; allow those who won't be taking up the meat option an extra corn cob.

---

8 sweetcorn cobs

MASALA BUTTER
250 g unsalted butter
2 spring onions, white parts only, finely chopped
4 garlic cloves, thinly sliced
2.5 cm ginger, thinly sliced
20 cardamom pods, lightly crushed (or, if you have time on your hands, scrape out the seeds)
10 green (or black) peppercorns
5 whole cloves
1 teaspoon fennel seeds
½ teaspoon cumin seeds
1 teaspoon ground turmeric
½ teaspoon ground mace
1 teaspoon curry powder

To make the masala butter, preheat the oven to 120°C (100°C fan). Place the butter in a cast-iron casserole over low heat. When there is a protective layer of melted butter on the bottom, add all the other ingredients and wait until the butter starts to foam. Keep a close eye on it – you don't want to burn this much butter! Let it bubble and foam for a minute or so, then clamp the lid on top and stick the casserole in the oven for about 1 hour. What should be happening behind that oven door is a gentle bubbling. After an hour, the garlic should be meltingly soft, and the flavours should have mellowed to give you something very tasty and a bit nutty. Fish out any cardamom pods you can find, let the butter cool slightly and then whizz the whole lot in a blender or food processor until smooth. Or just mash it well with a fork, then sieve out any stray pods and seeds. You won't need all the masala butter here – only about half, so pour the rest into itty-bitty containers and refrigerate until set, then transfer to the freezer, where it will keep for several months.

Once the butter is taken care of, you can make the sambol. Soak the desiccated coconut in just enough warm water to cover and leave for at least 10 minutes. Gently pour off the excess water, squeezing with the back of a spoon to remove as much as possible.

COCONUT SAMBOL

60 g (⅔ cup) desiccated coconut
1 large carrot, grated
2 spring onions, thinly sliced into rounds
80 g coriander, leaves and stalks, finely chopped
½ teaspoon fish sauce
finely grated zest of ½ lime
juice of 1 lime

Close to serving time, mix together all the sambol ingredients in a bowl, seasoning with salt and pepper to taste.

When you are ready to serve, bring a large pan of salted water to the boil. Add the corn cobs and boil for 4-5 minutes, then drain and transfer to a large serving platter. If you don't have a pan big enough to cook all the corn cobs at once, you can keep the first batch warm in a 160°C (140°C fan) oven.

Melt half of the masala butter, either in a small heavy-based pan over low heat or in the microwave (be careful, it won't take long - I do 5 seconds at a time in the microwave to avoid it splattering all over the inside. Pour the melted masala butter all over the corn cobs, spinning them around to make sure they're well covered, then scatter with spoonfuls of sambol. Bring the platter to the table for guests to serve themselves.

MORE MASALA BUTTER...

With a stash of masala butter in your freezer, a quick meal or snack is never far away: try a few spoonfuls on some roasted cauliflower with flaked almonds and greens, tuck a slice or two into a baked potato or onto a piece of grilled fish, or just guzzle it neat.

Salads for all

< CORN-COB SALAD
WITH MASALA BUTTER
& COCONUT SAMBOL

PUNCHED
CUCUMBER
SALAD >

PUNCHED CUCUMBER SALAD

SERVES 4-6

Cucumber: always a side option. But here it is honoured as the principal ingredient in a salad (pictured on the previous page). This needs to be eaten within an hour of making or it will lose its crunch. Luckily, there isn't much to its construction, and it's refreshing yet - thanks to the cashews - filling on a warm evening. With a fillet of baked salmon or a grilled chicken breast, and maybe some steamed rice, you are in summer-food heaven; and some thin strips of tempeh sizzled under the grill for 3-5 minutes will keep your vegetarian guests happy.

½ garlic clove, finely chopped
2 tablespoons rice wine vinegar
2 teaspoons tamari sauce
   (or light soy sauce)
1 teaspoon caster sugar
generous pinch of chilli flakes
   (or ground black pepper)
2 long cucumbers
2 teaspoons sesame oil
1½ tablespoons olive oil
100 g asparagus spears, woody
   ends snapped off
100 g raw cashews
1 large ripe avocado (or 2 small ones)
juice of ½ lime
20 g chopped coriander, leaves
   and stalks
chilli oil, to serve – optional

The first thing to do is to get your garlic into a vinegar bath to calm down its flavour a little. Put it into a large bowl with the vinegar, tamari sauce, sugar and chilli flakes. Mix together and set aside until the sugar has dissolved. This is your dressing.

Here comes the fun part! Wash the cucumbers and place them on a board or bench. Now whack seven bells out of them with a wooden rolling pin. Well, actually, just whack once in each spot, working your way along the length of the cucumbers: you will see the flesh visibly soften and sag under the skin. Ouch.

Now carefully cut the battered cucumbers in half lengthways and use a teaspoon to scoop out the seeds. (Here I offer my usual suggestion to get those cucumber seeds straight into a pitcher of cold water for the table - or quick smart to the bottom of your gin and tonic.)

Give the cucumbers a pat and a squeeze dry with paper towels. Slice on the diagonal, to get some sharp shapes, then transfer to the bowl with the dressing. Drizzle with the sesame and olive oils.

Let the cucumber sit in the dressing for 15-60 minutes, so it has time to pickle. Cut the asparagus into very thin, diagonal slices and add to the cucumber while it's pickling. (If your asparagus is on the gnarly side you could blanch it first, but otherwise it's fine to go in raw.)

Meanwhile, preheat the oven to 200°C (180°C fan). Tip the cashews onto a baking tray and toast in the oven for about 10 minutes. You're after a deep brown colour - but watch them carefully so they don't burn. When they are done, spill them out onto a plate to cool.

Just before serving, cut the avocado into chunks and arrange over the cucumber and asparagus. Squeeze over the lime juice, aiming, as best you can, for the avocado. Sprinkle with coriander and cashews, then toss together. If you like things fiery, add a stripe of chilli oil.

MOZZARELLA SALAD WITH BROCCOLI, ANCHOVIES & OLIVES

SERVES 6 AS A GENEROUS STARTER

If you are reading this at the height of summer, when the markets are full of perfect tomatoes and cheap fistfuls of basil leaves, please do use your finest mozzarella in the salad it was born for: the Caprese - just tomato, basil and mozzarella, simply dressed with olive oil and a few drops of excellent balsamic. Because there is no more delicious salad to start a meal, and there never will be. However, if the days are drawing in, and the taste of summer produce is on the wane, it's time to switch over to this more autumnal option.

---

about 3 tablespoons olive oil
4 anchovy fillets, roughly chopped
3 garlic cloves, thinly sliced
1 small red chilli, seeds removed, finely chopped
2 generous sprigs of rosemary, leaves stripped and finely chopped
4 tablespoons chopped black (or purple) olives
juice of ½ lemon
600 g purple sprouting broccoli or broccolini, any tough parts trimmed
3 x 125 g balls of buffalo mozzarella, thickly sliced or torn
toasted almond flakes, for sprinkling
crusty bread, to serve

Pour the olive oil into a frying pan over low heat and add the anchovies, garlic, chilli and rosemary. When the garlic is soft and the anchovies have disintegrated to make a sauce, and the smell is making you want to eat straight from the pan, remove from the heat. Stir in the olives, then leave to cool. You shouldn't need any salt - those anchovies will take care of that - but squeeze in the lemon juice and set the pan aside. (You can press 'pause' at this point if you are preparing ahead.)

When you are almost ready to serve, plunge the broccoli or broccolini into a large pan of salted boiling water and cook for a minute or so until it has softened slightly, but still has some bite. Meanwhile, set your pan of deliciously pungent, herby oil over low heat to gently reheat.

Drain the broccoli thoroughly, then add to the frying pan for a few turns through the tasty oil. Now tip out the contents of the pan onto a large serving platter, arrange the mozzarella on top and sprinkle with toasted almond flakes. Don't shy away from another glug of olive oil to finish. Serve warm or at room temperature, with some bread for dredging through the sauce.

EVEN EASIER
Serve the mozzarella with those irresistible black figs that appear right at the end of summer, and some peppery rocket. Dress with browned butter, toasted pine nuts and a few drops of balsamic vinegar on the figs.

MAKE IT GLUTEN-FREE
Use gluten-free bread.

WARM GOAT'S CHEESE SALAD WITH GRAPES & WALNUTS

SERVES 6–8

This starter is on just about every prix fixe lunch menu in French bistros - and for good reason; it's easy to forget just how good cheese on toast with some perky leaves can be.

If you're not keen on grapes, replace them with slices of firm pear; matchsticks of tart apple also look and taste lovely. Likewise, do exchange the goat's cheese for a mild blue cheese - a perfect match with pear and hazelnut - if that's what you have in the fridge.

You can toast the bread and make your vinaigrette in advance. And then, when you are ready to serve, you're looking at mere minutes of preparation.

---

500 g black seedless grapes, washed and de-stemmed
1 teaspoon caster sugar
1 tablespoon olive oil
1 tablespoon balsamic vinegar, plus a few drops extra
200 g baby spinach leaves, watercress and/or rocket, washed and spun dry
1 baguette, sliced, or 6-8 generous slices of sourdough or ciabatta
6-8 rounds white-rind goat's cheese (or fresh curd-style, if you – or your guests – prefer)
1 tablespoon runny honey
about 10 walnuts (or almonds), roughly chopped

VINAIGRETTE
1 teaspoon dijon mustard
2 teaspoons red wine vinegar
2 tablespoons olive oil

EVEN EASIER
Skip the vinaigrette and splash some olive oil, a squeeze of lemon juice and a tablespoon of sweet balsamic vinegar or glaze over the leaves.

Preheat the oven to 200°C (180°C fan). Tumble the grapes into a baking dish with the sugar, oil and balsamic vinegar. Give them 10 minutes in the oven, until they have collapsed a little and the juices are slightly jammy. Leave to cool.

Arrange the salad leaves on a large serving platter and scatter over the grapes. Run the slices of bread through the toaster or under the grill, then lay them out in a single layer on a baking tray.

To make the vinaigrette, put the mustard in the bottom of a teacup or small bowl and slowly add the red wine vinegar, while mixing constantly with the back of a teaspoon. One you have a smooth mix, slowly dribble in the oil, keeping going with your spoon action, until you have a smooth emulsion. Set aside. If the vinaigrette splits before serving time, take to it again with your spoon until the dressing has recombined.

When you're ready to serve, dress the leaves with the vinaigrette and toss. Put a slice (or spoonful) of cheese on each slice of toast, then give them 1-2 minutes under a hot grill, or a 3-4 minute bake in a 220°C (200°C fan) oven.

Now lay the hot toasts on top of the leaves and drizzle with a quick zigzag of honey. Finish with a few drops of extra balsamic vinegar, a scattering of walnuts and plenty of pepper. Send to the table for guests to serve themselves. I go heavier than usual on the vinaigrette with this dish because I love the way that the toast soaks up the tangy dressing to become slightly 'good soggy'.

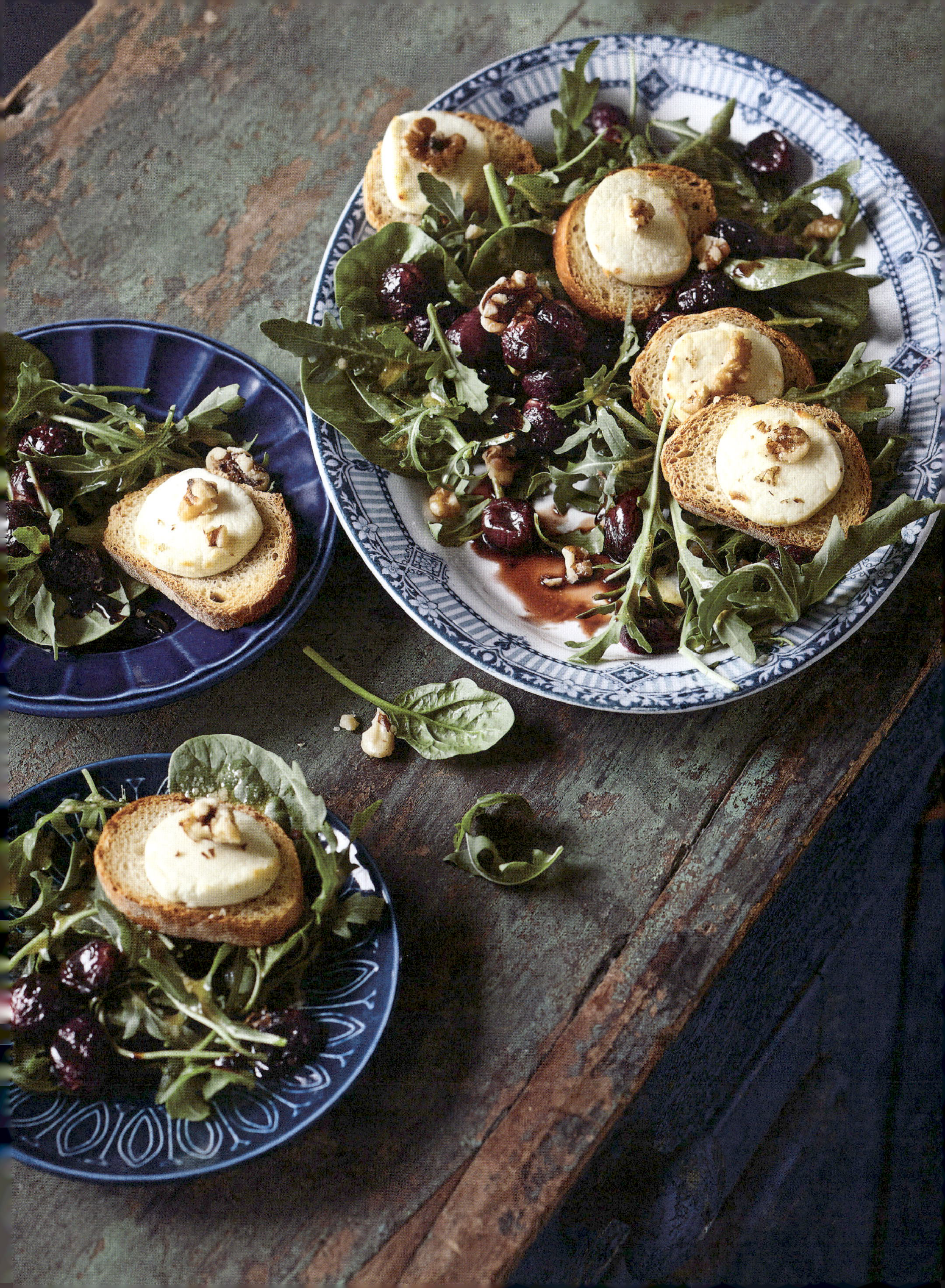

Bring back afternoon tea

If this book is about making entertaining easier, then what gives with four-tier filled cakes and plaited brioche? Yes, some of the recipes in this chapter are fiddly and fussy and take some time and technique. But viewed from another angle, they are a one-plate, plan ahead, make ahead, entertaining shortcut. You can cope with - and maybe even enjoy - making a spectacular cake just so long as you're not also doing a million other things. So while the multi-course lunch for ten with matched wines is off your calendar for the time being, a huge plate of biscuits or a tasty swirly cherry bundt? Yes, I think I could manage that! Try to resist the temptation to disappear down the rabbit hole of a full high tea with a vast spread of sandwiches and iddy bitty salmon bagels (unless your guests are bringing them). Do one cake and do it well and call the day a success.

PASSIONFRUIT CURD MERINGUE CAKE

SERVES 8

This is a cake that looks handsome on the plate. There are effectively six layers, but because the meringue-topped sponges are baked together, the assembly is simpler than it sounds. The passionfruit curd recipe makes about 320 g (1 cup), which is plenty to fill the cake. But do consider doubling it; passionfruit curd is a good thing to have in the fridge.

---

125 g unsalted butter, softened
330 g (1½ cups) caster sugar
4 large eggs, separated
70 g (¼ cup) Greek-style yoghurt
1 teaspoon vanilla paste
150 g (1 cup) plain flour
25 g cornflour
1½ teaspoons baking powder
½ teaspoon cream of tartar
125 ml (½ cup) thickened (whipping) cream
icing sugar, to decorate – optional

PASSIONFRUIT CURD

55 g (¼ cup) caster sugar
2 eggs, plus 1 yolk extra
60 g unsalted butter, cubed
pulp and juice from 4 passionfruit, strained
1 tablespoon lemon juice

Preheat the oven to 180°C (160°C fan). Grease and line two 20 cm springform or loose-bottomed cake tins.

Using an electric mixer, cream the butter and 110 g (½ cup) of the caster sugar until light and fluffy. Add the egg yolks and beat to the consistency of pale yellow shaving cream. Granted, this does not sound especially attractive, but it's the texture you want. Beat in the yoghurt and vanilla. Sift the flour, cornflour and baking powder together and fold into the batter, then spoon half into each tin.

Whisk the egg whites to soft peaks. Gradually add the remaining 220 g (1 cup) of caster sugar and whisk until the sugar has dissolved and the meringue is thick and glossy. Mix in the cream of tartar, then spread half the meringue over each cake base, swirling it to create a rippled surface. Bake for 25-30 minutes. Keep an eye on the meringue tops: if they seem to be browning too quickly, tent with foil. Leave the cakes to cool in their tins for 10 minutes, then carefully remove and transfer to a wire rack to cool completely.

To make the curd, put the sugar, eggs and extra yolk into a small heatproof bowl and whisk until pale. Set the bowl over a pan of simmering water and keep whisking as the mixture heats and starts to thicken. Add the butter, cube by cube, whisking until it melts and the mixture has a custard-like consistency. Add the passionfruit juice and lemon juice and keep whisking until it thickens up again. Leave to cool. (If not using right away, transfer the curd to a lidded jar and refrigerate for up to a week.)

When both cakes and curd are cool, it's time to assemble. Whip the cream until it's nice and pillowy. Whichever cake has the least visually pleasing meringue top will be your bottom half: invert a cake plate over it and flip so it's meringue-side down on the plate. Spread with curd, going right to the edges, then top with whipped cream. Use a wide spatula to help you lower the top cake into position, meringue-side up. Dust with icing sugar, if you like.

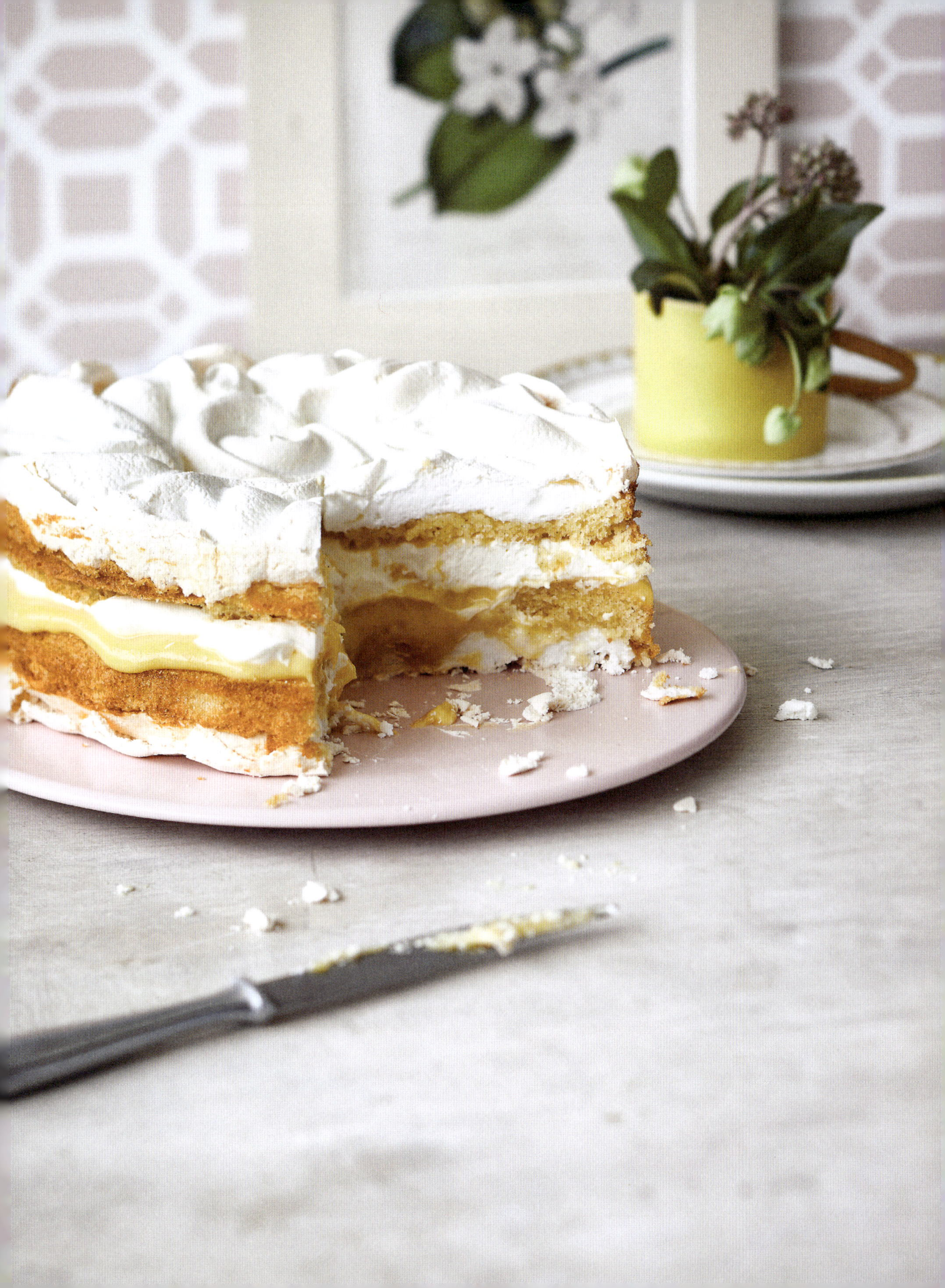

PEACH-LEAF VANILLA SLICE

SERVES 6–8

The notion of using the gentle marzipan flavour of peach leaves in cooking was a very recent one for me. Who knew? Happily, my discovery coincided with the emergence of a mop of leaves on the young peach tree right outside my kitchen. You want tender leaves that are a bit fragrant when you crush them; if you don't have a peach tree, you could substitute a vanilla pod, some lemon verbena or lemon balm leaves, or a sliver of lemon or mandarin zest.

---

70 g unsalted butter, melted
1 x 375 g packet of filo pastry
50 g icing sugar
1 teaspoon ground cinnamon

PEACH-LEAF CUSTARD
1 egg, plus 1 yolk extra
3 tablespoons white sugar
375 ml (1½ cups) full-fat milk
6–7 soft peach leaves, well washed
50 g fine semolina
30 g unsalted butter, cubed

A GREEK BREAKFAST

This version of vanilla slice is based on Greek bougatsa, which is eaten for breakfast, so don't be frightened to serve this early in the morning with some ferociously strong coffee. You can make it ahead of time and then refresh it for 1 minute in a preheated 200°C (180°C fan) oven. The icing sugar and cinnamon are not just for decoration here, but are essential to the taste.

For the peach-leaf custard, whisk the egg, extra yolk and sugar in a heatproof bowl until well combined and a bit fluffy. In a heavy-based saucepan, warm the milk and peach leaves over low heat. Depending on the type and state of the leaves, the flavour could infuse quite quickly, so taste at regular intervals. Once you are happy with the flavour, fish out the leaves and pour the warm milk onto the egg and sugar mixture, whisking as you go. Pour back into the saucepan and place over low–medium heat, stirring all the time, until it comes to a simmer. Turn the heat down to low and slowly scatter in the semolina, whisking all the while. There will be some graininess from the semolina, but keep whisking if it's lumpy. Once the custard has returned to a simmer, cook, stirring constantly, for 2 minutes or until the custard has thickened. Remove from the heat and whisk in the butter, then transfer to a shallow bowl and cover with plastic wrap, pressing it onto the surface of the custard to stop a skin forming. (The custard can be made a day ahead and kept in the fridge.)

When you're ready to put this thing together, preheat the oven to 180°C (160°C fan) and find a baking tray about 25 cm x 20 cm.

Generously brush the baking tray with melted butter. Lay in your first sheet of filo and brush with butter. Repeat until you have 6–8 layers of filo in the tray, then trim off any overhanging pastry. Now spread out the layer of peach custard, and add another 6–8 layers of filo and butter, finishing with filo. Take a knife and score the top layer into rectangles or squares, as though you were cutting into slices to serve. (If you like, use your fingers to give the filo a tiny scrunch around the edges for a more interesting and crunchy finish.) Brush any remaining melted butter over the top.

Bake for 25–30 minutes or until golden. Leave to cool to room temperature, then cut into slices along your pre-scored lines. Dust generously with icing sugar and cinnamon and eat with your fingers.

RHUBARB SYRUP CRUMB CAKE

SERVES 8–10

The idea of using breadcrumbs in a cake is apparently an Irish concept by origin – a thrifty way of recycling old bread. Its effect, when combined with almond meal, is quite magical, resulting in a cake with a nutty, slightly chewy texture that's a perfect foil for the bright colour and tartness of rhubarb.

Given its waste-conscious antecedents, this was a fine cake to take to Greens leader Richard Di Natale's farm, which is entirely solar powered and has beautiful orchards, a modest number of cattle and – appropriately enough – a rhubarb patch. If you don't have such a thing, you could try this with another slightly tart fruit, such as roast nectarines, peaches or plums. Or make the syrup with orange and/or lemon juice and serve the cake with fresh berries.

---

75 g raw almonds, skin on
50 g stale sourdough (or any other robust bread)
100 g (1 cup) almond meal
220 g (1 cup) caster sugar
½ teaspoon baking powder
4 eggs
185 ml (¾ cup) vegetable oil
crème fraîche, whipped cream or thick yoghurt, to serve

RHUBARB AND SYRUP
400 g rhubarb, as vivid pink as you can find, washed and any leaves trimmed off
100 g white sugar

Preheat the oven to 200°C (180°C fan). Grease and line a 20 cm cake tin.

For the rhubarb, chop the stems into pieces about the size of your middle finger. Arrange in a single layer in a baking dish, then flick over about 80 ml (⅓ cup) of water and sprinkle with the sugar. Roast for 10–15 minutes or until soft but still holding its shape.

Scatter the almonds over a baking tray and toast in the oven for 10 minutes. Slice the bread as thinly as you can, lay it on another baking tray and place in the oven for about 5 minutes to dry it out. Set aside the rhubarb, almonds and bread to cool.

Take to the dried-out bread with a large knife (or hand the job over to your food processor) and chop (or whizz) to very coarse crumbs. Same goes for the almonds: chop or blitz until you have a rubbly mixture with some pieces up to the size of a small pea. Tip the breadcrumbs and almonds into a large bowl. Stir in the almond meal, sugar and baking powder. Whisk the eggs and oil together, then pour into the dry ingredients and stir to combine.

Transfer the batter to the tin and slide it into the oven, then drop the temperature to 160°C (140°C fan) and bake for 45 minutes. When it's ready, the cake should look temptingly crispy at its edges, and a skewer inserted in the centre should come out clean. Leave to cool.

Meanwhile, drain the syrup from the rhubarb and then – up to an hour or so before serving – use a skewer to poke holes in the cake and slowly pour the syrup all over, giving it time to soak in as you go.

Serve each slice of cake with a substantial log-pile of the baked rhubarb and some crème fraîche, whipped cream or thick yoghurt.

Bring back afternoon tea

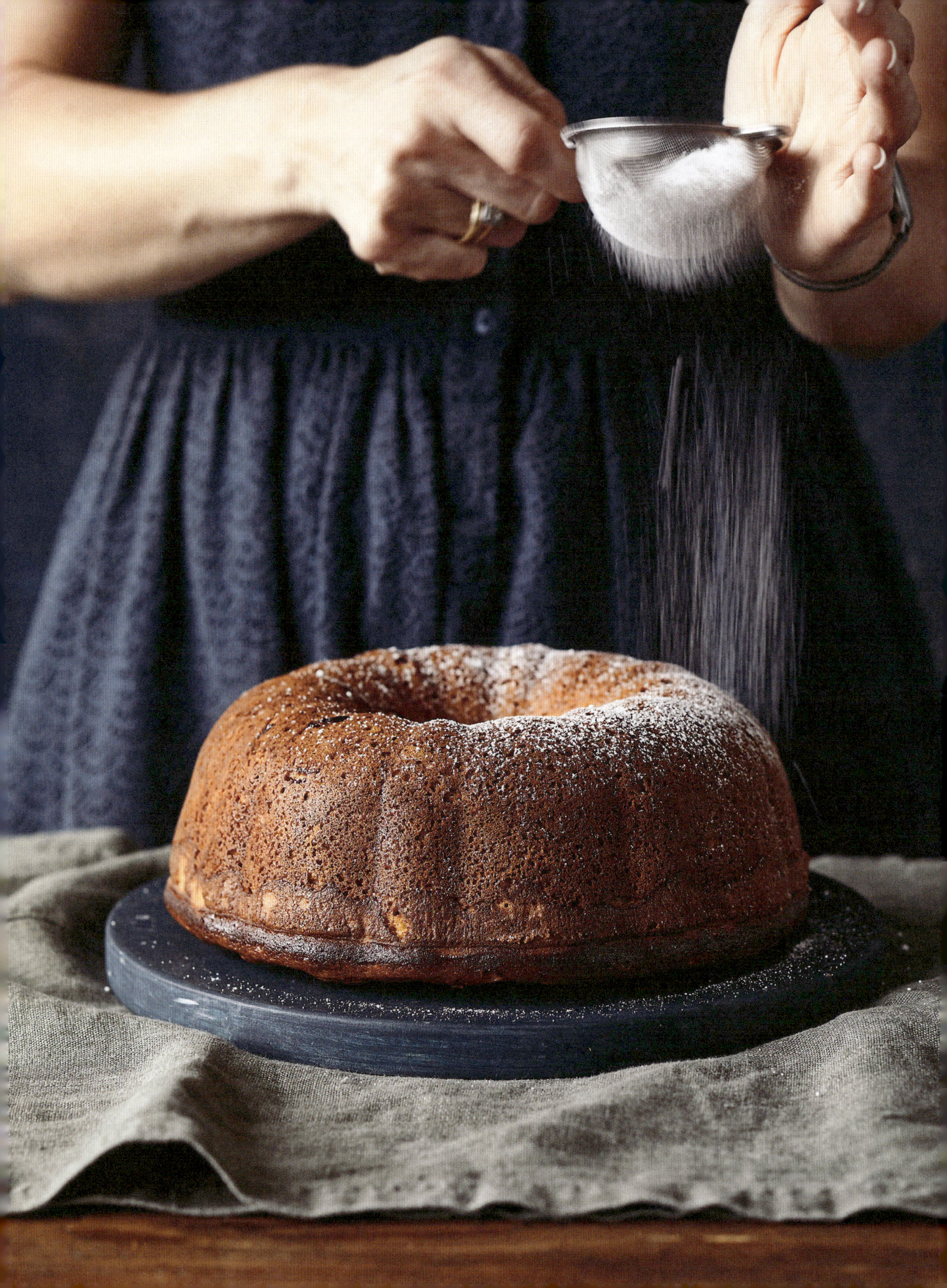

CHERRY RICOTTA BUNDT CAKE

SERVES 10

This is a cake that is, at heart, desperately auditioning for the shelves of a Barossa Valley bakery. The German fondness for cakes with fruit, cheese and/or crumble toppings is irrevocably baked into Wendy and me, simply through the geography of our shared childhood. Bienenstich (see page 158) is the queen of the genre, in my opinion, but this cake certainly deserves a spot at court.

It's a fairly simple pound-style cake with cherries, but the unique feature here is the ricotta custard, which is poured over the cake batter before it goes in the oven. During baking, the ricotta sinks through the cake, making for a marbled cheesecake surprise. *Wunderschön!*

---

200 g unsalted butter, softened
220 g (1 cup) caster sugar
1 teaspoon vanilla paste
3 eggs
260 g (1 cup) Greek-style yoghurt
375 g (2½ cups) self-raising flour, sifted
1 teaspoon baking powder
300 g (1½ cups) pitted sour or morello cherries (the kind in a jar), drained
2 tablespoons plain flour
icing sugar, for dusting – optional

RICOTTA CUSTARD
250 g ricotta
2 eggs
110 g (½ cup) caster sugar
1 teaspoon vanilla paste
2 tablespoons plain flour

Preheat the oven to 180°C (160°C fan). Grease and flour a 26 cm bundt tin – I use a pastry brush dipped into very soft (but not melted!) butter for this task. It's crucial that you get into every little crevice; otherwise you are on a one-way express train to bundtastrophe, and no one wants that.

Using an electric mixer, cream the butter and sugar together until pale and creamy, then mix in the vanilla paste. Now add the eggs one by one, beating as you go. When the eggs are fully incorporated, add the yoghurt, beat briefly, then gently fold in the self-raising flour and the baking powder. Toss the cherries in the plain flour, then fold them lightly into the batter – don't overmix. Spoon the cake batter into the tin, pushing down gently to make sure it gets into all the fluted bits. Smooth the top.

Now for the ricotta custard. In the same mixing bowl (this is probably slovenly, but I'm not very bothered and it saves washing up), beat the ricotta with the eggs, sugar and vanilla paste. Pour the mixture on top of the batter, then bake the cake for 35–40 minutes or until a skewer inserted into the deepest part comes out clean.

Let the cake cool in the tin for 10 minutes before turning it out onto a wire rack. When it's completely cool, dust your cherry cake with icing sugar, if you like.

CHOCOLATE CELEBRATION CAKE

SERVES 12

Pictured over the page, this is a cake for any special occasion. Its central charm lies in the mirror-like shine of its chocolate glaze, which can be left as is (perfection!) or gussied up with all manner of extra decoration. Inside, there is a cream layer, the tart thrill of raspberry and a reliable chocolate sponge. It really is the only celebration cake you'll ever need.

The shine and perfection of the glaze on this cake comes from gelatine. But there's also a note opposite to help you carry off a vegetarian or halal version, using agar agar. If I'm honest, the gelatine produces a superior result – glossy, perfectly set and smooth – but what fun is a shiny cake if your vegetarian or Muslim friends can't eat it?

---

50 g unsweetened cocoa powder
100 ml boiling water
100 g unsalted butter, softened
250 g caster sugar
3 large eggs
175 g plain flour
3¼ teaspoons baking powder
generous pinch of salt
1 generous tablespoon Greek-style yoghurt
apricot jam, for sealing – optional

CHOCOLATE GLAZE
6 titanium-strength gelatine leaves
85 ml thick (double) cream
1 tablespoon runny honey
175 g caster sugar
75 g unsweetened cocoa powder
50 g dark chocolate, chopped

FILLING
120 ml raspberry coulis (or 60 ml raspberry jam)
300 ml thickened (whipping) cream, whipped to soft peaks

Preheat the oven to 200°C (180°C fan). Grease and line two 20 cm cake tins.

Dissolve the cocoa powder in the boiling water and stir to a smooth paste. Using an electric mixer (or a good old-fashioned whisk), cream the butter and sugar until pale and creamy. Add the eggs one at a time, beating well each time, then beat in the cocoa paste. Sift together the flour, baking powder and salt, then add to the batter with the yoghurt. Fold in until combined.

Divide the batter evenly between the two tins (electronic scales are invaluable here). Bake the cakes for 15 minutes, then have a peek: in all likelihood, they will need another 5–10 minutes, but ovens vary so much that it is worth checking, rather than risking an overcooked sponge. You are looking for edges that are slightly pulling away from the tin, tops that spring back when gently pressed, and of course, a skewer that comes out clean when inserted into the centre.

Leave the cakes to cool in their tins for 10 minutes, then carefully turn out onto a wire rack to cool completely. (If you're not constructing the cake on the same day, wrap and refrigerate or freeze your sponge cakes at this point: they'll keep for a few days in the fridge and up to a month in the freezer.)

Now for the chocolate glaze. Soak the gelatine in a bowl of cold water for about 5 minutes. In a medium saucepan, whisk together the cream, honey, sugar and cocoa powder. Bring to the boil, whisking constantly, and let it bubble for 20 seconds or so, then turn down to a bare simmer and keep whisking until smooth. Stir in the chocolate and, one at a time, the squeezed-out gelatine leaves.

Special Guest

EVEN EASIER

I tend to stick to the steps listed here, superstitiously adding the eggs one at a time, but if you are seeking shortcuts, try the all-in-one method to make your cake batter: just plonk all the sponge ingredients in a bowl and beat until smooth. The only precautions you need to take are to sift the flour and baking powder together first, and to make sure your butter is softened but not starting to melt.

USING AGAR AGAR FOR THE CHOCOLATE GLAZE

Add 1½ teaspoons agar agar powder to 120 ml water in a saucepan, then bring to the boil, stirring well. Reduce the heat, cover and simmer gently for 5 minutes. Add the cream, honey, sugar and cocoa powder, then bring back to the boil and cook for 1 minute, whisking constantly until smooth. Take off the heat and fold through the chocolate until completely melted. Strain the glaze through a fine sieve.

QUICK RASPBERRY COULIS

If you have some raspberries in the fridge or freezer, make your own raspberry coulis: bring 150 g raspberries to a slow simmer and stir in a scant tablespoon of icing sugar. Mash with a potato masher, then strain out the seeds (or not, if you prefer a little crunch and texture to your coulis).

Once everything has melted and dissolved to make a smooth glaze, take off the heat and leave to cool slightly. This next step may seem fussy, but it makes for an extra-special finish. Strain the chocolate mix through a fine sieve to remove any lumps or undissolved gelatine. Your chocolate glaze should now look beautifully slick.

To assemble the cake, either cut each sponge cake in half horizontally for a four-layer cake or just leave them as they are and go with a two-layer cake. Spread each layer of cake with raspberry coulis, then sandwich together with a decent layer of whipped cream, bearing in mind that the sponge layers do tend to suck up a lot of the coulis and cream filling - so what looks like a lot at the start might not seem so much by the time you are cutting. But don't worry, if this cake becomes your go-to celebratory gateau, then you will have lots of practice and become an expert within the year. Think of it as your own cake journey, as they say these days. Use your hands to coerce the edges of the layers into the neatest arrangement you can, in preparation for the pouring of the glaze.

Transfer the cake to a wire rack and use a pastry brush to sweep off any excess crumbs. If you want a neat, professional finish, you can do what's called a 'crumb coat', which involves painting a kind of sealant (made from heated and strained apricot jam) all over the naked cake. It does add a tiny something extra - but for my money, not enough to warrant the time and effort it takes.

Pour the warm, but not hot, glaze - it should be the consistency of molten lava - over the cake, letting it run down the sides to cover the cake completely. Use a spatula or offset palette knife to encourage the glaze over the edges and smooth the sides. In a perfect world you would have not a peep of the underneath cake showing through, but in real life, no one is going to give a hoot if there are gaps; you might even choose to ride the trend for 'drippy' looks on the edge. Honestly, if there is one thing I have learned about cake making is that people love a homemade cake and so long as it looks a bit jolly, the imperfections will bother absolutely no one but you.

To transfer the cake to its serving plate, I use a couple of fish slices and, with beaded brow - and ideally the help of another adult - carefully manoeuvre it into position. But I do know there are such things as cake-shifters, which look like snow shovels, and there is one of those on my Christmas list this year. Patch up any dents or dings made during the procedure with a little bit of glaze and set aside until the whole cake is cool (at least 2 hours in the fridge or a very cool spot).

Decorate your cake with as much taste or kitsch as you like.

< CHOCOLATE
CELEBRATION
CAKE

On birthday cakes

Birthdays are supposed to be happy occasions: celebrations to mark a year of achievements and milestones. But the associated events can elicit a visceral reaction of horror, especially if you are going for the full catastrophe with a party, invitations, gifts, entertainment, snacks, party bags for the children... and, wait for it, the cake!

Birthday cakes, and the quest for decorating perfection, can be the match in the powder keg that finally blows a host's composure to a million tiny pieces. Some time into her parenting life, and after one too many instances of gently weeping into yet another very-late-night icing and cake-decorating session, Wendy did the maths: her children were still young and there were a lot of cakes left on the parenting horizon.

Because what any child or birthday celebrator wants just as much as a cake is for their dear cake-maker to be happy, not stressed, and involved with the fun of the big day, Wendy realised something had to change: 'For the good of everyone... I let go of the dream that I would ever be good at the fiddly cake - the clever shapes and the smooth sugar-paste icing. Anything spherical or in the form of a living creature, I will never make, nor even attempt to. I am at peace with that. Some people thrive on a cake challenge: I do not. My cakes will be very tasty but quite likely messy.'

So here's our two cents' worth: put aside visual perfection and concentrate on the simple delights of decent ingredients and a properly scrumptious sponge. If you suspect that you too are not a natural born cake-maker, follow our suggestions below for a birthday-cake-baking future devoid of frazzle and wonky fondant unicorns.

KEEP IT SIMPLE
Children, especially, have quite a low threshold for thrills when it comes to cake. A carefully crafted guitar-shaped cake will probably be no more impressive to a child than your standard chocolate cake with a clunky great plastic guitar wedged on the top and sprinkled with edible glitter from a packet. For adults, a mass of berries and chocolate shavings covers a whole range of cake errors beneath.

FIND A RELIABLE RECIPE & STICK TO IT
Once you find a sponge recipe that works, keep several copies of it in safe places, because it is precious. On the previous page is an easy chocolate sponge that is neither overly sweet nor dry, and produces two 20 cm round stackable cakes. The citrus sponge recipe on the next page, with the zest exchanged for ½ teaspoon of vanilla paste, could become your standby plain sponge. However, if you have Uncle Quentin's excellent family recipe and it works for you, then stick to it. After a few years, you'll virtually be able to make it in your sleep.

GET THE GEAR
Invest in two good same-sized tins if you are going to make layer cakes: the loose-bottomed anodised aluminium ones give an even bake and keep a good shape. Pre-cut reusable cake-tin liners can save time and paper, and a cake-cutting wire is worth every centimetre of space it takes up in your cupboard. If you calculate that you have a lot of cakes in your short- to medium-term future, set yourself up right from the start.

MAKE THE SPONGE IN ADVANCE
Sponge cakes can be made a few days ahead and kept, well wrapped, in the fridge. Or for weeks, even months, in the freezer. Slapping them together and decorating when you're ready will feel like less than half the work.

A 'SECRET' CAKE FOR A CROWD
Large cakes are difficult to bake evenly and tricky to manage and transport. Stick with a 20 cm cake for decorating, candles and ceremonial cutting. Have an extra in the wings for cutting and more cutting if you are catering for a crowd. It doesn't need to be pretty and it doesn't have to be decorated – add a few sprinkles for children or fruit for adults. The traybake format can be a practical solution for the background cutting cake.

And our final off-trend word on cakes is this: if at first you don't succeed, give up. Accept that some years you should just buy a cake for a birthday party. Although they can be maddeningly expensive, shell out for one if it allows you some breathing space. If it comes to a choice between enjoying your loved one's party and making a cake, we vote for quitting every time... and perhaps make a mental note to devote a slow weekend afternoon at a quieter time in your life to make a knockout over-the-top crazily decorated cake for them for absolutely no reason at all.

Bring back afternoon tea

CITRUS MASCARPONE LAYER CAKE

SERVES 12

Like its chocolate-y fraternal twin on page 146, this cake (pictured over the page) is suitable for any event that involves the popping of someone's cork. Dress it up with an asymmetrical arrangement of garden flowers. Spell out the appropriate birthday number in Smarties, if it's a younger demographic you're baking for. Sprinkle some citrus zest over the top cream layer! Forget about the top cream layer! Really, you can dress this cake up or down to suit your purposes: the basic elements are buttery sponge and zingy mascarpone cream; no one is ever going to complain once those two are on board.

---

225 g unsalted butter, softened
150 g caster sugar
50 g soft brown sugar
4 large eggs
finely grated zest of 2 citrus fruit (lemon and/or orange)
225 g (1½ cups) self-raising flour
1 teaspoon baking powder
pinch of salt
50 ml citrus syrup (I use the syrup from tinned mandarins) or reduced sweetened orange juice – optional

LEMON MASCARPONE FILLING
150–200 ml thickened (whipping) cream
1 tablespoon icing sugar
150 g mascarpone
2 tablespoons lemon curd, plus 2–3 tablespoons extra for spreading

Preheat the oven to 180°C (160°C fan). Grease and line two 20 cm cake tins.

Using an electric mixer, cream the butter and sugars until light and fluffy. Add the eggs one by one, beating well each time, then mix in the citrus zest. Sift in the flour, baking powder and salt, then fold into the batter until thoroughly incorporated.

Divide the batter evenly between the two tins (not usually one for precision, I do use an electronic scale here to help me get the same amount in each tin). Smooth the surface and bake for 20-25 minutes, until the cakes have a golden hue and a skewer inserted in the centre comes out clean.

When the cakes are cool enough to handle, carefully turn them out onto a wire rack to cool. As this is a slightly sticky sponge, be careful that the cakes don't stick to the rack: the trick is to move them once or twice on the rack before they are completely cool. (If you are splitting the work of making the sponges and constructing the cake, you can wrap and refrigerate or freeze them at this point: they'll keep for a few days in the fridge and up to a month in the freezer.)

A sponge cake that has been refrigerated will be much easier to cut than one that is straight out of the oven, so this is a good time to decide whether you want to cut each sponge in half horizontally for a four-layer cake, or stick with two layers.

To make the lemon mascarpone filling, whip 150 ml of the cream with the icing sugar until it has thickened slightly, stopping well short of soft peaks. Then fold in the mascarpone and the 2 tablespoons of lemon curd until smooth – thin out with a little extra cream if it seems too stiff – you're after an an easily spreadable consistency so you won't plough up the surface of the cakes.

To assemble the cake, use a pastry brush to dab some of the citrus syrup on the first layer of cake, concentrating on the edges (which may have dried out if you made the sponge in advance). Next use a spatula or offset palette knife to spread a very thin layer of the extra lemon curd over the sponge, followed by a generous layer of the lemon mascarpone cream, making sure to get it all the way to the cake edges. Gently sit the next layer of cake on top and spread it with syrup, curd and lemon mascarpone cream. Keep going until all your layers of cake are used up.

Spread a final layer of lemon mascarpone cream over the top of the cake and decorate. Or don't decorate. It's your party.

LEMON CURD

If you can't find lemon curd, you can make your own: follow the recipe for passionfruit curd on page 140, replacing the passionfruit pulp and juice with 4 tablespoons lemon juice.

< CITRUS
MASCARPONE
LAYER CAKE

APRICOT,
PISTACHIO &
ROSEWATER
CORONET >

APRICOT, PISTACHIO & ROSEWATER CORONET

SERVES 8

This is most definitely a tea-time project for when you have a free morning in which to indulge in the ruminative pleasure of baking. Essentially, this is a brioche stuffed with apricots and nuts, based on the French couronne. I first started thinking about this compelling bakery item when - in Melbourne, after a live 'Chat 10 Looks 3' show - a woman named Karen Gough slipped me a still-warm cardboard box, which turned out to contain some freshly made, hand-sized coronets of yeasty, apricot-laden delight. After several months of thrilled experimentation, here is my version (pictured on the previous page), which has a whiff of the Middle East about it. The filling contains rosewater, which goes so beautifully with apricots, and pistachio marzipan, which is shockingly easy to make. As indeed, incidentally, is almond marzipan. Why is that stuff so expensive in the shops? The scales have fallen from my eyes now; I'm never buying it again.

---

450 g (3 cups) strong white bread flour, plus extra for dusting
7 g active dried yeast (1 standard sachet)
2 tablespoons runny honey
150 ml lukewarm milk
1 large egg, lightly beaten
100 g unsalted butter, softened
handful of ice cubes

PISTACHIO MARZIPAN
150 g pistachio kernels
130 g icing sugar
1 egg white

APRICOT FILLING
150 g dried apricots
150 ml apricot nectar
1 tablespoon rosewater
50 g unsalted butter
50 g soft brown sugar
30 g plain flour

Tip the flour into the bowl of a stand mixer fitted with the dough hook. In a teacup or small bowl, whisk the yeast and honey into the warm milk and leave to stand for 5 minutes. When it is slightly foamy, add it to the flour and mix until combined, then add the egg. Mix for a minute, then add the butter. Mix on medium speed for about 5 minutes, or until you have a sticky, shiny, elastic dough. (You can refrigerate the dough overnight at this point and it will be fine - just allow it to return to room temperature before proceeding.)

Cover the dough with plastic wrap (I just leave it in the mixer bowl, but you could transfer it to a clean oiled bowl, if you like) and leave to rise in a warm place until doubled in size, about 1½ hours.

Meanwhile, to make the pistachio marzipan, blitz the pistachio kernels with the icing sugar and egg white in a small food processor or the bowl part of a stick blender. If you have neither, just use a big knife to chop the nuts to a coarse powder, then mix in the icing sugar and egg white, kneading at the end to bring it to a stiff paste. Wrap in plastic wrap and refrigerate until you're ready to use it.

For the filling, dice the apricots and put them into a small bowl. Stir in the apricot nectar and rosewater and set aside to macerate for about an hour, or until the apricots have swelled nicely. (If you want to speed things up here, you could gently heat the apricot mix in a small pan for a couple of minutes - just let it return to room temperature before the next step.)

TO FINISH

1 egg yolk, beaten with
    1 teaspoon water
2 tablespoons apricot jam or honey,
    warmed with 1 teaspoon rosewater
2 tablespoons slivered pistachios
1 teaspoon dried rose petals
100 g icing sugar and juice of
    ½ lemon – optional

Mash the butter, sugar and flour together, then add the apricots and nectar and squish everything together into a chunky paste.

Okay. Once your dough is risen, punch it down and roll it out on a large sheet of baking paper (sprinkled with flour if the dough seems sticky) into a rectangle – around 35 cm x 25 cm. Spread the filling over the dough, right to the edges.

Now roll out the marzipan into a thin, brilliant green sheet. Cut it to the same length as the rectangle of dough but about 3 cm narrower. Lay it over the apricot filling, leaving a strip of exposed apricot down one of the long sides. Starting from this side, roll up the dough into a sausage, pressing the dough to seal. Slice the sausage in half lengthways, cutting it right through the middle. Put the two halves next to each other, lining them up so they're parallel and touching. Dust the cut sides, and your hands, with flour. Now twist the two halves together, like a pair of pants you're wringing the water out of. Form the twist into a circle, folding the end under to keep the circle a uniform thickness. Your coronet will look wonky, but don't worry – another proving, and the baking, will mask a lot of the wonkiness. Slide the baking paper and coronet onto a baking tray and leave to prove for another hour or so, tented in oiled plastic wrap.

Preheat the oven to 200°C (180°C fan), slipping an empty roasting tin into the bottom to heat at the same time.

When your coronet is risen and springy to the touch, it's time to bake. Use a pastry brush to egg-wash all the visible bits of dough with the beaten egg yolk. Drop a handful of ice cubes into the roasting tin and put the coronet in to bake. After 5 minutes, turn the oven down to 180°C (160°C fan) and bake for a further 25 minutes. If the top is getting too brown, tent with foil.

The coronet is done when it's nicely browned on top, firm to the touch and the base is browned too. Remove from the oven, allow to stand for 10 minutes, then brush with the warm jam or honey glaze. You can either sprinkle the pistachio slivers and dried rose petals on now, or wait until the cake has cooled and make a basic runny lemon icing from the icing sugar and just enough of the lemon juice to give a pourable consistency. Drizzle the coronet with the icing, then do your sprinkling on top of the icing. Consume!

EVEN EASIER

Buy almond marzipan and use that instead.
Use apricot jam in the filling, rather than soaked apricots.
Omit all the post-baking icing and sprinkling palaver.

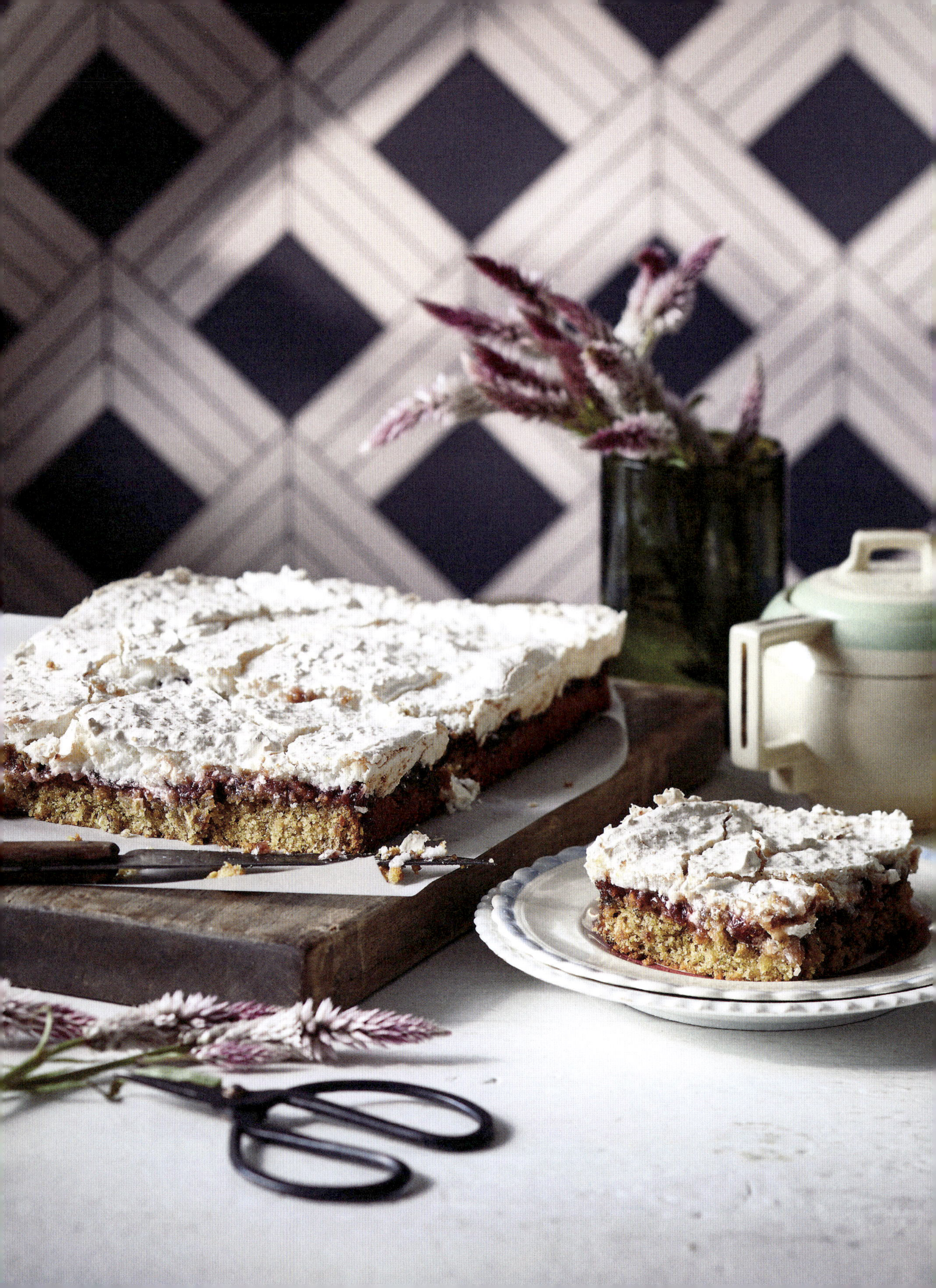

PISTACHIO LOUISE CAKE

SERVES 12

The Louise cake is an old-fashioned delight: it has elements of cake, but also elements of slice, regally inhabiting a broad shallow tin and incorporating a sponge layer, a raspberry jam layer and a top layer of crowd-pleasing coconut meringue. This variation has a pistachio sponge, which can easily be made gluten-free and adds a pleasingly festive green tinge to the whole affair. Pistachio paste can be found in fancy food shops: look for the sweet kind, not the pistachio-pesto sort. It's expensive but transcendentally delicious and you will immediately want to spread it on everything you own. If you can't find it, though, just leave it out – your cake will still be very nice.

---

300 g good-quality, deep-red raspberry jam

PISTACHIO CAKE
125 g unsalted butter, softened
50 g caster sugar
2 eggs
100 g marzipan
30 g pistachio paste – optional
110 g (¾ cup) plain flour
1 teaspoon baking powder
125 g unsalted pistachios, finely ground

COCONUT MERINGUE
4 egg whites
220 g (1 cup) caster sugar
90 g (1 cup) desiccated coconut

Preheat the oven to 180°C (160°C fan). Grease and line a 30 cm x 20 cm slice (traybake) tin.

For the pistachio cake, using an electric mixer, cream the butter and sugar until light and fluffy. Add the eggs one by one, beating well each time. Add the marzipan and pistachio paste, if using, and beat well. Combine the flour, baking powder and ground pistachios, then fold into the batter until thoroughly incorporated.

Spread the batter evenly over the base of the tin. Bake for 15 minutes or until firm and slightly golden. Leave to cool in the tin while you make the coconut meringue.

Whisk the egg whites to soft peaks. Gradually add the caster sugar and keep whisking until the sugar has dissolved. Fold the coconut through gently and evenly, being careful not to lose too much air out of the meringue.

Now, spread the jam in an even layer over the cake, taking it right to the edges. Top with the meringue, spreading it out evenly and smoothing the surface. Return to the oven and bake for another 30 minutes or until the meringue is nicely golden. Allow to cool in the tin, then cut into squares for serving.

MAKE IT GLUTEN-FREE
Use good-quality gluten-free flour and baking powder.

BIENENSTICH TRAY CAKE

SERVES 12

Two Wells, the Adelaide Plains town where we grew up, is close enough to the Barossa Valley that the fabulous yeasted cakes and streusel toppings of the German kitchen wafted across to our bakeries like the aroma of a just-out-of-the-oven pie. School fetes, church morning teas, they all bore the mark of the Teuton – and the cake I always looked for was Bienenstich, which translates as 'bee sting'. There's an absurd range of explanations for the name, including some cockamamie tale about fifteenth-century German bakers lobbing beehives at marauders and then inventing this cake in triumph. No one should care. This slab of Bienenstich (pictured over the page) – brioche baked in a slice tin, topped with honey and almond toffee and filled with custard – will feed an afternoon horde and is perfect with a cup of tea.

Custard purists will note the use of cornflour and gelatine. They are included because the custard here is a structural element and cannot afford to be runny.

---

450 g (3 cups) plain flour
pinch of salt
7 g active dried yeast
   (1 standard sachet)
2 tablespoons runny honey
200 ml lukewarm milk
1 large egg, lightly beaten
100 g unsalted butter, softened

TOFFEE TOPPING
75 g unsalted butter
3 tablespoons runny honey
75 g caster sugar
1 tablespoon cream
80 g flaked almonds

CUSTARD FILLING
2 gelatine leaves
250 ml (1 cup) milk
4 tablespoons custard powder
375 ml (1½ cups) cream
3 tablespoons caster sugar
260 g (1 cup) Greek-style yoghurt

Tip the flour into the bowl of a stand mixer fitted with the dough hook and add the salt. In a teacup or small bowl, whisk the yeast and honey into the warm milk and leave to stand for 5 minutes, or until slightly foamy, then mix into the flour until combined. Add the egg and keep mixing until it starts to come together. Add the butter all at once and mix on medium speed for about 5 minutes, or until you have a soft, shiny, elastic and sticky dough.

Cover with plastic wrap and leave in a warm place for 1–1½ hours until doubled in size. (If you're doing this ahead of time, you can chill the dough in the fridge overnight, then take it out and allow it to rise and return to room temperature in the morning.)

Punch the dough down (with floured hands – it will be sticky). Grease a 30 cm x 20 cm slice (traybake) tin and line with baking paper. Now gently press the dough out and stretch it to fit the tin, pushing it into the corners and trying to make it as even as possible. Cover with oiled plastic wrap and then a tea towel, and leave somewhere warm to rise for about an hour.

Preheat the oven to 200°C (180°C fan).

For the toffee topping, melt the butter, honey and sugar together in a small saucepan and cook until foaming and combined. Add the cream, followed by the almond flakes, then stir. Remove from the heat and allow to cool for about 5 minutes.

Now, your next task is to spread - very gently and as evenly as you can - the almond toffee mix all over the risen dough. Avoid dumping too much of the mix on at once as it can deflate the dough: I use a rubber spatula to transfer and distribute small amounts at a time.

Bake for 25 minutes, turning the oven down to 180°C (160°C fan) at about the 10-minute mark. When it's ready, the cake should be well-risen and have a dark golden-brown toffee crust. Set aside to cool.

Now for the custard filling. Soak the gelatine leaves in cold water until floppy. Use a splash of the milk to make a paste with the custard powder. Pour the rest of the milk into a saucepan with the cream and bring to a simmer. Now whisk in the custard paste and the sugar until smooth, and keep cooking gently until the custard thickens, stirring constantly. Take off the heat and whisk in the squeezed-out gelatine leaves. Finally, whisk in the yoghurt and then set aside to cool.

When both cake and filling are cool, cut the cake in half horizontally and spread a thick layer of filling in the middle. Replace the toffee 'lid' and serve, cutting into square pieces with a serrated bread knife.

< BIENENSTICH
TRAY CAKE

MANDARIN
& HONEY
MADELEINES >

MANDARIN & HONEY MADELEINES

MAKES 12

Hot, buttery, soft but crispy on the edges when straight out of the oven, these madeleines (pictured on the previous page) are one of the easiest options when you have a gang coming over for afternoon tea. They are quick to make in advance and take less than ten minutes to bake. Make up the batter and transfer to a piping bag, then chill for a few hours, or overnight if you can. When your guests' arrival is imminent, just pipe the batter into shell-shaped tins and slip the madeleines into the oven as your guests are pulling into the driveway. The only downside is that they don't keep especially well, but I doubt you will ever have to find that out.

---

100 g unsalted butter
3 tablespoons strong-flavoured runny honey
200 g (1⅓ cups) plain flour
1 teaspoon baking powder
75 g caster sugar
2 eggs
30 ml full-fat milk
finely grated zest of 1 well-washed mandarin (or 1 lemon or ½ orange)
icing sugar, for dusting

Before we get started, the issue of madeleine tins needs to be addressed. The classic tin with a dozen distinctive shell-shaped depressions is almost mandatory, but you could squeak in a result using a patty-pan tin with hemispherical cups. You want something shallow to give you a high ratio of crust to sponge, and non-stick will save you a lot of time. Once you have the hang of madeleines (and really, there isn't much to get the hang of) you can experiment with all different sorts and flavours. If you've been convinced and are now in possession of a madeleine tin... then let's proceed.

Keep back 1 tablespoon of the butter for greasing your tin later, then melt the rest in a saucepan over medium-high heat - let it bubble until it is just starting to show signs of turning brown, then remove from the heat. The residual heat should take the butter to just the right side of nut-brown. Stir in the honey.

Sift the flour into a large mixing bowl, then stir through the baking powder and sugar. In a small bowl, whisk together the eggs and milk, then add to the flour mixture. Mix until you have a thick batter without any visible clumps of flour left. Now pour in the warm melted butter and honey. Add a dash more milk if the mixture seems too thick: it should run lazily off the spoon rather than plopping off it; the batter will also thicken up a bit while it is waiting to be baked. Mix in the mandarin zest, then chill the batter in the fridge: a few hours is good, overnight is even better. Don't leave it much longer than that, though.

When you are almost ready to bake, melt the reserved butter and use a pastry brush to make sure all the little valleys and ridges of your 12-berth madeleine or patty-pan tin are well greased, including a decent perimeter around each depression to cater for any overflowing batter. Even with non-stick tins, greasing is important here.

My usual technique at this point is to decant the batter into a disposable piping bag and refrigerate. Then, all that remains to be done is to snip the corner off the piping bag and three-quarters fill each little madeleine shell with batter. Alternatively, you can simply use a spoon to drop the batter into depressions. Aiming to get just the right amount of batter in every time is a lost cause – better to accept that there might be some joined-up madeleines, and that this is no big deal.

There is much chat in madeleine circles about chilling the tin, re-chilling once filled, all in the quest of the feted little 'hunchback' that is the hallmark of a good madeleine. Personally, I have found that piping into a room-temperature tin and baking straight away works out just fine most of the time. And the little hump? Meh! If it doesn't appear, simply turn the cakes over to show the pretty corrugated side and douse the things with icing sugar.

But I digress. Preheat your oven to 200°C (180°C fan), then bake your madeleines for 6–10 minutes, depending on their size. Look for a golden colour and crispy-looking edges. Eat warm from the oven, lightly dusted with icing sugar.

MORE MADELEINES

For passionfruit or vanilla madeleines, swap the citrus zest for the sieved pulp of a passionfruit, or ¼ teaspoon vanilla paste.

MOROCCAN CHOCOLATE & ALMOND SURPRISE BISCUITS

MAKES ABOUT 24

The 'surprise' of the title is the filling at the centre of these crackly little chaps. A little shot of crystallised ginger, chewy dried apricot or sweet dark date... it's a rich biscuit that incorporates toothsomeness with chewiness. Very satisfying.

When preparing these, maybe choose a few different fillings so that in each batch there will be several flavours to keep things interesting – I'm particularly fond of crystallised ginger and, of course, apricot. A plate piled with ghribi (their Arabic name), a bowl of mandarins and a couple of steaming hot pots of fresh mint tea would be a lovely way to pass a winter's afternoon.

---

50 g unsalted butter
150 g dark chocolate (70% cocoa), chopped or grated
100 g caster sugar
2 eggs
a few drops of orange flower water (the strength can vary widely, so go easy)
125 g almond meal
100 g (⅔ cup) plain flour
1 teaspoon baking powder
icing sugar, for dusting

SUGGESTED FILLINGS
crystallised ginger
tart dried apricots
dates
dried peaches or pears
crystallised orange peel
dried barberries

EVEN EASIER
If you are pushed for time, skip the fillings completely. These biscuits stand alone very well.

Melt the butter in a heavy-based saucepan, then remove from the heat and sprinkle in the chocolate – there should be enough residual heat to melt it, but give the pan a short stint back on the heat if not.

Whisk the sugar and eggs until light and fluffy. Stir in the orange flower water, then fold in the almond meal, flour and baking powder. Fold in the melted chocolate and butter until just combined into a firm dough. Gather up into a ball, cover with plastic wrap and chill in the fridge for an hour or two.

Meanwhile, choose your fillings and cut all of them except the barberries into chunks just a bit smaller than 1 cm. Preheat the oven to 200°C (180°C fan) and line a baking tray with baking paper.

Take the dough from the fridge and use your hands to roll into small balls about 3–4 cm in diameter. (If I'm feeling pernickety, I use digital scales to weigh out 25 g per ball for perfectly uniform biscuits – the joy I derive from scoring a hat-trick of exact-target-weight balls of dough is probably greater than it should be.) Sneak a chunk of one of your fillings (or 2–3 barberries) into each ball of biscuit dough, re-rolling it so the filling is hidden roughly in the middle of the sphere. Gently roll in icing sugar, then lay out on the baking tray. Use the palm of your hand to ever-so-gently squash each ball of dough from round to ever-so-slightly flat-ish.

Bake for about 10 minutes: when the biscuits are ready, they should be crackled on top. Let them cool on the tray for a few minutes, then transfer to a wire rack to cool completely. These guys keep quite well in an airtight container but are best on the day of making.

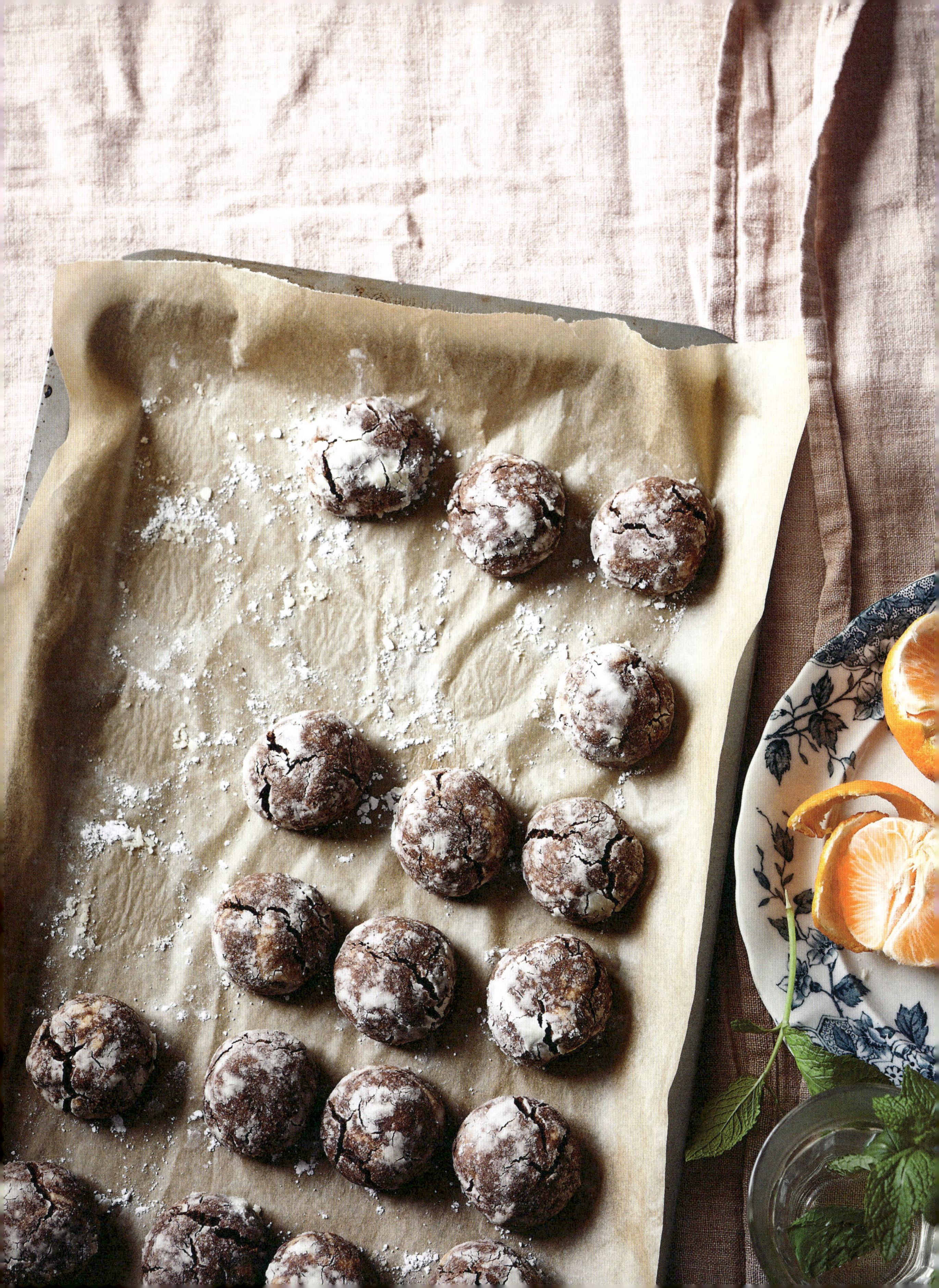

STICKY PUMPKIN GINGERBREAD

SERVES 12

I'm not going to pretend that this recipe was born of anything but an open-pored, panic-stricken attempt to get rid of excess pumpkin after a Halloween-era procurement malfunction. Who outside the United States takes the pumpkin and spice obsession quite so seriously anyway? Come late October in those parts, everything from coffee to biscuits wears a little garland of nutmeg and cinnamon. And I generally have no urge to get involved. However, I'm fairly committed to Nigella Lawson's sticky gingerbread, owing to its inclusion of both fresh and ground ginger. And when I experimented with adding pumpkin purée, I was completely delighted with the result. Think dark, sticky and moist, with a pungent ginger presence - and the secret thrill of withholding information from the children, who love this cake and have no idea just how much pumpkin is in it.

---

300 g (2 cups) plain flour
1 teaspoon ground cinnamon
½ teaspoon ground allspice
1 teaspoon baking powder
125 g unsalted butter
110 g (½ cup) dark brown sugar
175 g (½ cup) treacle
175 g (½ cup) golden syrup
3 cm ginger, finely grated
1 teaspoon ground ginger
1 teaspoon bicarbonate of soda
2 eggs, lightly beaten
125 ml (½ cup) milk
250 g (1 cup) pumpkin purée

MAKE IT GLUTEN-FREE

I have had success with gluten-free flour here. The one I use for baking – and that seems to work well for cakes – is Bob's Red Mill Gluten Free 1-to-1 Baking Flour, which you should be able to find at health food shops and gourmet grocers. You may have another trusted brand, in which case use that. Remember to check that your baking powder is gluten-free.

Preheat the oven to 200°C (180°C fan). Grease and line a 30 cm x 20 cm slice (traybake) tin.

Sift the flour into a mixing bowl with the cinnamon, allspice and baking powder.

In a large heavy-based saucepan over low heat, melt the butter, sugar, treacle and golden syrup with the grated and ground ginger. When everything is incorporated, remove from the heat and whisk in the bicarbonate of soda - it will fizz up, which will be fun for a moment. Whisk in the eggs, milk and pumpkin purée until smooth.

Now add the contents of the pan to the bowl and mix well. It will be a very liquid batter, but don't despair: all will be well. Pour into the tin and consign to the oven. After about 25 minutes it will be done. Keep an eye on it - the gingerbread should be sticky, so don't wait until it's too risen and cracked, but a skewer inserted in the centre should come out clean.

Scout's honour, this cake is nicest just as it is. What's more, it keeps well in the fridge for a few days in an airtight container.

PUMPKIN PURÉE

For this gingerbread, you need pumpkin purée that's not too wet. I baked half a Queensland Blue, cut-side down (seeds scooped out with spoon), on a lined baking tray at 200°C (180°C fan) for about 40 minutes. When it was cool enough to handle, I scooped out and mashed the flesh. That did the trick, and moreover saves the annoyance of peeling the bugger, which has long been ranked #1 in the list of pumpkin's most annoying attributes. If your mash looks a bit wet, spread it out on the tray so it dries as it cools.

SEEDED OAT, DARK CHOCOLATE & BARBERRY COOKIES

MAKES 18–20

We are definitely on team nuts in the cookie world, but if you need to play it safe with nut allergies, then give seeds a chance. These cookies aren't terribly sweet, and the tartness of the barberries with the dark chocolate is quite a grown-up taste, which is handy if you have a team of in-house biscuit-scoffing juniors who would otherwise hoover them up in a sitting. That said, Wendy makes these a lot, and her children have never refused one to date. These biscuits have become firm favourites for us both – they just seem to tick all the boxes, and are great to have on standby for drop-in guests.

The sweet-sour flavour of barberries works equally well in savoury dishes, such as salads or in a chicken stuffing, as it does in these cookies. Or try them sprinkled on your morning muesli or granola. If you can't find barberries, use tiny pieces of candied orange or dried apricot instead.

---

150 g unsalted butter, softened
80 g light brown sugar
80 g caster sugar
1 egg
150 g (1 cup) plain flour
½ teaspoon baking powder
150 g (1½ cups) rolled oats
100 g dark chocolate, chopped
50 g pumpkin seeds and sunflower seeds (in whatever ratio you like)
25 g sultanas
15 g dried barberries

Preheat the oven to 200°C (180°C fan). Line a large baking tray (or two smaller ones) with baking paper.

Using an electric mixer, cream together the butter and sugars, then add the egg and beat until combined. (It's also perfectly possible to do this by hand, as long as your butter is at room temperature and you're prepared to put in a few minutes of beating with a wooden spoon.) Now sift in the flour and baking powder, then stir in the rest of the ingredients until just combined into a firm dough.

Using your hands, roll the dough into golfball-sized rounds, then flatten slightly. Set on the baking tray, spacing them about 2 cm apart, to give them room to spread. Bake for 12–15 minutes until golden, then leave to cool and firm on the tray for a few minutes before transferring to a wire rack to cool completely. These cookies will keep in an airtight container for several weeks – or as long as you can resist them.

Crowded house

Of course we're all happy for friends and family when they partner up and then, perhaps, reproduce. But that sort of behaviour can play havoc with catering numbers. What might have started out in your twenties as a tight-knit group of four flatmates enthusiastically cooking whatever could be found in the fridge, now runs to around eighteen people. Feeding the masses sounds terrifying, but with a change of format you can come out of the panic room and back in to the kitchen. Choose food that doesn't require a table to eat at or cutlery to eat with. Rely on the self-serve or self-assembly format and go for recipes that can be scaled up and up and up…

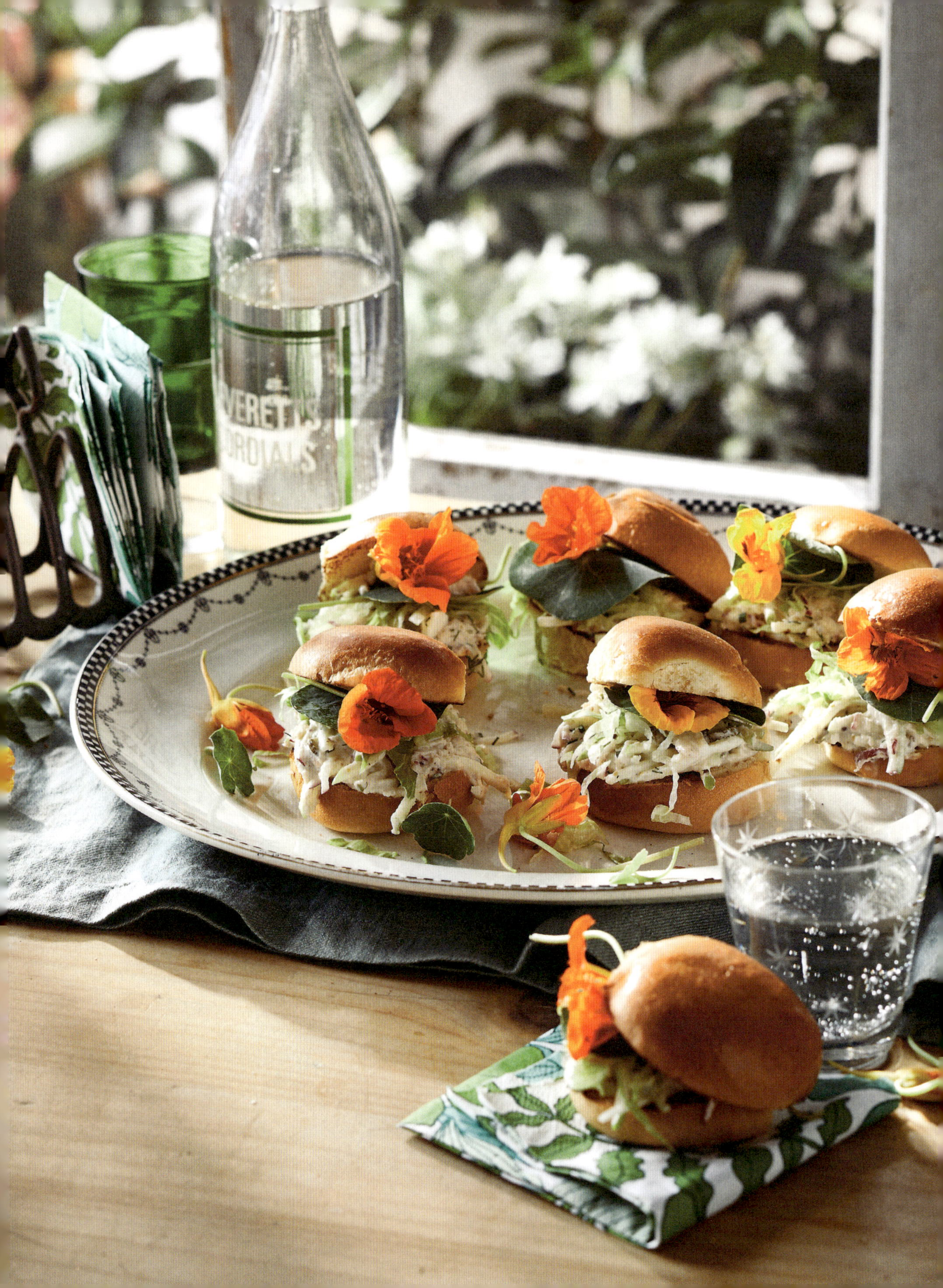

CRAB & NASTURTIUM SANDWICHES
SERVES 12 AS A HAND-AROUND APPETISER, OR 6 AS A SIT-DOWN STARTER

Blue swimmer crabs and nasturtiums: two summer staples from our part of the Adelaide Plains, brought together *at last* in sandwich form. This had its genesis in a delicious whiting sandwich, cooked live on stage for me and Leigh Sales at the Adelaide Festival in 2016, by MasterChef winner Adam Liaw (a genius whose cookbooks you should definitely add to your collection). On the day, my mum, Christobel, brought a big bag of nasturtiums in from the farm, and Adam used them to make his platter of sandwiches look amazing. Adam teamed his whiting with a crab tartare, but here the crab has become the main event, in a crunchy apple and radish remoulade that can be prepared in advance. Because their pepperiness works so well with crab, I've gone the whole hog and stuck the nasturtiums in the sandwiches too. This would be a perfect starter for a Christmas lunch, I fancy.

If you can't find nasturtiums, use watercress instead, and a colourful plate. If you can find nasturtiums, wash and dry them very carefully and of course check for hidden proteins. (Crab and caterpillar remoulade doesn't quite have the same ring to it.) On the matter of the brioche rolls: Adam let me in on a chef's secret, which is that you really don't need to bother making them. Head to a purveyor of ultra-sweet, ultra-soft Asian milk breads (such as Breadtop) and get yourself a couple of packs of plain small buns, or try your luck in a sizeable supermarket, as many now sell brioche burger rolls.

---

12 small soft brioche-style buns
¼ iceberg lettuce, shredded
2 large handfuls of nasturtium leaves and flowers

CRAB REMOULADE
2 granny smith apples
8 radishes
juice of ½ lemon
120 g (½ cup) mayonnaise
125 g (½ cup) crème fraîche
1 teaspoon dijon mustard
1 teaspoon wholegrain mustard
1 teaspoon horseradish cream sauce
2 hard-boiled eggs, chopped
2 tablespoons chopped cornichons
1 tablespoon tiny capers, rinsed and drained well
2 tablespoons chopped dill
2 tablespoons chopped chives
200 g picked crab meat – 4 cooked blue swimmers will see you right

For the remoulade, cut the apples and radishes into fine matchsticks and immediately toss with the lemon juice to prevent discolouration. Stir in all the other ingredients except the crab, then finally fold in the crab meat. You can make this up to 6 hours ahead; any longer and the apple will lose its crunch and the radish colour will bleed.

When you're ready to eat, split the buns and toast their cut sides, either by placing them cut-side down on a hot barbecue flatplate or chargrill pan, or cut-side up under a hot grill, for about 3 minutes. Watch closely, as brioche buns go from toasted to burnt pretty fast.

Place a generous spoonful of remoulade on the bottom half of each bun. Top with shredded lettuce and one or two nasturtium leaves and a flower, then close the bun. Arrange all the buns on a large platter liberally strewn with nasturtium flowers and leaves.

MAKE IT VEGETARIAN
Use charred sweetcorn instead of crab: grill two generous cobs of corn on the barbecue (or directly on a gas hob) until tender, then shave the kernels into the remoulade.

CHILLI BEANS WITH LIME LEAVES & AVOCADO SALSA

SERVES 8-10

This is a dish born of pleasant misadventure. A while back, Wendy read a recipe for chilli con carne that called for lime leaves. Despite her deep (and accurate) suspicion that the recipe didn't mean kaffir lime leaves, Wendy - being an avid enthusiast of these fragrant shiny double leaves - threw them into this chilli and has never looked back. The result of all the herbs, spices and imposter leaves here is a deeply savoury bowlful that works well for large groups of people, and you can scale up the recipe as far as your pot size will allow. Even better, children of all levels of fussiness and appetite seem drawn to this dish (hmmm, or perhaps that's the mysterious power of the hot cheesy corn chip).

---

125 g Puy-style lentils (or similar), picked over
1 teaspoon coriander seeds
olive oil, for frying
2 onions, coarsely chopped
3 celery stalks, finely diced
4 garlic cloves, finely chopped
1 heaped tablespoon ground cumin
1 tablespoon smoked paprika
2 teaspoons ground cinnamon
1 tablespoon dried oregano
2 tablespoons tomato paste (concentrated purée)
2 x 400 g tins of tomatoes
1 x 400 g tin of red kidney beans, rinsed and drained
1 x 400 g tin of black beans, rinsed and drained
125 g red lentils, picked over
3 large kaffir lime leaves
3 tablespoons finely chopped coriander stalks
1 scant tablespoon cocoa powder (*not* drinking chocolate!)
1 vegetable stock cube
3-4 dried red chillies (but see note opposite)
2 x 200 g packets of tortilla chips
300 g grated cheddar
sour cream, to serve

Tip the Puy-style lentils into a small saucepan, cover with cold water and bring to the boil, then reduce to a simmer and cook for 10 minutes.

Take your hugest, heaviest pan or flameproof casserole and set it over medium heat. Just as it is heating up, add the coriander seeds and wait for the first one to pop. Once this has happened, add a swirl of olive oil and the onions and celery. Fry gently until they are starting to soften, then add the garlic, keeping it moving so it doesn't brown or burn. Add a bit more oil and the cumin, paprika, cinnamon and oregano, and stir for a moment or two before sending in the tomato paste to join them. Next, empty out your recycling bin in preparation for all the used tins... first, the tomatoes, swirling almost a full tin of water around each tin to chase out the last of the juices. Next, in go both types of beans. Rinse and drain the red lentils and the par-cooked Puy-style lentils and add those, along with the lime leaves, coriander stalks, cocoa powder, stock cube and chillies (if using). Give it a good stir and bring to the boil, then cover the pan.

You now have three options: tuck it away in a 180°C (160°C fan) oven for 40 minutes; speed through the process in a pressure cooker (10-12 minutes will see you right); or keep cooking it on the hob, at a slow simmer, for 45-60 minutes. Give it a stir every now and then, but don't worry too much if it catches slightly - any browned bits will only add to the flavour when stirred back in.

This chilli is really best made the day before, then cooled and refrigerated overnight to let the flavours develop. But if you need to serve up right away, just remove the lid and boil off any excess liquid until the chilli is the consistency you like.

AVOCADO SALSA
3 avocados, roughly chopped
250 g cherry tomatoes, roughly chopped
handful of coriander leaves
juice of 2 limes

Just before your crowd arrives, preheat the oven to 200°C (180°C fan). Spread out the tortilla chips on a lined baking tray (or two) and mix through the cheese. Make the salsa by mixing the avocado with the cherry tomatoes, coriander, lime juice and salt to taste.

Once you have your crowd assembled, put the tortilla chips in the oven for about 5 minutes or until the cheese is bubbling and golden. Let guests serve themselves the chilli and the avocado salsa, together with a dollop of sour cream and some of the cheesy tortilla chips.

WE NEED TO TALK ABOUT CHILLI

As the size of your crowd increases, so does the likelihood that you will be hosting those from opposite ends of the chilli-tolerance spectrum – and, quite possibly, children with tender palates. Unless you know that you have a homogenous group of fire-loving guests, you might want to leave out the chillies from the main recipe and instead, provide a bowl of chilli flakes and another of chopped pickled jalapeños from a jar. That way, each guest can customise their bowl according to their desired heat level.

FOR THE MEAT-EATERS

You don't really need meat with this, but if you have a crowd of eaters with mixed dietary preferences, by all means slow-roast a shoulder of pork and then go at it with two forks to make a small mountain of pulled pork.

MAKE IT GLUTEN-FREE

Use gluten-free tortilla chips.

LIMEY CORNY SALMON BAKE

SERVES 6

Half an hour of preparation in advance will yield this colourful, spicy, zesty crowd-pleaser (pictured over the page), which is happy to wait in the fridge until required. When the time comes, you just put it in the oven and twenty minutes later, all done! Thank you, Elsa Santo, for serving this to me years ago and instantly installing it in my favourites file.

Whole cumin and coriander seeds are specified here just because they are so superior - in their coarsely milled and fragrant presence - to the ready-ground variety. If you're in a hurry, you can of course use powdered; maybe just toast briefly to ignite the flavours.

―――――――

6 sweetcorn cobs
1 tablespoon cumin seeds
1 tablespoon coriander seeds
1 teaspoon salt
1 teaspoon ground ginger
1 teaspoon ground turmeric
½ teaspoon ground black pepper
6 x 250 g skinless salmon fillets
4 limes
3 tablespoons olive oil
large handful of coriander leaves
1 chilli, sliced – optional

First: chargrill your corn cobs. I find that the easiest way to do this quickly is on a gas cooktop. Put an old wire rack over a medium flame and crowd your cobs onto it, so they're right in the flame. Turn them as they brown and blister, ensuring all sides of them get a bit of the heat. You can balance them directly on the hob but it's messier, plus you get red-hot corn cobs rolling everywhere - good comedy potential, but annoying if you're pushed for time. Once all the cobs are done, set them aside to cool. (If you don't have a gas cooktop but you do have a barbecue, use that instead. And if you have neither, just cook the cobs under a hot grill, turning regularly.)

Toast the cumin and coriander seeds in a dry frying pan until fragrant, stirring often so they don't burn, then tip the lot into a large mortar and pestle, along with the salt. Grind to a powder, then stir in the ground ginger, turmeric and black pepper.

Choose an ovenproof dish that will hold your salmon fillets snugly, obliging them to overlap each other a bit; overlap is key here. Line the dish: no greasing or anything, you just want a big sheet of baking paper scrunched up then straightened out and laid over the dish. Now, take half of your spice mix and rub it all over the salmon fillets. Lay them - you guessed it - overlapping on top of the baking paper.

Back to the corn. With a big sharp knife, cut the kernels from the cobs. (I keep the cobs because they make an excellent addition to stock for Chinese soups, but you need not share this particular behavioural quirk.)

With luck, some of the kernels will come off in big sheets. Tuck these between, under and on top of the salmon fillets. Don't feel all teary and inadequate if the kernels just crumble off, though; it's no biggie.

Put the rest of the corn into a bowl for the salsa. Zest one of the limes into the bowl, then juice that lime and one of its friends and add that too. Stir in half of the olive oil and the rest of your spice mix. If you're prepping in advance, cover with plastic wrap and chill until needed.

Juice the other two limes and whisk with the rest of the olive oil. Drizzle this over the salmon in the dish, which is now oven-ready: you can cover the dish with plastic wrap and consign it to the fridge, or cook it straightaway. Either way, it needs about 20 minutes in a preheated 200°C (180°C fan) oven, or until the salmon is just starting to brown around the edges - be careful not to overcook it.

At the last minute, toss the coriander leaves through the salsa and add the chilli, if using. Top the baked salmon with large dollops of salsa: you want a riotously colourful and loaded look, not just a sprinkle. Serve straight from the dish at the table, with any remaining salsa on the side so people can help themselves.

WHY WE ALL NEED A SIGNATURE DISH

If you don't relish experimentation in the kitchen, or just flat out don't love cooking, and the prospect of cooking a new recipe for guests raises your pulse but not in a good way, that doesn't mean you can't be a terrific host. All you need is a handful of simple, reliable dishes you have made before. Dispense with any idea that you need to offer your friends variety – cooking the same really tasty dish every time they come is not unimaginative, it is your signature dish! Or, if you really aren't up for a full meal, then find out how to bake a round of cheese (see page 226) or whizz up a bowl of tapenade (see page 88) to have with a glass of wine or fancy cordial. See? You are now a natural entertainer.

< LIMEY CORNY
SALMON BAKE

MEXICAN
WINTER SOUP >

MEXICAN WINTER SOUP

SERVES 4 GENEROUSLY

Wendy has been making versions of this soup (pictured on the previous page) for about twenty-five years now. And nobody is sick of it. Its brilliance is that it can be scraped together even from most midweek crisper drawers; all you need is half-decent knife skills and an eye for colour. Furthermore, all guests, irrespective of dietary requirements, can mix and eat seamlessly: vegan, gluten-free, halal, chilli-fiends and the spice-averse, you have the world covered with this one. While the fire and zip of this soup are undeniably cheering on winter days, it is delightful in the heat too. So if you're a Queenslander or top-ender, don't wait for grey skies - just add lots of chilli and sweat it out.

2–3 tablespoons olive oil
1 small red onion, cut into 5 mm dice
1 small brown onion, cut into 5 mm dice
2 carrots, cut into 5 mm dice
3 celery stalks, cut into 5 mm dice
2 tablespoons ground cumin
1 tablespoon ground coriander
2 teaspoons dried oregano
1 kaffir lime leaf, finely shredded
3 large tomatoes, roughly chopped
1–2 peppers (capsicums), cut into 5 mm dice – a mix of whatever colours you have to hand
750 ml (3 cups) vegetable stock or water
5 tablespoons finely chopped coriander stalks (leaves reserved)
200 g (1 cup) frozen sweetcorn or 1 x 200 g tin of sweetcorn, drained
5 spring onions, thinly sliced
100 g grated cheddar
6–10 pickled jalapeños, chopped
sour cream, tortilla chips and lime wedges, to serve
handful of finely shredded purple cabbage – optional

MAKE IT GLUTEN-FREE
Use gluten-free tortilla chips.

Use a good heavy-based stockpot or large saucepan, to avoid burning - you want to keep the flavours fresh and the vegetables quite sprightly. Set it over a gentle heat and pour in 2 tablespoons of the olive oil. Start with the onions: get those frying away, and when they're starting to soften, add the carrots and celery and cook for another 2–3 minutes, stirring frequently. Now add the spices and herbs, together with a bit of extra oil to prevent sticking, and stir for another minute or two, taking care not to let them burn (add a splash of water if you need to cool things down a little).

Tip the tomatoes and peppers into the pan, then add the stock or water and bring to a low simmer. Next add the coriander stalks, corn and spring onions. Let the soup bubble away for about 5 minutes, then have a taste and add some salt if it needs it. (You can make the soup up to here a few hours ahead of time and gently reheat it later.)

One small snag to be aware of with this soup is that the ground spices can feel quite gritty in the thin broth. But to my mind a hint of grit is a small price to pay for such a winter treat. In any case, the spices will sink to the bottom, and so you can avoid the worst of the grittiness by not scraping the bottom of the pan with your ladle, or at least serve your fussiest guests from the top layers first.

When you're almost ready to serve, get together the grated cheese, jalapeños, sour cream, tortilla chips and lime wedges. Ladle some hot soup into each large bowl, then sprinkle over the reserved coriander leaves - and the purple cabbage, if you are using it (I add this at the end because cooking it with the other vegetables turns the soup a bright shade of hippie violet, which sometimes settles down to a weird grey blue/green...). Let your guests help themselves to all the delicious extras.

EGG SALAN

SERVES 6

This is a dead-easy curry – a popular staple in Pakistan – whose mild, yoghurty sauce makes it extremely popular with children and adults alike after a trying day. It also involves peeling many boiled eggs, which is one of my favourite kitchen tasks, confirming my suspicion that I would have made quite a good Victorian under-scullery maid. This recipe comes via my sister-in-law's mother, Jennifer Zulfiqar. She recommends two boiled eggs per person, so if you are expecting more than six people – scale up! Having only a few years ago discovered that poppadums are easily cooked in the microwave without the use of oil (place each one on a paper towel and give it about 45 seconds on full blast), I serve this with a big plate of them.

---

1 small brown onion, finely chopped
1 tablespoon rice bran oil
1 garlic clove, finely chopped
2 cm ginger, finely chopped
1 x 400 g tin of tomatoes
2 tablespoons cumin seeds, toasted in a dry frying pan then ground
1 teaspoon chilli powder (omit if cooking for children)
1 teaspoon ground turmeric
1½ teaspoons garam masala
90 g (⅓ cup) tomato paste (concentrated purée)
300 g Greek-style yoghurt
125 ml (½ cup) vegetable stock or water
12 hard-boiled eggs, peeled
juice of ½ lemon
handful of coriander leaves, roughly chopped
steamed rice, to serve

I use a cast-iron casserole for this, but you could use a heavy-based saucepan or even a deep frying pan or a wok, if you like.

Fry the onion in the oil over low–medium heat until it's translucent and soft, but not brown. Add the garlic and ginger and fry for a further minute, then add the tomatoes and mash everything about with a wooden spoon. Now add the spices and fry for another minute or so, stirring and prodding as you go.

Next add the tomato paste and yoghurt and stir until combined, then thin with the stock or water until you have a sauce consistency that makes you happy. Halve the boiled eggs and slip them into the pan, then gently stir in the lemon juice.

Allow the eggs to warm through in the sauce, then garnish with the coriander and carry the entire pan to the table. Serve with rice.

SRI LANKAN BUTTERNUT & CASHEW CURRY WITH BEETROOT SAMBOL

SERVES 6

This dish (pictured over the page) is the product of Wendy's patient, repeated attempts to get into a particularly popular London restaurant specialising in Sri Lankan street food; you know, one of those places that is totally relaxed and laid-back, apart from the fact that you've got to wait three hours before even getting in. Anyway, her persistence is our gain here, as it got Wendy thinking about the delicious salad-cum-side dishes called sambols that are a vital part of virtually every Sri Lankan meal.

There seem to be as many recipes for sambol as there are Sri Lankan kitchens, but at its essence it is a simple mix of coconut and/or vegetables with a hint of lime and, sometimes, dried fish. This modest recreation of a sambol is pretty to look at and is the perfect foil for a rich, spicy butternut and cashew curry.

---

1 butternut pumpkin (squash), peeled and cut into wedges
vegetable oil, for roasting and frying
10 curry leaves
1 teaspoon black mustard seeds
1 teaspoon cumin seeds
1 teaspoon fennel seeds
8 cloves
8 cardamom pods
1 cinnamon stick
2 red onions, finely chopped
2 teaspoons ground turmeric
8 garlic cloves, thinly sliced
20 g ginger, finely chopped
1 green chilli, some seeds removed, thinly sliced
1 x 400 g tin of coconut milk
tiny dash of tamarind paste
squeeze of lime juice – optional
170 g unsalted raw cashews
4–5 tablespoons finely chopped coriander
steamed rice, to serve

Preheat the oven to 200°C (180°C fan).

Lightly coat the pumpkin wedges with oil, sprinkle with salt and roast for about 25 minutes. (This step can be done a day in advance and the pumpkin kept refrigerated.)

Heat a glug of oil in a wok or large frying pan over medium heat and add the curry leaves, mustard seeds, cumin seeds and fennel seeds. When they start popping, add the cloves, cardamom pods, cinnamon stick, onions and turmeric. Keep stirring – and turn down the heat if the spices are in danger of burning and becoming bitter. Next add the garlic, ginger and chilli, again keeping it on the move to avoid burning and sticking.

Now stir in the coconut milk and tamarind paste and simmer for a couple of minutes. Taste and adjust the seasoning with lime juice and salt if needed, keeping in mind that Sri Lankan curries typically celebrate the woody flavours of clove and fennel rather than the zing of citrus.

When you are more or less happy with the flavour, add the pumpkin and cashews and gently heat through. (Roasting the pumpkin and adding it to the curry at the last minute helps it to hold its shape, rather than dissolving into a puddle of glorious orange.)

BEETROOT SAMBOL

30 g desiccated coconut

3 small cooked beetroot, cut into matchsticks

1 lime

1 handful of kale, well washed and any tough stalks removed

½ teaspoon fish sauce – optional

About half an hour before you want to serve, make the sambol. Soak the desiccated coconut in water for about 10 minutes, then drain off the excess liquid. Add the beetroot and the finely grated zest of the lime, plus the juice of half the lime, a pinch of salt and a good grind of pepper. Scrunch up the kale in your hands to tenderise it, then cover with boiling water and leave for a few minutes until just wilted. Drain, rinse under cold running water, then tear up and add to the beetroot and coconut. Just before serving, stir the fish sauce into the sambol, if using.

When you are ready to eat, scatter the coriander over the curry and serve with the sambol and plenty of steamed rice.

EVEN EASIER

Given how many good pre-made curry pastes and spice mixes there are, may I suggest you eschew the carefully constructed list of spices here and buy yourself a high-end Sri Lankan curry paste instead? Perk up your bought paste with a few cardamom pods, maybe some extra garlic and ginger – and some curry leaves, if you have a stash in the freezer – then sink your energies into making a really cracking sambol.

MAKE IT VEGAN

Opt out of the fish sauce in the sambol.

< SRI LANKAN
BUTTERNUT &
CASHEW CURRY WITH
BEETROOT SAMBOL

HOT-SMOKED SALMON WITH PEA-GREEN SALAD >

HOT-SMOKED SALMON WITH PEA-GREEN SALAD

SERVES 10

This dish (pictured on the previous page) honours two acts of extraordinary kindness. At the 2017 Sydney Writers' Festival, Leigh Sales and I did a 'Chat 10 Looks 3' event at the Ros Packer Theatre, from which I optimistically estimated I could escape in ample time to attend a netball game with my family in Homebush. You will be stunned to learn that things ran on a bit, and by the time we got to the book-signing afterwards I was so late that I barely noticed when someone shoved a parcel in my hand. I ducked outside to run for the train, but: Vivid! The streets were choked with pedestrians. I was whining to Leigh about this when, miraculously, an audience member materialised, offering to give me a lift. She and her mum and girlfriend drove me *all the way* to Homebush, and were hilarious company from start to finish.

It was only when I bade them farewell and was frisked by the security guards at ANZ Stadium, that I suddenly recalled the parcel from the event. Somehow I'd held onto it, and when I opened it - ravenous, and with only hot chips and pies on offer from the stadium food stands - I found the most delicious and well-thought-out salad imaginable. It came in a homemade cold pack, and featured a piece of hot-smoked salmon wrapped in greaseproof paper and carefully kept separate from a profusion of greens: broccoli, peas, asparagus, shaved zucchini (courgette). There was also a cunning jar of avocado-pale dressing. And a fork. It was an actual physical delight to eat. I later properly met its maker, Kate Knott, who kindly shared the recipe - an approximation of a dish she once ate at a Balmain cafe called The Hunter Works. I've twiddled the recipe further and scaled up the proportions, so you can share the delight of this dish with your crowd. All of its elements can comfortably be made in advance, too.

You can hot-smoke your own salmon if you have a barbecue with a lid - otherwise, just buy it. I've allowed 150 g of salmon per person; a full side of salmon weighing 1.5 kg will comfortably feed ten, especially if you make Glass potatoes (see page 193) to go with it.

1.5 kg salmon fillet, skin off
160 g (½ cup) salt
100 g (½ cup) soft brown sugar
2 large handfuls of smoking chips

First: the salmon. In a non-reactive bowl or container, dissolve the salt and sugar in 1.5 litres (6 cups) of water and immerse the salmon. Cover and leave in the fridge to cure for 4 hours or overnight. Soak the smoking chips in water for the same amount of time.

Remove the salmon from the brine and place on a rack set over a baking tray. Return to the fridge to dry overnight - the drier it gets, the better.

Drain the wood chips and put them in a foil tray (you can make one by scrunching up the sides of a large sheet of foil).

PEA-GREEN SALAD

olive oil, for cooking
4 zucchini (courgettes), cut lengthwise into 5 mm slices
20 asparagus spears, woody ends snapped off
500 g green beans, topped and tailed
1 head of broccoli, sliced into long, 1 cm wide florets
200 g sugar snap peas, trimmed
200 g frozen peas
200 g pea shoots

DRESSING

200 g frozen peas, thawed
125 g (½ cup) sour cream
130 g (½ cup) Greek-style yoghurt
60 g (¼ cup) good-quality mayonnaise
1 tablespoon horseradish cream sauce
1 tablespoon finely chopped preserved lemon rind
large handful of dill fronds
4 spring onions, thinly sliced into rounds
juice of ½ lemon
dash of milk to thin, if necessary

Fire up your barbecue, igniting the grill but leaving the flatplate part, if it has one, switched off. Place your foil container of smoking chips over the heat. Once it starts to smoke (about 10 minutes), place the tray of salmon on the flatplate part (or grill) of the barbecue and close the lid, trapping the smoke and heat inside. Smoke the salmon for about 20 minutes, or until a knife pierced into the flesh reveals that the salmon is cooked, but still moist in the middle. Remove, and leave to cool to room temperature.

For the pea-green salad, lightly oil the zucchini slices and asparagus spears. Sear the vegetables on the barbecue (or on a chargrill pan over medium-high heat) until they are just tender, with pleasing char-marks. Remove and refrigerate. Next, steam or boil the green beans and broccoli for about 4 minutes, adding the sugar snap peas and frozen peas for the final minute. Blanch them all in cold water and drain, then refrigerate.

For the dressing, just use a blender to blitz all the ingredients until smooth. Taste and season with salt and pepper as required.

Once all the greens are ready, gently toss them all together with the pea shoots, then tip out onto a huge shallow serving platter (use two if you only have smaller ones – one for each end of the table). Flake over the salmon in big chunks. Zigzag the dressing over the top and you're good to go.

EVEN EASIER

If you or your friends have a hot smoker, then for god's sake use it. They are terrific. And if you're cooking for a smaller group, you can just buy ready-made hot smoked salmon. It's widely available at supermarkets. Just don't confuse it with ordinary pre-sliced cold-smoked salmon – which somehow always makes me feel a tiny bit squeamish, and will definitely not work in this salad.

MAKE IT VEGETARIAN

Swap the salmon for barbecued halloumi or chunks of feta cheese.

MAKE IT GLUTEN-FREE

Check the label on your mayonnaise to make sure it's a gluten-free one.

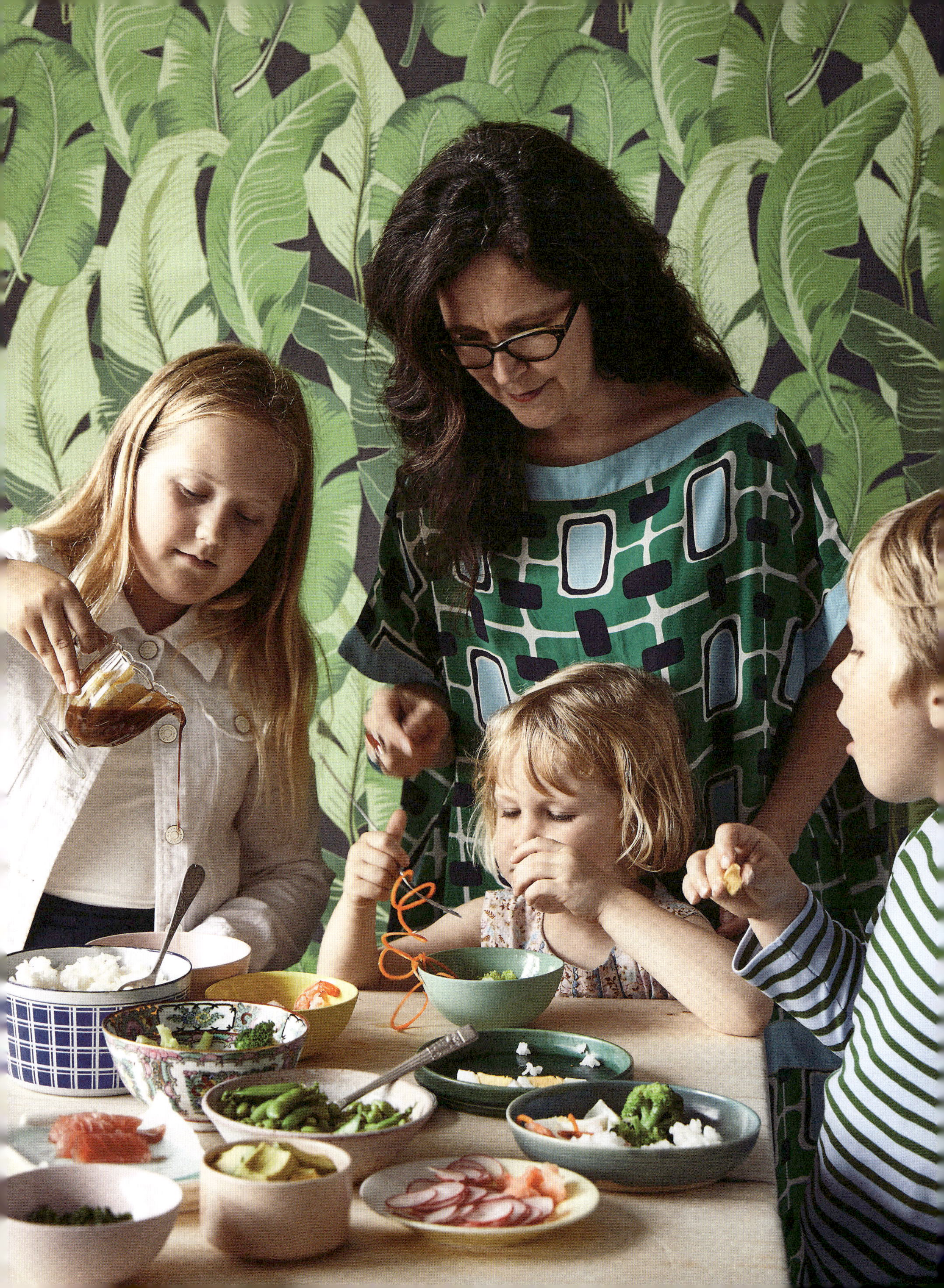

POKE-BOWL BUFFET

SERVES 12

Ah, yeah. I know. The poke bowl is a very hot takeaway lunch item right now. The Hawaiian-derived combination of sushi rice with raw fish and various accompaniments seems to tick a lot of boxes. But have you considered offering a poke buffet at home to feed a crowd? It's very simple. You supply an industrial quantity of sushi rice, an array of accompaniments and garnishes, plus a memorable dressing and some bowls, and your guests help themselves. There are many advantages to this approach. First, you can do the prep in advance. Second, your ingredients will resemble a Yayoi Kusama installation (no bad thing). Third, your guests can load up on the things they love, while discreetly eschewing those they've always secretly despised. Fourth, and most importantly, you can elegantly cover a lot of dietary requirements with ease.

---

840 g (4 cups) sushi rice
125 ml (½ cup) rice wine vinegar
2 tablespoons caster sugar

PROTEINS (PICK TWO OR THREE, DEPENDING ON DIETARY NEEDS)
200 g sashimi-grade tuna, salmon or kingfish, diced
200 g marinated tofu or tempeh, pan-fried and sliced
200 g cooked prawn meat
6 hard-boiled eggs, quartered

VEGETABLES
250 g frozen podded soy beans (edamame), steamed until tender
1 head of broccoli, broken into florets and steamed
6 curly kale leaves, stripped from their stalks, steamed and shredded
6 radishes, thinly sliced
2 carrots, cut into matchsticks
120 g (½ cup) pickled ginger slices
1 large avocado, diced

DRESSING
90 g (⅓ cup) white miso paste
125 ml (½ cup) rice wine vinegar
80 ml (⅓ cup) tamari sauce
80 ml (⅓ cup) olive oil
60 ml (¼ cup) mirin

Rinse the rice and put it in a large saucepan over medium heat with 1.5 litres (6 cups) of water. Place over medium heat, cover and cook until the water is absorbed, about 15 minutes. Remove from the heat and leave, covered, for 10 minutes. In a small saucepan, heat the rice wine vinegar and dissolve the sugar in it. Add to the rice and stir thoroughly, then transfer the rice to a large serving bowl.

In the meantime, whisk or whizz your dressing ingredients together until smooth. Consign to a jar and screw the lid on firmly. That way all you'll have to do before serving is give the thing a brisk shake.

Prep the rest of your ingredients: cook and/or cut up the proteins, and steam or slice the vegetables. Arrange them attractively on platters or in bowls.

When your guests are ready to eat, just lay everything out, shake the dressing and pour it into a jug, then see about a refreshment for yourself.

MAKE IT GLUTEN-FREE
This recipe specifies tamari sauce because it's gluten-free. If you're cooking for coeliacs, make sure you buy gluten-free miso; some miso is grain-based, so you'll need to check.

MAKE IT VEGAN
Leave out the eggs and fish, and just stick to tofu and vegetables.

FALAFEL WRAPS

SERVES 4-6

Back in the old days, before having children, I might have presented each guest with a carefully assembled wrap full of all these goodies in perfect proportions. But that was then, and this is now - and you and the many other people in your house are hungry. These falafels should probably be called chickpea balls, since they deviate so wildly from traditional falafel: they are baked rather than deep-fried (for practical reasons, not health reasons - if you have the facilities to deep-fry, then run don't walk); also, they have ginger in them, plus egg and ricotta... oh, and did I mention parmesan? I love the crunch of whole coriander seeds (I've even been known to nibble on them as I work) - but if you think I'm the only one, feel free to use ground coriander instead.

Pre-make the hummus (or use bought) and the yoghurt mint sauce, have your mock falafels ready to reheat in the oven. On the day, just whip up a huge fresh herby salad. For meat-eaters, there might be a leg of lamb in the oven or on the barbecue, slow-cooking for shawarma, but that's entirely up to you.

1–2 flatbreads per person
hummus (see page 14), to serve

YOGHURT MINT SAUCE
500 g thick yoghurt
2 small garlic cloves, finely chopped
pinch of salt
1 cucumber, halved and seeds removed, thinly sliced
handful of mint leaves, finely chopped

FALAFELS
1 red onion, finely chopped
olive oil, for frying and drizzling
2 garlic cloves, finely chopped
1 teaspoon finely grated ginger
1 teaspoon ground cumin
½ teaspoon coriander seeds
1 x 400 g tin of chickpeas, rinsed and drained
finely grated zest of 1 lemon
3–4 tablespoons chopped coriander stalks and/or parsley stalks
2 tablespoons seeds – sunflower or pumpkin
1 egg
3 tablespoons firm ricotta
30 g parmesan, finely grated

First, make the yoghurt mint sauce, since it benefits from a couple of hours' rest before serving. Mix together the yoghurt, garlic and a pinch of salt, then stir through the cucumber and mint. Check for seasoning, then set aside in the fridge.

For the falafel, fry the red onion with a glug of olive oil in a large frying pan over low heat until soft. Add the garlic, ginger, cumin and coriander and stir for a moment until aromatic, then stir in the chickpeas and cook for a few minutes, stirring every so often, to dry them out a bit. Once you have a fragrant-smelling mess in your pan, stir in the lemon zest and herbs. Scrape the mixture into a bowl and let it cool down slightly before taking to it with a potato masher: you want to squash most, but not all, of the chickpeas. When you're happy with the texture, stir through the seeds, egg and ricotta and season well with salt and pepper. (The seeds are in lieu of pine nuts, which are ten types of delicious, but since they are so bloody expensive, I am suggesting a cheaper alternative this time. The ricotta? I know, not traditional, but I don't like dry falafels, and I think the added fat helps to make them more flavoursome; feel free to leave it out if it offends you.)

Preheat the oven to 220°C (200°C fan). Line a large baking tray with baking paper and lightly oil the baking paper.

Drop walnut-sized blobs of your falafel mixture onto the tray: you will probably end up with about a dozen. Trickle a few drops of olive oil on top of each one, then sprinkle with a teaspoon or so of parmesan –

HERBY SALAD

any salad greens you have to hand, shredded or chopped
masses of coriander leaves, parsley and mint (dill too, if you fancy it)
ripe and tasty tomatoes, roughly chopped
juice of 1 lemon
glug of olive oil
sprinkle of sumac

these two measures both help to bring a bit of crispness to the falafels and compensate for the lack of deep-frying. Bake for 20-25 minutes until quite firm and golden. (They can be easily reheated when you're ready to serve – just give them 10 minutes at 180°C/160°C fan.)

Meanwhile, assemble your herby salad in a large serving bowl and dress with lemon juice, olive oil and sumac. Season with salt to taste and gently toss everything together.

Transfer the baking paper, laden with the falafel, onto a serving platter (to avoid eager fingers getting burnt on the hot baking tray). Pile up some rounds of flatbread, with a big bowl of hummus and the bowl of yoghurt mint sauce and the herby salad alongside. Since the chef has to eat, lead the way with your own plate: a warm flatbread, a stripe of hummus, a few hot falafels, a dash of yoghurt mint sauce and some salad on top, then deftly rolled up. Not elegant, perhaps, but hopefully delicious.

EVEN EASIER

If you have a purveyor of quality falafel nearby, then for goodness sake go ahead and buy it, and just reheat gently when it is time to eat. If you have a spare jar of pickled turnips or packet of chilli flakes, or some finely shredded sauerkraut, set those out for guests too. Put your effort into the salad and sauce being as fresh and herby as can be, and you will end up with a low-effort but delicious shared meal.

Crowded house

OLD-FASHIONED VEGETABLE PASTIES

MAKES ABOUT 8-10

In the eastern states of Australia, pasties - tragically - play humble understudy to the meat pie. But if you were raised in South Australia, then pasties rule, and they always will. Thanks to the mass emigration of tin miners from Cornwall to South Australia, our part of the world really knows how to do a hand-held hot snack. And while a commercial meat pie is essentially a gastronomic lottery, in which a tarry brown sauce shields from our trusting eyes the exact nature of what beast might lurk within, the pasty boasts a profusion of fresh and identifiable ingredients, enlivened by a generous seasoning of pepper. Okay, they might take a bit of work to get together, but they can be baked in advance and then reheated the next day. Or frozen for a rainy afternoon in front of the footy. A pasty make an awesome school lunch, too.

---

2 brown onions, finely chopped
1 large leek, pale parts only, shredded
knob of butter
1 large potato
2 carrots
1 small swede (or celeriac)
generous pinch of curry powder
140 g frozen peas, any excess ice rinsed off
125 g cooked brown lentils (use tinned or start with 50 g dried)
3 tablespoons chopped flat-leaf parsley
100 g grated cheddar
1 egg, lightly beaten

PASTRY
160 g butter
250 g plain flour
90 g self-raising flour
pinch of salt

For the pastry, cut the butter into small cubes, spread out on a plate and then give it 5 minutes in the fridge - or better still, in the freezer. In a large bowl (or a food processor), mix together the two types of flour and the salt. (I sometimes take out 2 tablespoons of the plain white flour and sub in 2 tablespoons of wholemeal flour, to give a hint of extra flavour and texture without making the dough difficult to work with.) Add the cold butter and rub into the flours using your fingers (or the food processor) until you have fine crumbs. Pour in about 2 tablespoons of cold water and use a knife to cut through the mixture (or pulse) until the dough starts to form; you might think you need more water, but keep cutting for a few minutes before you make the decision to add more water. Once it looks all knobbly, bring the dough together with your hands, but try to avoid handling it too much. Pat the dough into a disc, cover with plastic wrap and chill in the fridge for at least 30 minutes. (And if you are reading this and thinking, what a palaver, then please go ahead and buy ready-made savoury shortcrust pastry.)

Put your onions and leek in a large frying pan with a knob of butter over low heat. While they are softening, peel and dice the potato, carrots and swede - the size of your cubes is a personal matter, but be aware that smaller cubes allow you to pack more filling in. Add the diced vegetables to the pan as they are ready, letting them sweat and soften for about 5 minutes, giving them a stir every so often. Add the curry powder and a couple of tablespoons of water to the pan, then cover and cook for a minute of two. The veg should be partly cooked, but still holding their shape; remove the lid and cook off any excess water. Now stir through the peas, lentils, parsley and cheddar.

Season generously with salt and both black and white pepper – it's this, the pepper, that really makes a pasty, so don't hold back. Set the filling aside to cool completely.

Preheat the oven to 220°C (200°C fan). Line a large baking sheet (or two smaller ones) with baking paper.

Take the pastry from the fridge and let the pastry warm up a little, until it is obliging and pliable. Roll it out to about 5 mm thick, then use a cup to trace circles about 10 cm across. (Originally, pasties were designed to take down the mines in a worker's pocket, so don't roll the pastry too thin – the finished shell should be good and robust.) I find it easier to cut smaller circles from a slightly thicker sheet of dough and then roll out each circle a bit more than to try and get the 'mother sheet' uniformly thin; keep rolling your cut circles until they are slightly thinner and larger.

Spoon a decent amount of filling in the middle of each circle, brush the perimeter with egg wash, then fold one half of the pastry over to make a half-moon shape; pinch the edges together with your fingers, making sure everything is contained. Patch up any holes with egg-wash glue and pastry off-cuts. For my money, this is the easiest shape to effect, but by all means fuss about with a crimped top, if you like. In South Australia, this shape signified that there were peas inside and was known as the 'Cornish pasty' – like there was any other kind. Transfer your pasties to the baking sheet and brush liberally with egg wash. Bake at 220°C (200°C fan) for 15 minutes, then turn the oven down to 200°C (180°C fan) and bake for another 10 minutes. The pasties should be lightly golden and crisp all over, including underneath.

Serve on a huge platter with a pile of brown paper bags on the side. Totally acceptable to eat these with tomato sauce or ketchup.

MEATY PASTIES
If you are not a fan of pulses, you can swap them for a bit of left-over shredded chicken, or roast beef or lamb, without any hard feelings.

MAKE IT GLUTEN-FREE
Follow the gluten-free pastry recipe on page 14 for the pastry.

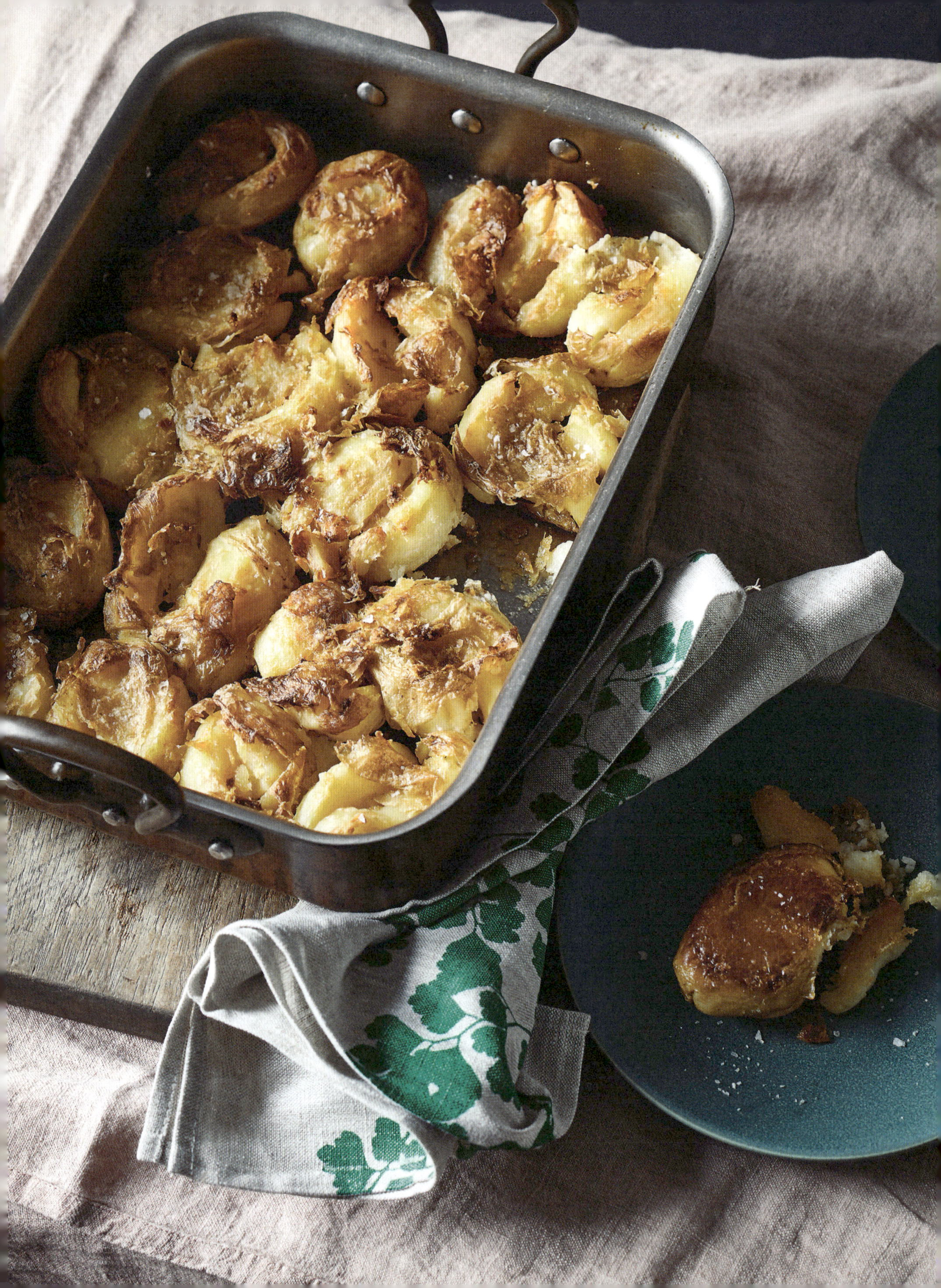

GLASS POTATOES

SERVES 6

I will go to my death arguing that potatoes can be a meal in themselves. Ironically, that argument would probably be conducted with the inventor of this dish, my friend Alice Ryan, who would never contemplate serving potatoes without a brontosaurean rib-eye.

When it comes to roast potatoes, these really opened my eyes. They're called 'glass potatoes' because the bottoms are a translucent, crackling, toffee-coloured brittle delight. Alice cooked them at a dinner party at her place in Melbourne; the following day, a surreptitious text message from another guest ('Did Alice say they were *kestrel* potatoes?') confirmed that, just like me, he was immediately trying them out himself. They were *that* good. If you can't find the kestrel variety – though really, try your best – substitute plain white washed potatoes; do not use a waxy kind.

'What's the catch?' I hear you ask. Well: oil. And salt. If you're planning to skimp on either, then just don't bother. While we're being frank, I disclose that I will likely sprinkle even more salt on my potatoes later, but that is because I am a salt-monster who was quite possibly an antelope in a previous life.

---

2 kg large potatoes (ideally kestrel), skin on
250 ml (1 cup) olive oil
1 tablespoon salt flakes

Preheat your oven to 220°C (200°C fan) and dig out a suitable roasting tin. The heavy cast-iron type is ideal, but use what you have; no ceramics, though, please. My 40 cm x 28 cm tin fits 2 kg of potatoes nicely.

Put the potatoes, whole, into a large saucepan and cover with water. Bring to the boil and cook for about 30 minutes, or until the potatoes are soft and a knife goes to the heart with ease. The skins will have split a little. Drain and tip into your *unoiled* roasting tin.

Okay. With a big spoon, press down on each potato to crush it slightly. What you're looking for is a big dent in the top of each spud, which will obligingly split a bit. Now pour over your scandalous, Exxon-Valdez quantity of oil, sprinkle with the salt flakes and put the whole thing into the oven. After 10 minutes, turn the oven down to 200°C (180°C fan), and let the potatoes go for another hour. Don't poke or baste or shake or otherwise interfere with them.

The ancillary beauty of these spuds is that they are very laid-back. If an hour goes by and you suddenly remember that you need to make a salad and you haven't yet, or you were going to cook some steaks and were so busy chatting that you plain forgot, just turn the oven temperature down to 180°C (160°C fan) and the potatoes will coast along for another half an hour while you catch up.

To serve, just bring the roasting tin to the table.

Pudding club

If you struggle to coordinate work or children's bedtimes with having people for dinner, how about inviting them for dessert? Just because 9pm is the best time to catch up. Think of it as book club, but without the last-minute cramming. Or consider this model for Children's Pudding Club... of course children should eat green vegetables, but others' offspring aren't your problem tonight. Have their own parents coerce a square meal into them beforehand, then serve up what they really want: SUGAR. While the children scoff pudding, parents enjoy pre-dinner drinks. Then children watch a movie while the adults eat a proper grown-up meal with spices and green things. As a provider of pudding, you have become every child's favourite adult friend. Adults love you because they haven't had to pay a babysitter. And you love yourself because you have dodged the minefield of who doesn't eat white food, or only white food, or food with corners.

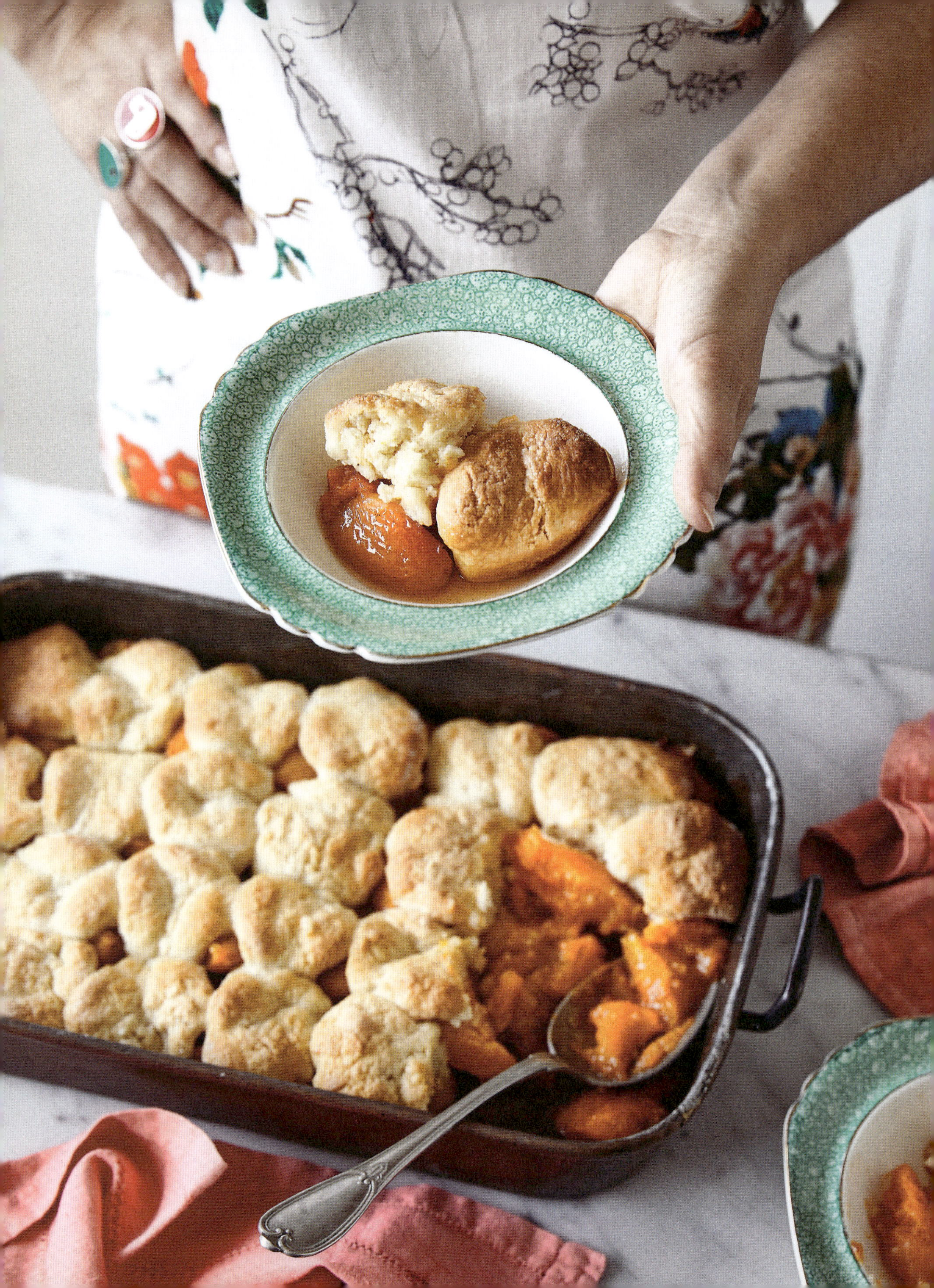

APRICOT COBBLER

SERVES 8

The cobbler is very popular in the United States but, like many other fads in that country (rendition, rampant gun ownership, aerosol cheese and so forth), it hasn't spread to the other side of the globe. This is a real pity, as cobbler - essentially, a scone topping atop a bubbling mass of fruit - is a dessert that is rich in delight but cheap in terms of effort. A crowd-pleaser that can be made ahead, it also reheats nicely for the late-night grazer. This recipe calls for Armagnac, because brandy and apricots are meant for each other, but if you want to keep it G-rated just use a squeeze of lemon juice and a tablespoon of maple syrup instead.

---

butter, for greasing
1.5 kg ripe apricots
55 g (¼ cup) raw sugar
1 tablespoon cornflour
1 teaspoon vanilla paste
2 tablespoons Armagnac
    (or regular brandy)
vanilla ice cream, Greek-style yoghurt
    or cream, to serve

SCONE TOPPING
300 g (2 cups) self-raising flour,
    plus extra for dusting
55 g (¼ cup) raw sugar, plus
    2 tablespoons extra
250 ml (1 cup) cream
130 g (½ cup) Greek-style yoghurt
milk, to loosen if necessary and
    for brushing

Preheat the oven to 180°C (160°C fan). Butter a roasting tin or large ovenproof dish.

Halve the apricots and remove the stones, then cut into quarters, putting them into a large bowl as you go. Sprinkle with the sugar and cornflour and toss gently, then stir in the vanilla paste and Armagnac. Tip the lot into the buttered tin or dish.

Now for the scone topping. Sift the flour into a mixing bowl and stir in the sugar, then fold in the cream and yoghurt until just combined. Don't overmix. Turn out the dough onto a floured board and press out with floured hands to about 1.5 cm thick, sprinkling more flour on top if things start to get sticky. Using an 8 cm cutter, cut out rounds (slightly bigger or smaller is fine here; an egg ring will work nicely too). Arrange the rounds on top of the apricots, overlapping them slightly. Brush with milk and sprinkle with more sugar.

Bake for 45 minutes or until the cobbler is golden brown and the fruit is cooked. Serve with vanilla ice cream, yoghurt or cream.

SALTED CARAMEL 'CRACK'

SERVES 10

This is a very wrong sort of dessert concept, involving as it does a salty cracker that was promoted during our youth for its easy snappability into 'bite size, snack size and *man* size' portions. However, it turns out the Salada biscuit is gnawingly addictive when blanketed with hard caramel and given a shiny topcoat of dark chocolate. I'm not going to waste any time trying to reason with you as to why it's good. I'm just going to testify that when a 'Chat 10 Looks 3' podcast listener sent in a box of this stuff, I briefly scoffed at it before taking a cautious bite. Next thing I remember is being found semi-comatose under the empty box. It's not called 'crack' for nothing.

You can serve 'crack' just as it is, but this version is tarted up with some festive pistachio slivers and dried raspberries. You could use any sort of nuts. Or use half dark, half white chocolate and swirl to mix! You can use other saltine-style crackers for this recipe; I've also had good results with Schär gluten-free crackers. For pudding club, I would dole out bowls of bought ice cream with a couple of crack shards stuck in like wafers.

---

1 x 250 g pack of Salada biscuits
200 g butter
185 g (1 cup) soft brown sugar
1 teaspoon vanilla extract
generous pinch of salt
200 g dark chocolate, chopped
50 g slivered pistachios
15 g dried raspberries

Rummage through your baking trays to find one that will fit three Salada crackers in one direction and four in the other. You can of course snap them to fit if you can't find quite the right tray, but this is the sort of surface area you're after. Line your baking tray with foil and then baking paper, and lay out the Saladas in a single layer.

In a saucepan, melt the butter and sugar together over medium heat, then cook, stirring occasionally, for about 5 minutes. The caramel should be thick and gloopy, and bubbling away sullenly. Stir in the vanilla and salt. Take the caramel off the heat and quickly pour it all over the Saladas. Smooth with an offset palette knife or spatula, if you have one; if you don't have one, get one immediately - for real, it will change your life. (Also, this would be an awesome time to remember that you forgot to preheat the oven. All is not lost: jack it up quickly - 180°C/160°C fan, okay?)

Now, into the oven with the lot for 15 minutes, or until the caramel has darkened to a deep gold. Keep an eye on it, as the caramel can quickly turn. When it's a good dark colour, remove from the oven and let it cool for a few minutes, then sprinkle the chocolate over the toffee. As the chocolate melts, use your spatula to spread it out evenly - this is extremely satisfying. While the chocolate is still soft, sprinkle over the pistachios and raspberries.

Allow your salted caramel 'crack' to cool (not in the fridge, please), then snap into pieces and store in an airtight container.

LORD HOWE ISLAND STICK INSECT
GIANT JUNGLE NYMPH
BED BUG
CASSAVA MEALYBUG
MYDAS FLY
MONARCH BUTTERFLY

MARMALADE BAKLAVA

MAKES ABOUT 36 SMALL PIECES

For *Kitchen Cabinet*, this is a dessert we took with us all the way to Kakadu, in the Northern Territory. Nova Peris had kindly invited us to visit her father's country, and we filmed for hours near Cannon Hill in the blistering heat, with crocodiles peering out from beneath waterlilies in the East Alligator River. All day, Nova patiently warned us: 'We've got to wrap this up before the sun goes down. Any later and the mozzies'll kill you.' Of course, things ran late, as they always do, and the very second the sun set, a Biblical plague of mosquitoes the size of Shetland ponies descended and began to tear us limb from limb. The packing and wrapping of cameras, lights and sound gear – ordinarily at least an hour-long affair – was accomplished in about six minutes flat.

Baklava was one of the best treats available in our childhood community, thanks to the Greek contingent of the first-generation migrants who ran small businesses, farms and market gardens around Two Wells and Virginia in that era. Baklava was an Ottoman Empire concept, but the Greeks have been making it for so long that it has become part of their cultural furniture. For Nova, we incorporated Australian macadamias instead of the usual walnuts, and quandong jam, but here we've gone for marmalade.

---

250 g almonds
100 g macadamias (or walnuts or pistachios)
1 teaspoon ground cinnamon
1 x 375 g packet filo pastry
200 g unsalted butter

MARMALADE SYRUP
250 g tart marmalade (or quandong jam, if you want to keep your guests guessing)
175 g (½ cup) runny honey
110 g (½ cup) caster sugar

In a 180°C (160°C fan) oven, toast the almonds for 10 minutes, and the macadamias (or other nuts) for 5 minutes.

Let the nuts cool slightly, then chop in batches, using a sharp knife (or whizz the whole lot in a food processor, again working in batches if necessary). Don't go too fine – you want the nuts to be about small-gravel sized. Stir through the cinnamon, then set the chopped nuts aside for filling the baklava, keeping 2 tablespoons separate in a small bowl.

Now make the syrup. Gently heat the marmalade, honey and sugar with 125 ml (½ cup) of water in a small saucepan, stirring intermittently, until the sugar has completely dissolved. Let it cool a bit, then sieve the syrup, pressing with the back of a spoon to extract as much as possible. Return the syrup to the pan.

If you like, you can chop the peel you sieved out of the syrup and sprinkle it through the main part of the nut filling, adding it a little at a time, to avoid clumps. If you are not a peel fan (and I know there are a lot of you out there), just skip this step. Personally, if I suspected fussy guests on the horizon, I would keep these peel leftovers in the fridge, ready to stir through my next bowl of yoghurt.

Preheat your oven to 180°C (160°C fan) and dig out a non-stick baking tray about 26 cm x 21 cm, and at least 5 cm deep.

Now it is time to construct your baklava: count out 16 sheets of filo pastry and cut them to the exact size of your baking tray. Melt your butter. (Yes, it *does* look like a lot of butter – and that's because it is a lot of butter.) Generously brush the bottom of the baking tray with melted butter, then lay in your first sheet of filo, brush with butter and sprinkle over a pinch of the 2 tablespoons chopped nuts (this will allow a tiny bit of air in-between the layers to help keep the pastry flaky). Repeat until you have eight layers of filo in the tray.

Spread the nut filling evenly over the base, along with whatever is left of the sprinkling nuts, then make the top by alternating filo and butter until all your filo sheets are used up. Finish off with a final flourish of butter. Now take a sharp knife and make confident diagonal cuts through the layers to make diamond shapes, making sure you cut all the way to the bottom of the tray. Bake for about 30–40 minutes until golden.

Just before the baklava comes out of the oven, warm up the syrup. Pour the syrup all over the baklava, making sure plenty of it runs down between the cracks. The warm syrup will sizzle as it hits the hot baking tray and crackly pastry, and you will want to gobble it up immediately. But if you can bear to wait a day or two, the syrup will sink in properly and the result will be more cohesive and all the tastier. Your patience will be rewarded!

PLUMBLE

SERVES 10

This is an incredibly pleasing dessert, not least because of how much fun it is to say 'plumble'. In fact, if you can persuade your kids to yell 'Let's get ready to *plumble*!' before it's served, that is more than worth the making of the thing. Use blood plums, if you can, for their beautiful colour and flavour.

This is easy to make ahead. Keep your nutty topping in reserve and sprinkle over just before baking. Speaking of toppings, this one is suitable for your Bondi gluten-free type – but not for coeliacs, since in Australia there is no such thing as a certified gluten-free oat. Other countries have gluten-free oats. This conundrum has all the hallmarks of a fight to be avoided. So, if you are cooking for a bona fide coeliac, use quinoa flakes instead.

Serve your plumble hot with ice cream or custard, depending on the season. Or snaffle some cold later, straight from the fridge.

---

2 kg plums
1 tablespoon butter
2 tablespoons sugar (or more, if your plums are super-tart)
2 tablespoons Pimms (substitute orange juice, if you want to go booze-free)
1 cinnamon stick
3 star anise

NUTTY TOPPING
100 g almond meal
55 g (⅓ cup) rice flour
½ teaspoon ground cinnamon
100 g butter
100 g rolled oats
100 g raw sugar
45 g (⅓ cup) slivered almonds
finely grated zest of ½ orange

MAKE IT VEGAN
Switch the butter for solid coconut oil and serve with coconut yoghurt or vegan ice cream.

MAKE IT GLUTEN-FREE
Sub out the oats for quinoa flakes.

Preheat the oven to 200°C (180°C fan). Lightly butter a casserole or enamel dish – I like to use a wide, shallow one, about 30 cm x 20 cm, for maximum crumble acreage.

Halve and stone your plums. And if they're the sort of plums that will not obediently pop out their stones at your behest (there are many such plums, sadly), do not stoop to swearing and wrenching at them tearfully until they're ruined. Cut off their cheeks with a sharp knife and remove as much flesh as you can, discarding the stones.

Now take a large frying pan, add the butter and place over high heat. When the butter is sizzling, add the plums, skin-side down, in a single layer and cook for a few minutes until the skins start to split and the juices start to emerge (you will need to do this bit in batches). Return all the plums to the pan and sprinkle the sugar over, then the Pimms, and poke the cinnamon and star anise in among the plums. Give them 2 minutes more, then scrape the whole panful into your buttered casserole or enamel dish.

Time for the topping. If you have a food processor, just pulse all the ingredients together. If you do not, mix the almond meal, rice flour and cinnamon in a bowl, then use your fingers to rub in the butter until the mixture resembles breadcrumbs and readily clumps together. Stir in the oats, sugar, almonds and orange zest. Reserve until you're ready to bake, whereupon you should sprinkle the topping over the plums and bake your plumble for 20 minutes or until browned, with sticky plum juices bubbling around the edges.

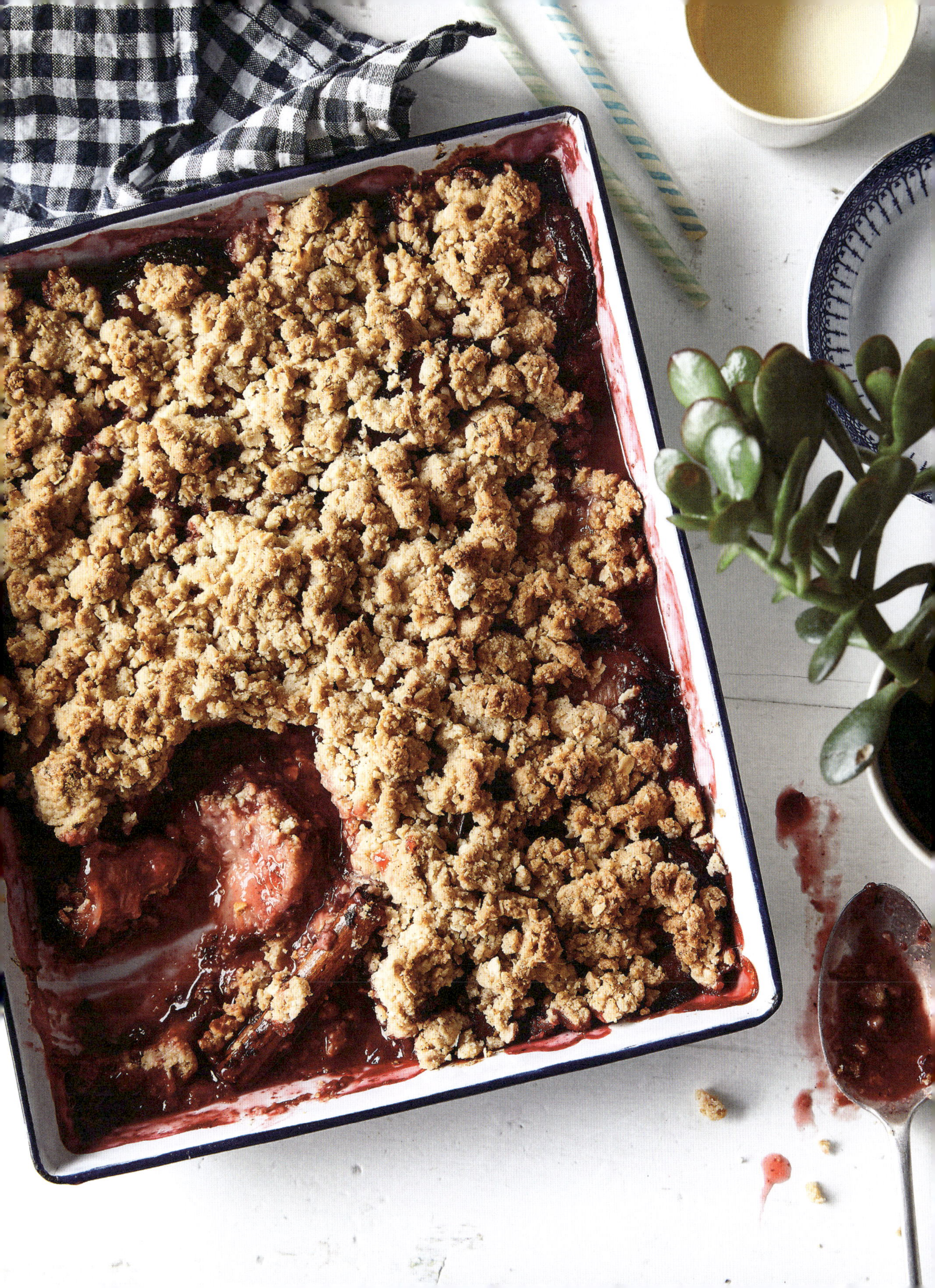

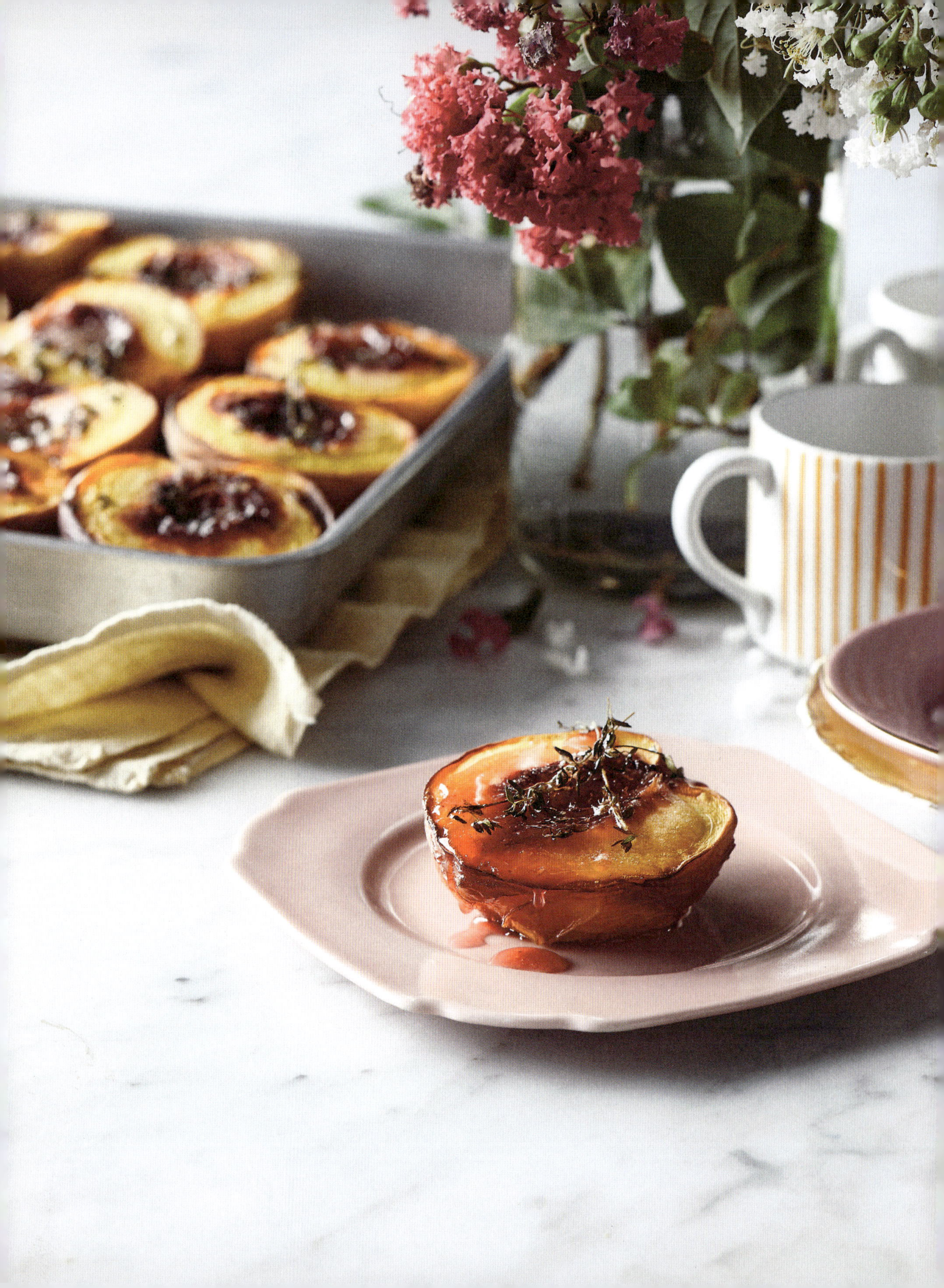

ROASTED THYME PEACHES

SERVES 6

A roasted fruit is possibly the easiest of desserts. The elements can be prepared ahead, and even those steps take mere minutes. They're good both hot and cold, so any leftovers from the kids' dessert can be hoovered up without reheating. If serving these cold later for the adults, I would plop one on a plate for each person, flanked by a glass of sweet dessert wine and a couple of almond cantuccini biscuits. A wine-dunked biscuit alternated with bites of peach will really put some fizz in your pop.

The other sneaky thing about roasting peaches is that it really can help out in cases of Disappointing Stonefruit Syndrome. You know the feeling: you buy a peach that feels and looks okay, and seems to have about the right heft in the hand, and then when you cut into it you're confronted with something doughily bland. (I'm always reminded of Evelyn Waugh's outwardly perfect peaches in *The Loved One*, which when bitten into reveal 'a ball of damp, sweet cotton-wool'.) Obviously, you're always going to be better off with fruit that starts out luscious, but roasting elicits a caramelly richness that will often carry a lacklustre fruit over the line.

The roasted peach was a favourite of my late mother-in-law, Jennifer Storer; I've made it even easier by spreading the fruit with a butter and sugar mixture spiked with thyme, a herb with which peaches enjoy an inexplicable affinity.

---

6 large peaches
50 g butter, softened
55 g (¼ cup) raw sugar
1 teaspoon thyme leaves
thyme sprigs and vanilla ice cream, to serve

Preheat the oven to 200°C (180°C fan).

Halve the peaches and remove the stones, then lay them cut-side up in a deep baking tray (I like mine to be stable, so I take a tiny slice off the base of each one; can't stand the thought of butter or sugar loss through fruit tiltage).

Mash the butter and sugar together with the thyme. Spread a teaspoon of the sweet thyme butter over each of the peach halves, then roast for 20 minutes or until tender and caramelised.

Top with thyme sprigs, then serve warm with vanilla ice cream.

MAKE IT VEGAN

Mix the sugar with a tablespoon of nut oil (hazelnut would be nice) instead of butter, and serve with vegan ice cream.

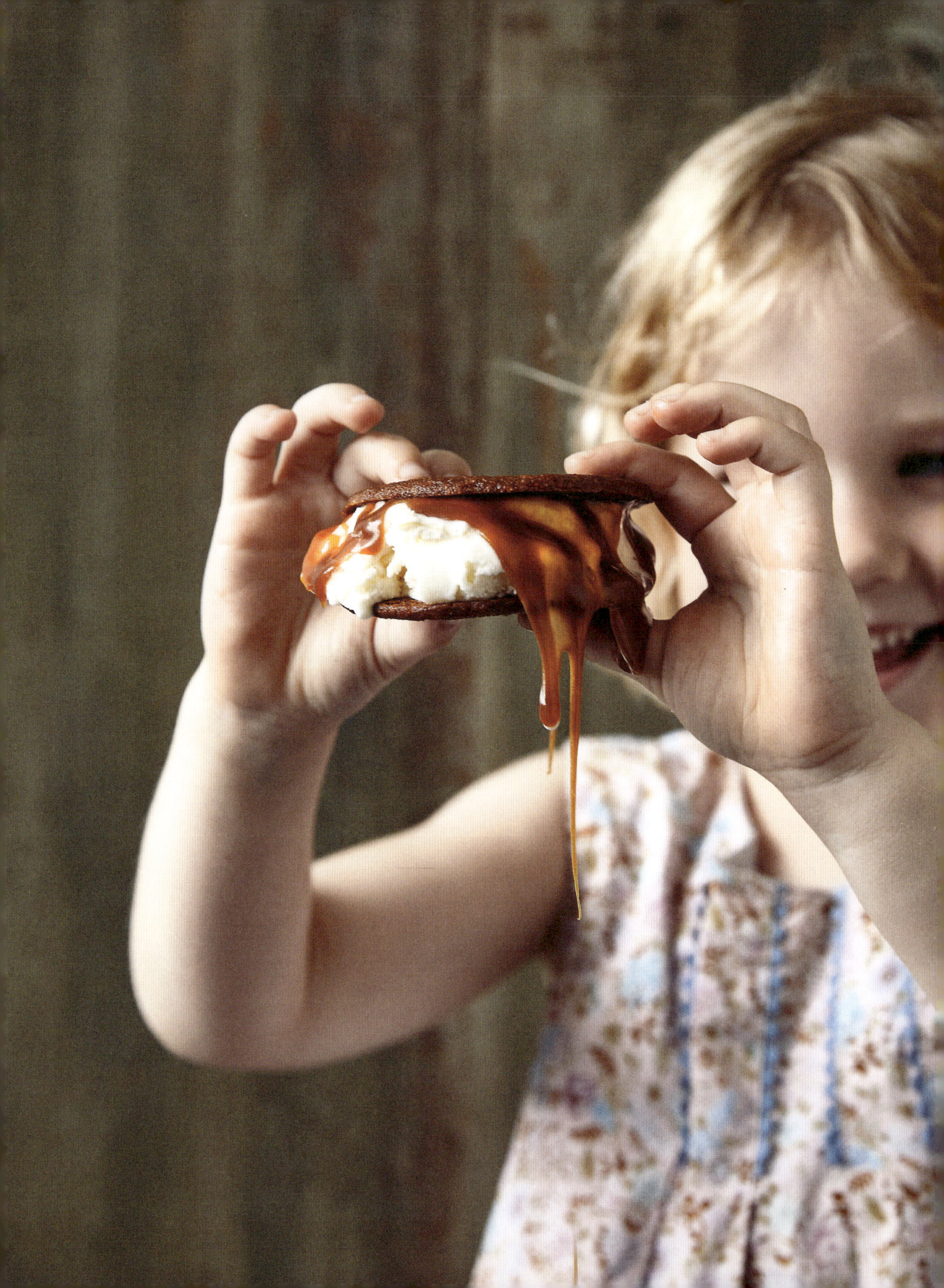

GINGERNUT ICE-CREAM SANDWICHES

MAKES ABOUT 24

The ice-cream sandwich – two biscuits with a wodge of ice cream in between – is the perfect solution for the pudding club operator. It's quick to assemble, always popular, and very amenable to guest numbers that swell at the last minute.

These may be called gingernuts, but they are unlike the commercial biscuit of the same name, which I've always suspected of being owned by some nebulous global-dentistry syndicate, so risky is it for even relatively hardy choppers. These gingernuts are chewy enough to give some ground and not squirt your ice cream everywhere. Make the biscuits the day before, then buy in some good-quality vanilla ice cream and assemble. Kids can be sent outside with a platter of ice-cream sandwiches and a roll of paper towel. Adults can enjoy a grown-up version of the sauce with a shot of bourbon.

---

225 g (1½ cups) plain flour
1 teaspoon ground ginger
½ teaspoon ground allspice
½ teaspoon ground cinnamon
125 g salted butter
100 g (½ cup) soft brown sugar
175 g (½ cup) golden syrup
1 teaspoon finely grated ginger
1 teaspoon bicarbonate of soda
1 egg, beaten
vanilla ice cream, to serve

CARAMEL SAUCE
220 g (1 cup) caster sugar
125 ml (½ cup) thick (double) cream
25 g butter
2 tablespoons orange juice (or bourbon if catering for adults)

First, make the gingernuts. Sift the flour, ground ginger, allspice and cinnamon together into a mixing bowl. In a small heavy-based saucepan over low-medium heat, melt the butter, sugar, golden syrup and grated ginger together. When it begins to bubble, remove from the heat and sprinkle in the bicarbonate of soda: excitingly, the mixture will fizz up. Pour the foamy liquid into the dry ingredients and stir, adding the egg to bring everything together. When you have a smooth and glossy dough, leave it to cool to room temperature.

Preheat the oven to 200°C (180°C fan). Line two baking trays with baking paper.

Take teaspoonfuls of the soft dough and roll into balls with your hands, spacing them out evenly on the trays and allowing plenty of room for the biscuits to spread – six to a standard-sized baking tray is prudent. Bake each batch of gingernuts for 8–10 minutes or until dark golden-brown. Remove and cool on a wire rack, then seal in a container until you're ready for the sandwiching.

Caramel sauce next. Put the sugar into a dry heavy-based saucepan over medium heat. Heat the sugar until it melts, swirling all you like. When the caramel is a deep golden colour, carefully pour in the cream: it will make an awful fuss, but keep stirring, at arm's length, and it will settle down. When you have a smooth sauce, stir in the butter and juice. Leave to cool, then pour into a jar – it will keep in the fridge for a week, so you can disgrace yourself with leftovers.

To serve, squish a good scoop of ice cream onto a gingernut and drizzle with the caramel sauce before applying its gingernut lid.

SNOWBALL SUNDAES

SERVES 8

Hot chocolate sauce lavishly poured on ice cream, coated with tasty crunchy stuff and topped with banana has to be one of the most famous desserts the Western world has to offer. And it must be a cinch, right? Careful now. Dispensing ball after ball of ice cream with toppings for sundae-eager guests is a messy and time-consuming exercise when you are catering for numbers. So here's the answer: you pre-scoop before your guests arrive, then roll the ice-cream balls in a crunchy coating – think toasted nuts, hundreds and thousands, coconut, or a combination thereof. Refreeze the balls, make a Class A gloopy chocolate sauce, and let the hordes descend!

---

2 x 500 ml tubs of ice cream (each one should give you about 16 scoops)

CHOCOLATE SAUCE
90 g dark brown sugar
75 g unsweetened cocoa powder
50 g dark chocolate, roughly chopped
125 ml (½ cup) thickened (whipping) cream
2 tablespoons golden syrup

FOR COATING AND TOPPING
100 g desiccated coconut or almonds
2 bananas or other fruit – optional

SUNDAE MADNESS

Other coatings you might like to consider are chopped pistachios, hundreds and thousands, little bits of freeze-dried strawberry, banana chips or chocolate chips. You can keep your coatings separate to give different-flavoured scoops, or just mix them all together for crazy mixed-up sundaes.

FOR THE GROWN-UPS

If you are catering for a purely adult crowd, a pinch of instant coffee powder added to the chocolate sauce at the start gives a good flavour.

Start with the chocolate sauce, since it will keep for at least a week in the fridge. Put 125 ml (½ cup) water into a medium heavy-based saucepan. Add the sugar and place over low-medium heat, then sprinkle in the cocoa powder, and whisk until smooth and lump-free. Bring to a gentle simmer and cook for 1 minute, stirring constantly. Turn the heat down as low as it will go and sprinkle in the chocolate – it should relax right into the hot cocoa mixture. Stir to combine, then add the cream and golden syrup and whisk until smooth. This isn't especially sweet, so add more golden syrup or a teaspoon of honey if you think your guests (children!) are sweet of tooth.

For the coating, spread out the coconut or almonds on a baking tray and toast in a 180°C (160°C fan) oven: coconut will take about 4 minutes to turn a nice deep golden colour, while almonds will need 10–15 minutes. Leave to cool, then finely chop the almonds (but not to dust). Put your coating into a wide shallow bowl, ready to go.

Use an ice-cream scoop or spoon to fashion the roundest balls you can. Toss into the bowl of desiccated coconut or almonds – and/or other coatings (see left for suggestions), shaking the bowl and using a spoon to get them turned, sprinkled and covered. Set the coated scoops on a baking tray lined with baking paper and freeze quick sharp. If your freezer space doesn't admit a tray (and Lord knows mine seldom does), stack them, interleaved with baking paper.

Just before serving, gently reheat the chocolate sauce, whisking until it's smooth again. Transfer to a jug. Drop two or three coated ice-cream scoops into each small bowl or serving glass.

Slice some bananas on top, if you like, then pour over the warm chocolate sauce at the table. And amazingly, everyone can eat at once!

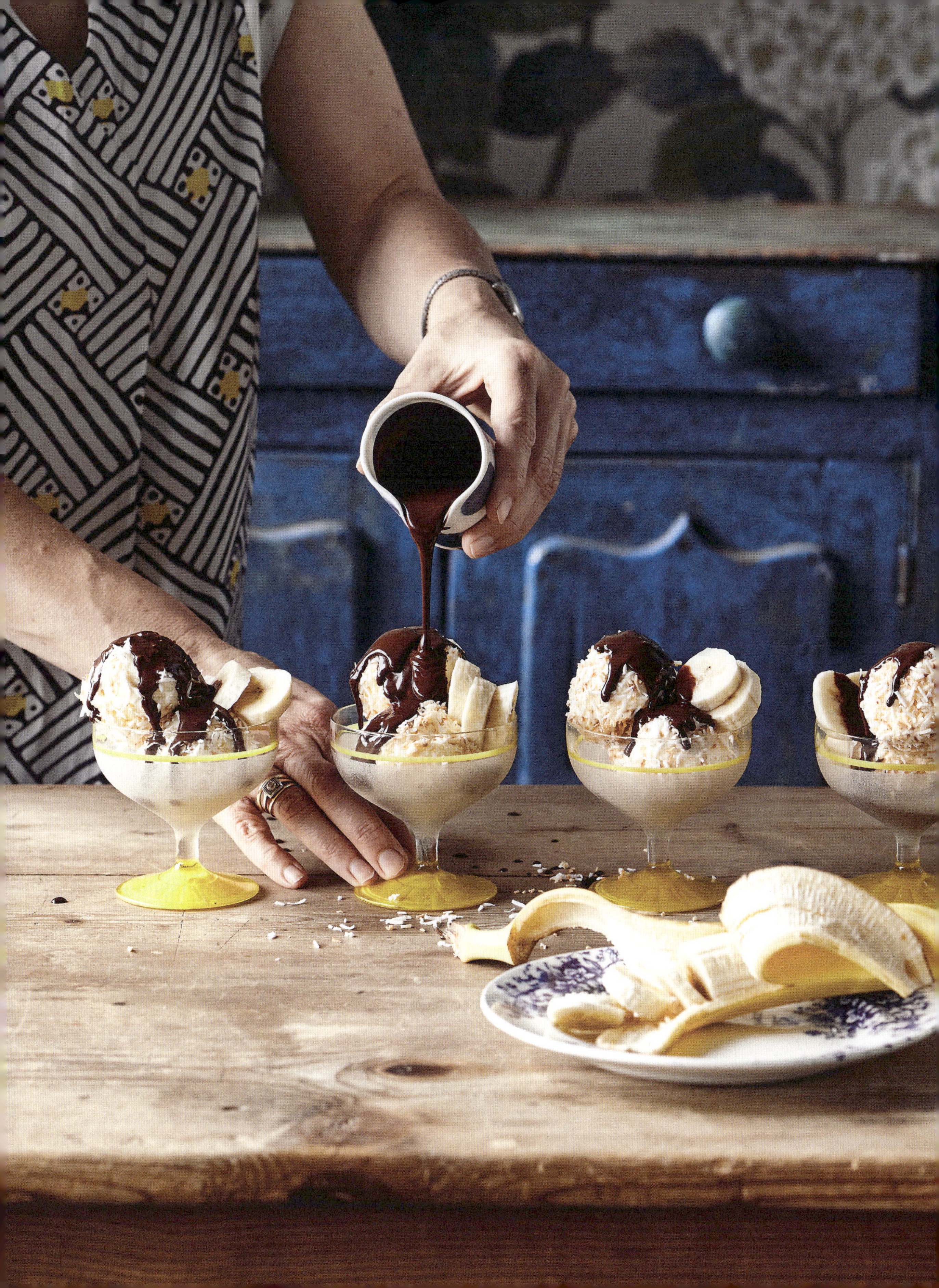

TOFFEE & ORANGE PANNA COTTA

SERVES 6

This is a dessert for anyone who's ever been defeated by a caramel. There is something so liberating about burning sugar and then dumping cream and milk in, watching it seize and yet knowing that it's all going to be okay. It feels like beating the system.

It takes ten minutes to make this recipe. You can do it ahead of time. It doesn't even take up much fridge space. It wobbles, so children love it. So many reasons.

---

300 ml cream
200 ml milk
100 g caster sugar
2 large strips of orange zest (removed with a potato peeler)
2 teaspoons gelatine powder

Combine the cream and milk in a jug or bowl. Set a heavy-based saucepan over high heat and fling in the sugar. It will start to melt and bubble. Stand and watch it, swirling to get all the sugar involved. Continue until the sugar is bubbling and a deep gold colour.

Turn the heat down to low and immediately add the combined cream and milk – be careful and stand well back, as the toffee will protest violently at this development, spitting and seizing. You will think it has all ended in a debacle. But you will not panic, because you know *everything will be all right*. Add the orange zest and stir and stir, and after a few minutes the toffee will magically dissolve in the cream and milk and you will be left with a smooth caramel-coloured liquid.

Remove from the heat and slowly scatter in the gelatine powder, whisking as you go. When the gelatine has dissolved, strain the panna cotta into six 125 ml (½ cup) ramekins or other moulds and refrigerate until set, about 4 hours.

MAKE IT VEGETARIAN

You can make this with agar agar, a seaweed-derived gelling agent that's available in powdered form. But beware – agar agar is much stronger than gelatine and you will only need ½ teaspoon here. Also it needs to be boiled to activate its setting properties, so add the agar agar at the same time as the cream and milk.

MANGO, COCONUT & PASSIONFRUIT PUDDING

SERVES 6

How glum is the lot of the vegan at dessert time? Truly, there are only so many poached pears a responsible human can trudge through in this minefield of eggs and butter. And, even within the humble jelly (an apparently uncomplicated and transparent proposition), untold trotter-horrors can lurk. So this is a straightforward and irreproachable pudding that is entirely vegan, while also being bright, festive and joyous. It can be dressed up with all manner of berries. It is unquestionably something that will make everyone at the table happy, and will not make your vegan friends feel like beggars at the feast.

---

2 mangoes
3 heavy passionfruit
juice of 1 lime
300 ml coconut cream
55 g (¼ cup) caster sugar
½ teaspoon agar agar powder

Slice the cheeks off the mangoes and scoop out the flesh into a blender. Scrape the pulp out of the passionfruit and strain into the blender as well. Squeeze in the lime juice. Blitz. Measure out 300 ml of your mango and passionfruit purée – precise proportions are important in this recipe. Return the 300 ml of purée to the blender (save any excess and drink it with rum on the quiet).

Meanwhile, put the coconut cream, sugar and agar agar in a saucepan. Bring to the boil and let it bubble for 1 minute – it will thicken a little. Unlike its hoofy cousin, gelatine, agar agar needs to be boiled to become active: it really doesn't get out of bed for much under 100°C. The ancillary news is that agar agar doesn't melt at normal hot-day temperatures, so any pud or jelly you make with it will be ruggedly picnic-proof.

Once you've boiled the coconut cream mix, it's game on. Take it off the heat and add to the purée in the blender, then give it another whizz before decanting into six 100 ml moulds.

These puddings will set in a few hours at room temperature, but that's just showing off really – refrigerate for faster results. To unmould, you will need to dip the mould in freshly boiled water for about a minute to loosen before upending.

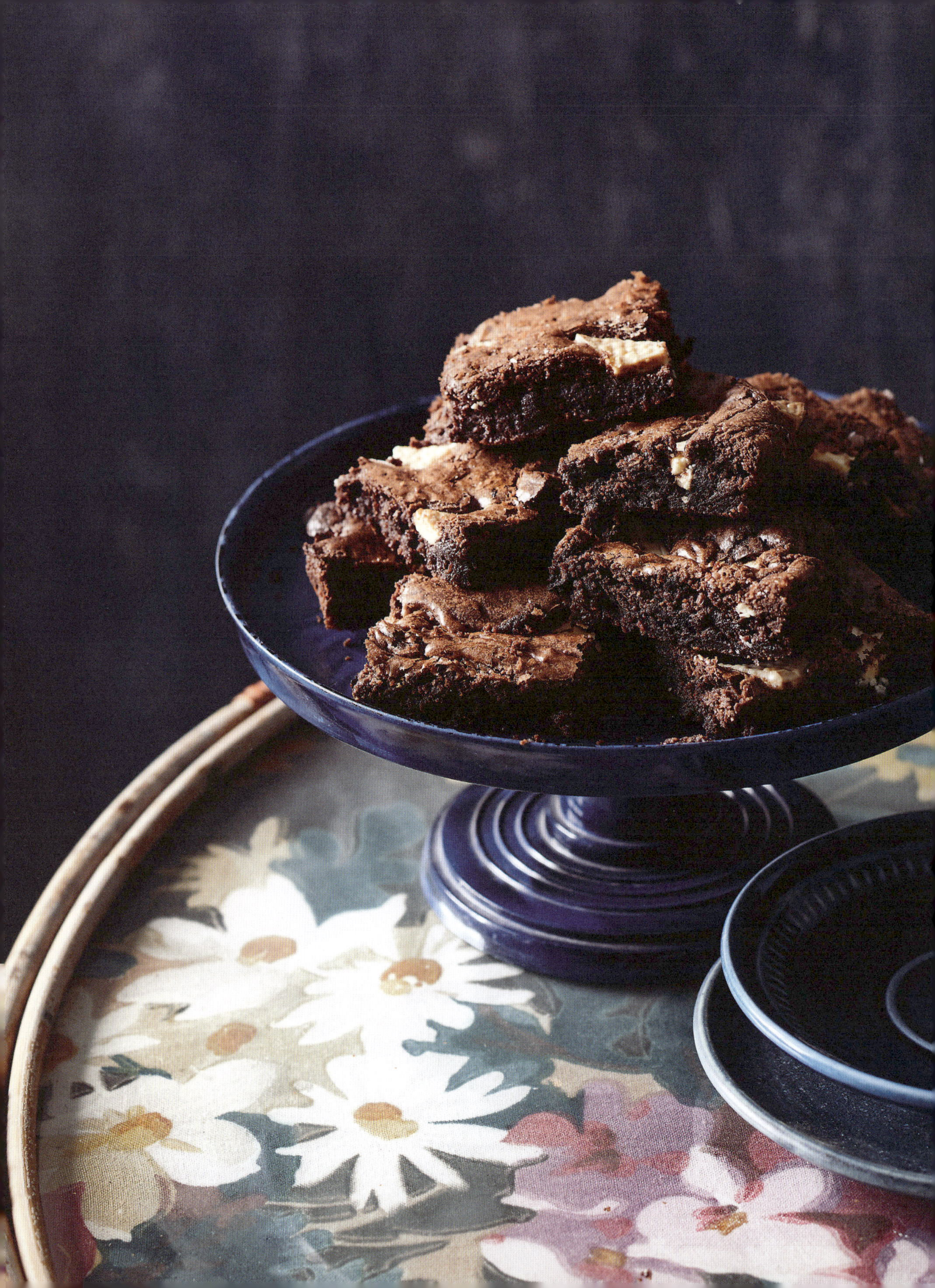

HIBISCUS BROWNIES

MAKES 12

Everyone has their favourite brownie recipe, I know, but I urge you to try this one, because it might just succeed to the throne and become your king of *all* brownies. The idea of slipping hibiscus into chocolate brownies could only have been thought up by a home-worker, really. Here, for your enjoyment, is Wendy's first-person account of inventing the hibiscus brownie: 'During a particularly scrambled chaotic week and with the cupboards in crisis, I consumed little outside kimchi and coffee, but when that was gone, I moved on to nibbling the dried petals of hibiscus tea. And, actually, those things are surprisingly delicious – tart and tangy. If you can't find them, or this combo sounds like a step too far into weird-food world, then stick with some muscaty sultanas and walnuts: old school, maybe, but just right, especially with a dash of cream.'

---

125 g unsalted butter, softened
250 g caster sugar
2 eggs
75 g (½ cup) self-raising flour
2 tablespoons unsweetened cocoa powder
100 g dark chocolate (70% cocoa), finely chopped
20 g dried hibiscus flowers, finely chopped
thick (double) cream, to serve

A FINAL FLOURISH

If you don't mind white chocolate, sprinkle about 40 g of the stuff, chopped into chunks, on top of the brownie before it goes into the oven. It caramelises and becomes rather terrific. I'm a fan.

MAKE IT GLUTEN-FREE

Use gluten-free flour.

Preheat the oven to 180°C (160°C fan) and dig out your baking tin that best approximates 25 cm x 20 cm. Tear off a sheet of baking paper roughly the same size and, using wet hands, screw it up into a ball, then unfurl and use to line your tin (this neat little trick helps to stop the baking paper jumping around so much).

Using an electric mixer, cream 100 g of the butter with the sugar until light and fluffy. Add the eggs, one at a time, beating on high speed until combined. Sift in the flour and cocoa and fold in gently.

Melt the remaining 25 g of butter in a small heavy-based saucepan over low heat. Add the chocolate, then immediately remove from the heat. There should be enough residual heat to melt the chocolate, but you might need to swirl the pan a bit, or give it another 5 seconds on the heat to melt the last bits. (This is my way of melting chocolate without a double boiler: the butter acts as a protective buffer to shield the chocolate from the hot pan, and also helps the chocolate to glide out of the pan more easily.) Pour the melted chocolate into the batter, then add the hibiscus flowers and fold everything together until just combined.

Scrape the brownie batter into your tin and use a palette knife to spread it out to the edges of the tin. Bake for about 20–25 minutes until mostly set but still with a slight wobble in the centre. Leave to cool in the tin before cutting into squares. Over time, you will work out whether you like your brownies gooier or chewier and adjust the cooking time accordingly (less for gooey, more for chewy). Me, I like them both ways. Serve at room temperature, or ever so slightly warm, with cream.

The happy hour

If you really need to slim down your hosting time but would still like to have your friends and family over on a regular basis, then give the happy hour a go. Provide a start and finish time for an updated 'at Home' invitation, letting guests know what time you will be free to receive them each week. RSVPs are not required. Have a nice bottle of wine, a soft drink, plus one back up, ready to go and - if you have time - just one snack. Some weeks there will be a crowd. Other weeks, it might just be one stalwart. Invite new neighbours, old friends, anyone who you wouldn't mind seeing more often. Wendy observes a drinks hour every Friday between 6.30 and 7.30 pm. Suddenly, all those aimless 'We must catch ups' have become 'Drop round Friday at 6.30'. If your guest can come - terrific. If they can't - oh well. Maybe next week, but at least you don't feel bad about not having tried.

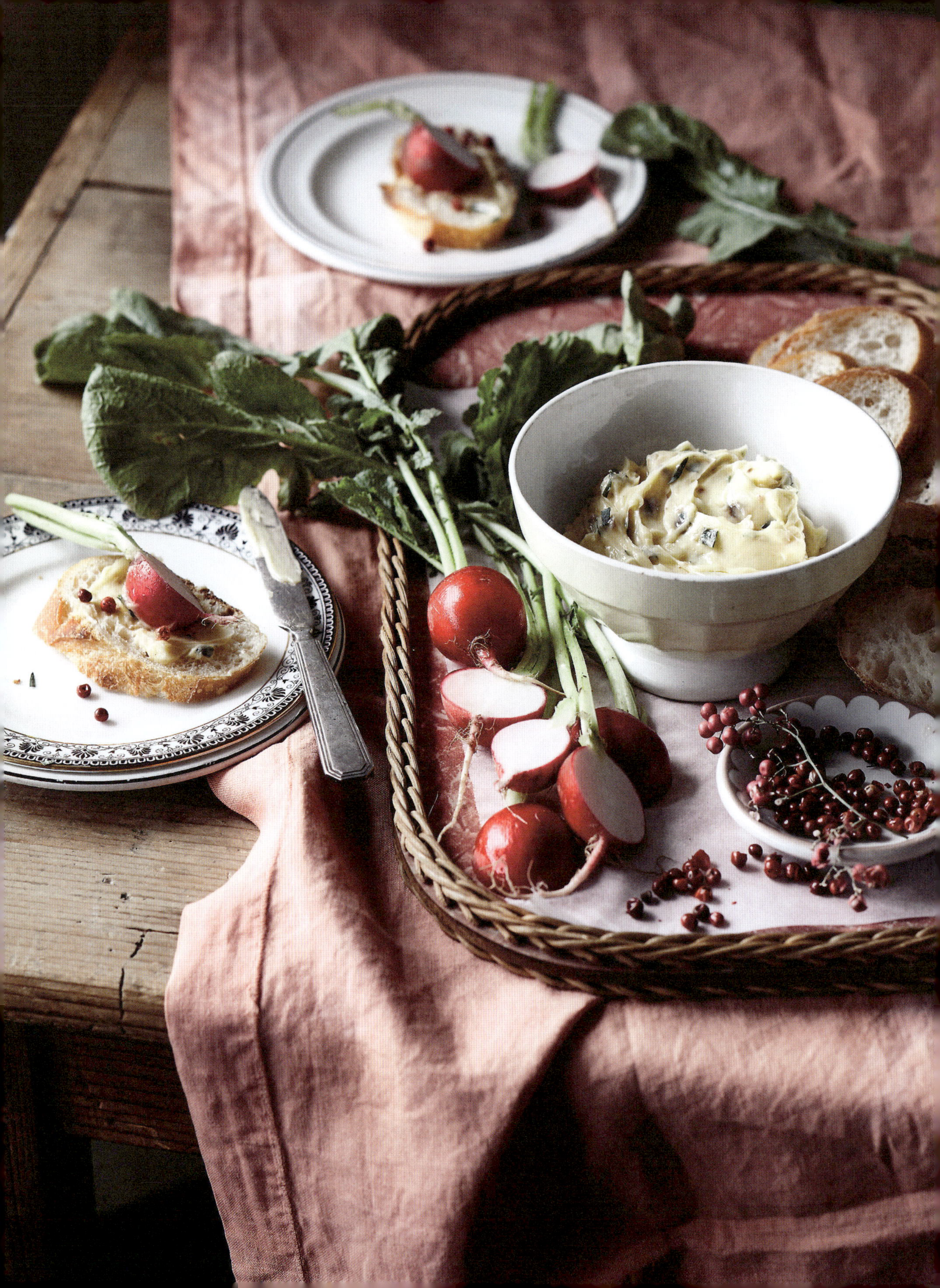

BAGNA FREDDO WITH TARRAGON & PINK PEPPER

SERVES 4

Traditionally a hot, buttery, anchovy-spiked dip to dunk your crudités and bread in, this update to the bagna cauda is rather easier to manage and can be prepared well in advance. We deviated to a more solid format to avoid the prospect of melted butter all over the chin and splashes of garlicky butter all over the sofa. If you really can't abide the aniseedy taste of tarragon, use parsley instead - it's the umami flavour of the anchovies that carries the dish. A baguette and a pile of radishes is all you need with this. Oh, and a frosty glass of nice white wine.

---

5 anchovy fillets
1 garlic clove (or ½ clove if your garlic is especially pungent)
pinch of pink peppercorns (green would also be fine)
125 g unsalted butter, softened
juice of ½ lemon
1 tablespoon olive oil
2 teaspoons chopped tarragon (or parsley)

Using a small food processor or a large mortar and pestle, mash up your anchovy fillets with the garlic and peppercorns until smooth-ish. Then add the butter, lemon juice and olive oil and whizz or pound until really smooth and a bit fluffy (a food processor is definitely an advantage here).

Sprinkle in the tarragon and mix until just combined. Chill until ready to serve - it will keep well for a few days in the fridge.

CACIO E PEPE GOUGÈRES

MAKES ABOUT 36

The speed with which cacio e pepe - the cult pasta sauce that is an emulsion of parmesan, pasta-cooking water and industrial quantities of pepper - has colonised the world in recent years is a stark demonstration of just how desperate adults have become for an excuse to eat macaroni cheese. But if you don't fancy standing around whisking cheese and water while your guests shift anxiously from foot to foot, try transferring the flavours of cacio e pepe to that immortal French canapé, the gougère.

Gougères are savoury cheese puffs - choux pastry piped or spooned onto a baking tray and baked for immediate consumption. Obviously, you are at this point thinking: uh huh, choux pastry. The easy entertainer. *Riiiggghhht*. But stay with me. The dough is easy and fun to make. Shove it into a piping bag and into the fridge (or freezer, if you're working ahead), then when your guests arrive all you have to do is squeeze out a tray's worth of doughy dobs and twenty minutes later you have a crowd-pleasing hot canapé that will - I guarantee it - disappear quickly.

---

125 g salted butter
150 g (1 cup) plain flour
4 eggs
100 g (1 cup) finely grated parmesan, plus 25 g (¼ cup) extra for sprinkling
1 tablespoon freshly ground black pepper, plus extra for sprinkling
salt flakes, for sprinkling

EVEN EASIER
Make this recipe ahead and freeze the batter in its piping bag or container, defrosting it in the fridge overnight before piping and baking. Warning: once the batter is thawed, use it within the day. If left to languish in the fridge for more than a day, it will discolour and go grey.

Put the butter into a heavy-based saucepan with 250 ml (1 cup) of water and bring to the boil. Sift the flour onto a large sheet of baking paper. Once the butter is melted and the water is bubbling, pick up the baking paper and use it as a chute to deliver the flour into the pan in one hit. Stir with a wooden spoon over low-medium heat for about 2 minutes until fully incorporated. The mixture will become thick and doughy, and will come away from the sides of the pan as you stir. Remove from the heat and leave to cool for a few minutes.

Now, using your wooden spoon, beat in the eggs one by one. You could do this in an electric mixer, but it's more of a physical challenge this way, giving a sense of satisfaction when your batter is thick, yellow and glossy. Now stir in your parmesan and pepper, mix well, then load the batter into a piping bag fitted with a wide plain nozzle. Seal the nozzle by wrapping foil around it and refrigerate until required. (If you don't have - or can't be bothered with - a piping bag, you can just put the batter in an airtight container and make slightly more rustic gougères with spoonfuls of batter instead.)

About half an hour before serving time, preheat the oven to 200°C (180°C fan). Line two baking trays with baking paper and pipe dobs of the batter onto them - aim for 3 cm in diameter with a 5 cm gap between them. With a wet finger, pat the tops so they're shapely, then sprinkle a pinch of extra grated parmesan, a grind of black pepper and a few salt flakes on each one. Bake for 15 minutes or until puffed and golden, then serve immediately.

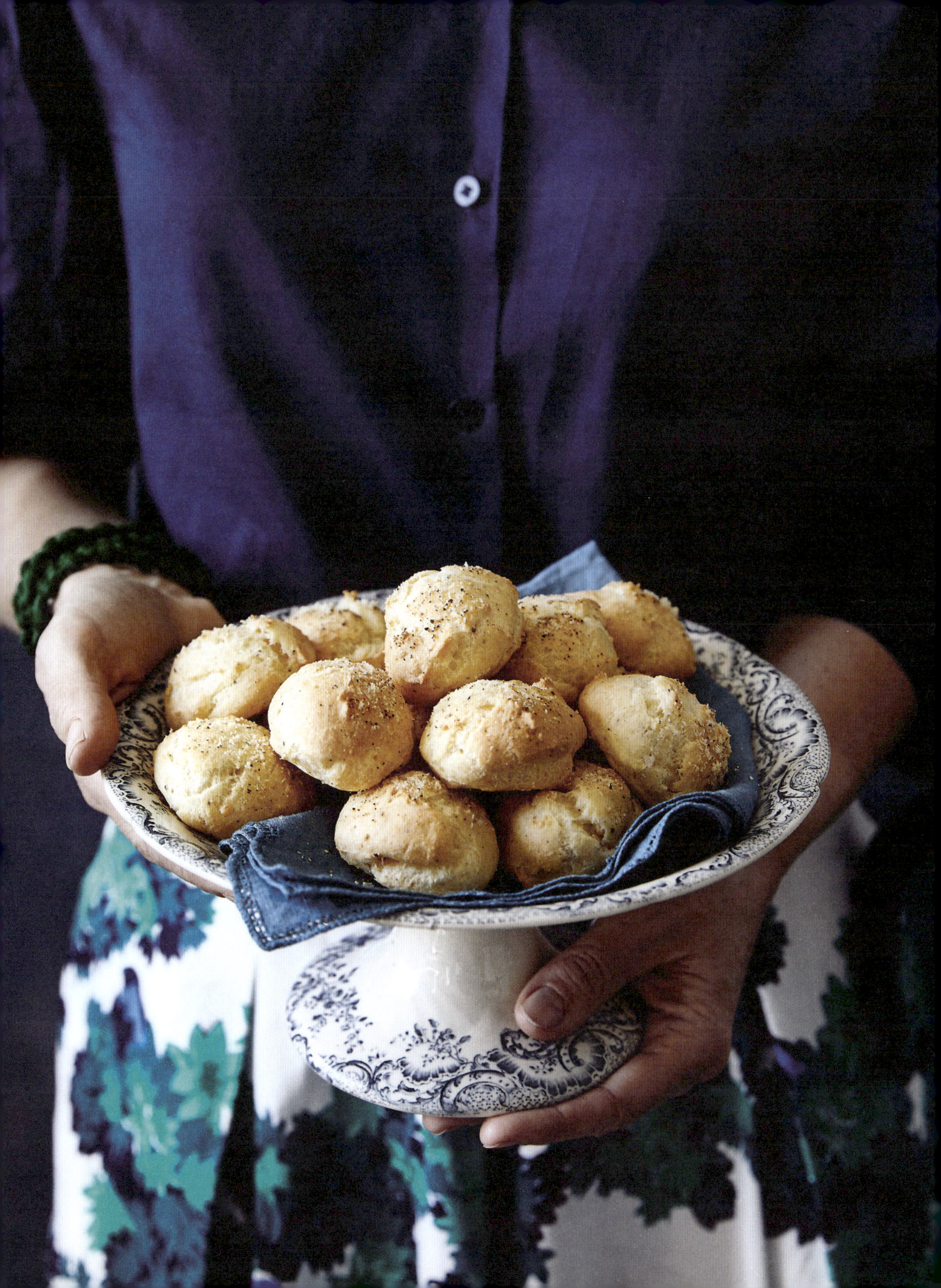

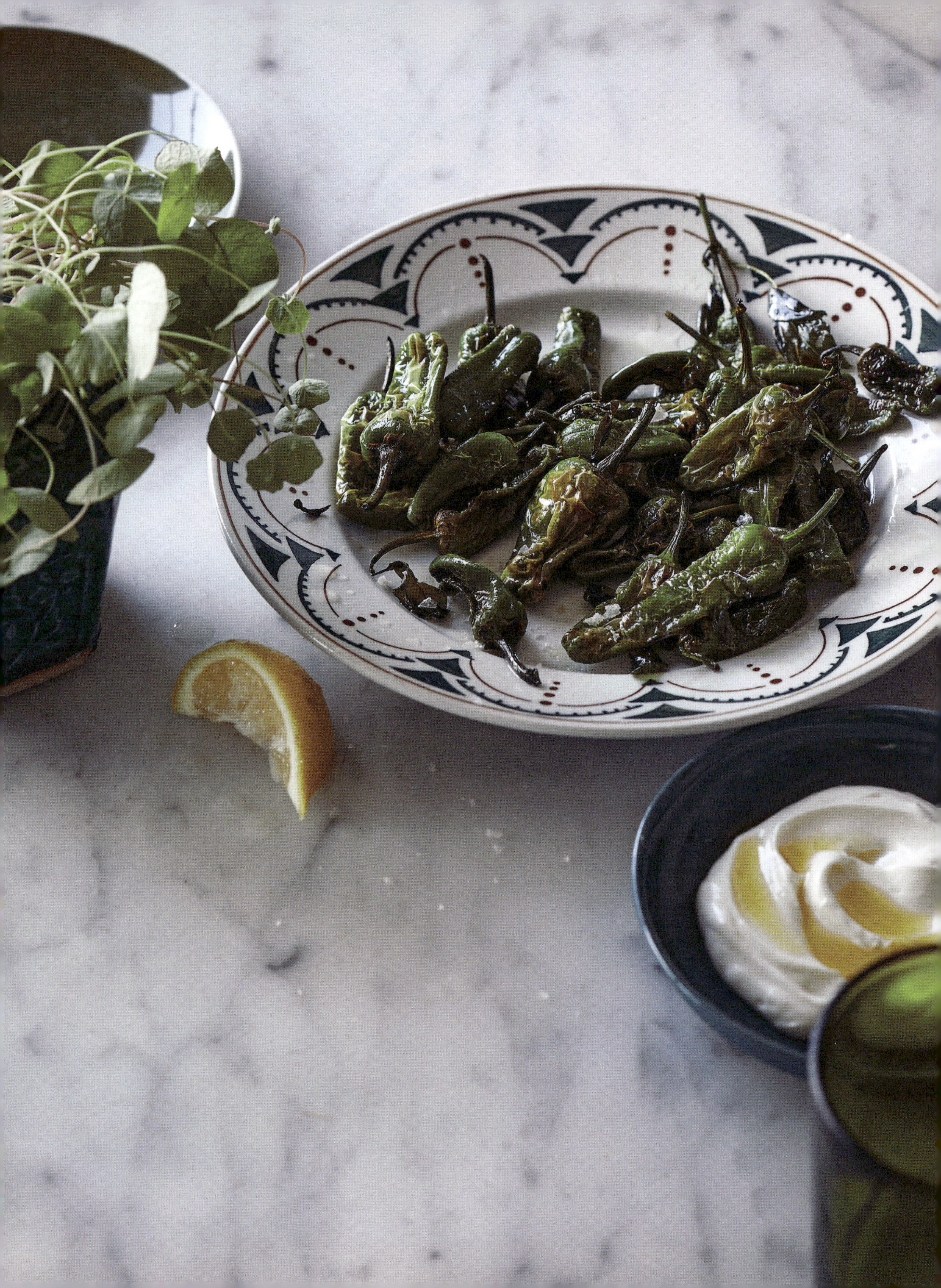

LUCKY-DIP PADRÓN PEPPERS WITH STRAINED YOGHURT

SERVES 4–6

The idea of serving just one perfect thing with a drink enters shaky ground here, since these little things are so addictive that it might be near impossible to keep up with demand. After their sheer deliciousness, the second-best thing about padrón peppers is that about one or two in every ten will be fiery hot, while the rest will be just mild and super-tasty. How can you tell which is the spicy one? You can't! Which is part of the utterly brilliant theatre of eating these. And for those who win the lucky-dip lottery, rescue is at hand, in the form of cooling strained yoghurt, or labneh. I never stop being surprised at how different this is to plain straight-from-the-pot yoghurt – it feels very special and is such an easy win.

Padrón peppers are becoming more widely available in Australia: ask your greengrocer; or there's a grower in Queensland who will ship them to you (www.midyimeco.com.au) during their December–May season. Or you could always get your hands on some seeds and grow your own – I am going to have a crack at self-sufficiency in the novelty mini-pepper category next year.

---

200 g Greek-style yoghurt
olive oil, for drizzling and frying
pinch of sumac
350 g padrón (or shishito) peppers
salt flakes
1 lemon

MAKE IT VEGAN
Omit the yoghurt.

For the strained yoghurt, line a sieve set over a bowl with a clean piece of cheesecloth (or an unsullied Chux or J-cloth), then spoon in the yoghurt. Set aside to drain for about 30 minutes and you'll have a slightly thickened yoghurt; the longer you leave it, the thicker it will get – but if leaving for longer than an hour, pop the lot in the fridge. (You can make this the day before, and keep it in the fridge.) I like to stir through a few drops of olive oil and sprinkle with a pinch of sumac just before serving.

Rinse your peppers and pat them dry. Heat a large frying pan (not non-stick) over medium-high heat, add a small glug of olive oil and swirl to coat the pan. Now throw as many peppers into the hot pan as will fit in a single layer. Let them cook, undisturbed, for about 30–60 seconds – that should be long enough to blister the skin and blacken it here and there, then give the peppers a stir to turn them over and cook for another 30–60 seconds. Once the peppers have collapsed and are a bit charred in places, tip them out onto a plate and sprinkle with plenty of salt flakes and a squeeze of lemon juice.

Serve on a big plate, with a small bowl of strained yoghurt alongside. Good luck!

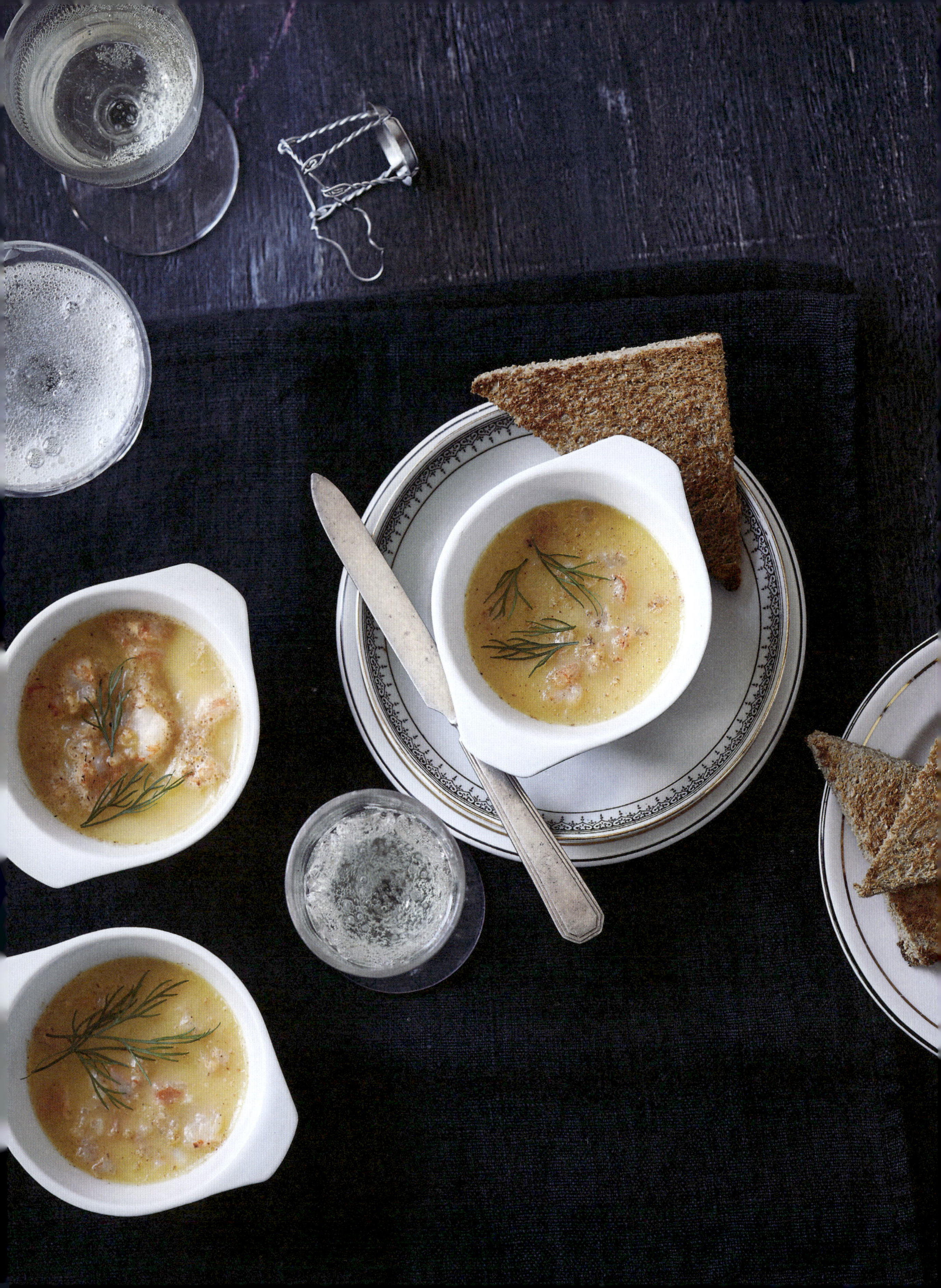

POTTED PRAWNS

SERVES 2–4

In the days long before refrigeration, cooks had to rely on canny ways to preserve food - burying it in the ground, salting and brining. There was also potting food. While the French were keeping duck under gallons of its own fat for months at a time, folk in the British Isles were busy preserving tongue and other squishy meats under slabs of clarified butter. For pretty obvious reasons, the technique's overall popularity has waned. However, potted shrimp is still a British favourite, especially in chic Mayfair restaurants, since it goes with Champagne so beautifully. The dish originates from the north-west of England, where the delicious, tiny brown shrimp come from.

This version, using prawns in place of the shrimp, is a make-ahead favourite. It is also a lesson in resisting the urge to automatically look to the Mediterranean for flavourings: when potted shrimp was first made, lemon wouldn't have been an option, nor garlic. The delicacy of mace and nutmeg turns out to be quite a revelation with seafood.

---

150 g butter
½ teaspoon ground mace
a few gratings of nutmeg
2 pinches of white pepper
pinch of cayenne pepper
150 g cooked, peeled and deveined prawns
dill sprigs and wholemeal toast, to serve

Melt the butter in a small saucepan and when it just starts to bubble, take it off the heat and wait for a minute to allow the milk solids to settle on the bottom of the pan. Now, very carefully pour off the top layer (the clear liquid, AKA clarified butter) into a heatproof bowl. Skim any white stuff from the surface, then clean the pan and pour the clarified butter back into it - you should be left with about two-thirds the amount of butter you started with. Add the mace, nutmeg and both peppers and set the pan over the lowest-possible heat to let the flavours infuse for a couple of minutes. Set aside to cool slightly.

Meanwhile, chop the prawns quite finely - you want a similar texture to coarse mince. Stir the prawns into the butter, then spoon into four 100 ml ramekins, or two slightly larger ones, squashing them down a bit so as to have as little wasted space as possible. Pour any clarified butter still in the pan over the prawns to cover. In the days when food was potted for more practical reasons than 'this is going to be delicious with Champagne', a thick layer of butter would have been essential to keep air out, and so prevent spoilage of the foodstuff beneath. But thanks to refrigeration, there's no need to worry if the odd bit of prawn is poking out. Leave to cool for about 20 minutes, then sprinkle with cayenne and refrigerate for up to 2 days.

When your guests arrive, give the ramekins a few minutes out of the fridge to soften the butter ever so slightly. Garnish with dill sprigs, then serve with triangles of brown-bread toast - and your best Tasmanian sparkling wine.

CHEESE & CARAWAY BAKED OLIVES

MAKES ABOUT 48

In the first series of *Kitchen Cabinet*, a long time ago now, we went to Tanya Plibersek's house and cooked with her. Her kitchen is a galley-style one with a mirrored splashback, so one of my main memories is of having to stifle fits of giggles every time I noticed a member of our camera crew stuffed into a stairwell or cupboard in an attempt to keep out of the reflections in shot. But Tanya is a spectacularly good cook and I do still make several of her recipes – most regularly these olives baked in cheese pastry, which are now a stalwart of mine for anything from drinks parties to wakes. The best thing is that you can make them ahead of time and keep them in the freezer, then bust them out whenever the occasion calls for baked olives, which is far more often than you might imagine.

---

500 g olives – kalamata or stuffed green olives work best

CHEESE PASTRY
1 teaspoon caraway seeds
185 g cold butter, cubed
350 g (2⅓ cups) plain flour
large pinch of salt
1 teaspoon mustard powder
2 egg yolks
250 g cheddar, grated
4 tablespoons iced water

First up, the pastry. Briefly toast the caraway seeds in a dry frying pan until fragrant, then crush roughly using a mortar and pestle. In a food processor, pulse the butter with the flour, salt, mustard and caraway seeds until the mixture resembles breadcrumbs. Add the egg yolks and cheese, pulsing to combine. Add the water, 1 tablespoon at a time, pulsing until the mixture just comes together. Don't overmix. (If you don't have a food processor, rub in the butter with your fingers, then cut in the wet ingredients with a knife.) Divide the pastry in half, then shape each half into a log about 5 cm in diameter. Wrap in plastic wrap and chill for half an hour.

If you're using kalamata olives, remove the stones. This is easily done by crushing each one with the flat of a heavy knife: the stone should twist out, leaving you with a cracked but highly serviceable olive.

Line a large baking tray with baking paper. And if you're going to bake your olives straightaway, preheat the oven to 180°C (160°C fan).

Now take out your rolls of cheese pastry. Cut off a 5 mm slice, and use your hands to flatten it into a sort of concave circle: a pastry lens, if you will. Now shape your pastry lens around one of your olives so it looks like a cheese football. Lay it on the baking tray and repeat until all your olives are gone and/or you've run out of pastry. If you have any spare pastry, roll it out and make cheese straws. If you have olives left over, eat them!

Right. You can now bake these for 15 minutes or until golden brown. Or you can freeze them for later: put the pastry-wrapped olives in the freezer on their tray – once they're frozen you can transfer them to a snap-lock bag. When you need them, bake at 200°C (180°C fan) for a little longer than the fresh ones, let's say 20 minutes.

FENNEL & PECORINO GLUTEN-FREE CRACKERS

MAKES ABOUT 10 LARGE CRACKER SHEETS

If coeliac disease has condemned you to a life without wheat and its cognates, you may as well have a sign around your neck at parties that says: 'I would like, with my cheese, something that resembles a communion wafer, please, only less fun.' This seems unfair. Why should a gluten-free person be denied a deliciously savoury cracker that's enjoyable with or without cheese? There really is no earthly reason. It's as bad as airlines who decide that just because you are vegetarian, what you really want with your indigestible bread roll is margarine. (*Not true*, airlines, in case you are reading this. Yours sincerely, Enraged of 22C.)

The below-outlined crackers are intensely flavoursome and can be put out for your guests to eat with cheese or spreads, breaking off bits at will, just like they do in Sardinia with the beautifully named but invariably gluten-harbouring carta di musica. You'll need to bake the large sheets of dough in batches.

---

1 tablespoon fennel seeds
300 g (2 cups) gluten-free plain flour
2 teaspoons mustard powder
1 teaspoon salt
½ teaspoon cayenne pepper
100 g cold butter, cubed
1 egg yolk
1 tablespoon white wine vinegar
150 g cheddar, grated
150 g pecorino, grated
iced water
salt flakes

Briefly toast the fennel seeds in a dry frying pan until fragrant, then crush roughly using a mortar and pestle. In a food processor, pulse the flour, mustard, salt, cayenne and fennel seeds with the butter until the mixture resembles breadcrumbs. Add the egg yolk and vinegar and pulse again. Add both cheeses, pulse again, and then gradually add iced water, teaspoon by teaspoon, until the dough just comes together. Scrape it out onto plastic wrap, divide in half and shape each half into a log, then wrap and refrigerate for half an hour. (You can freeze the dough if you are working fiendishly far ahead.)

If you're baking right away, preheat your oven to 180°C (160°C fan).

This is the point where a lot of gluten-free dough runs into bother. It's tricky because when firm out of the fridge, it's hard to roll, but when it gets warm it falls apart. Working with the stuff can be rage-inducing. Not for you, however. Because you're going to do it the easy way. Take your chilled, firm dough out of the fridge and lay out a sheet of baking paper on your bench. Take a coarse grater and grate the dough over the baking paper: you want an even layer of gratings over a roughly rectangular area. Cover with another sheet of baking paper and – with a rolling pin – roll the dough into a thin (about 1 mm) sheet. Peel off the top layer of paper and slide the bottom layer, with its sheet of dough, onto a baking tray.

Sprinkle with salt flakes and bake for 10 minutes or until golden brown. Allow to cool, then immediately store in an airtight container.

BAKED CAMEMBERT WITH WITLOF & WALNUTS

SERVES 4-6

A baked cheese is a thing of comfort. But you needn't go the whole hog and deep-fry a camembert wedge. (Remember those crumby chunks, with cranberry sauce? They used to dish them up at The Lodge's Christmas drinks for the media, and every year some unwitting hack would be caught out and burnt by the oozing cheese, which was as hot as the surface of the sun. I always suspected they were planted by Janette Howard, seeking revenge on the press for the disobliging coverage of her husband.)

Don't splash out on high-end cheese here - this has a marvellously redemptive effect on the chalkiest supermarket camembert, so if you are one of those people with a constant eye out for reduced-price cheeses 'for immediate use', this is your moment! The only requirement is that the cheese is whole, so it will stay contained in its rind in the oven.

---

1 whole camembert (or other white-rind soft cheese)
1 garlic clove, thinly sliced
a few sprigs of rosemary
3-4 witlof (chicory)
handful of walnuts, lightly crushed
crusty bread, to serve

DIJON VINAIGRETTE
1 scant teaspoon dijon mustard
2 teaspoons red wine vinegar
25 ml olive oil

MAKE IT GLUTEN-FREE
For a gluten-free fest, skip the bread and the vinaigrette and just use a spoon to scoop the cheese straight onto the conveniently structural witlof leaves with half a walnut, then eat!

Use a small knife to make 8-10 tiny slits in the top of the cheese and slide a slice of garlic into each one. Push them down some way, but it is fine if the garlic still sits partly above the surface of the camembert like so many little sailing boats on a cheesy pond. If the cheese is fridge-cold, you might need to make some tiny wee divots with the tip of your knife to help you push the garlic in. Now use the stems of the rosemary to push little sprigs into the cheese, arranging them in between the garlic. And that's the cheese ready.

About half an hour before you want to eat, preheat the oven to 200°C (180°C fan).

If you have, despite best advice, shelled out for a fancy camembert, it might well come in an all-wooden box suitable for baking it in. If so, set it directly on a baking tray. If not, no problem, just place our spiky round of cheese on a baking tray lined with baking paper. Bake for about 15 minutes, or until flecked with brown and molten inside.

Meanwhile, to make the dijon mustard vinaigrette, put the mustard in a small bowl with a pinch of salt. Slowly add the vinegar, while stirring with the back of a teaspoon. Once it's smooth, slowly add the oil and keep going with the back of the spoon until you have everything combined into a creamy emulsion.

Separate the witlof leaves. Dress with as much of the vinaigrette as you like, then scatter with the walnuts. Serve the witlof and walnut salad alongside the ooey-gooey cheese, with plenty of crusty bread.

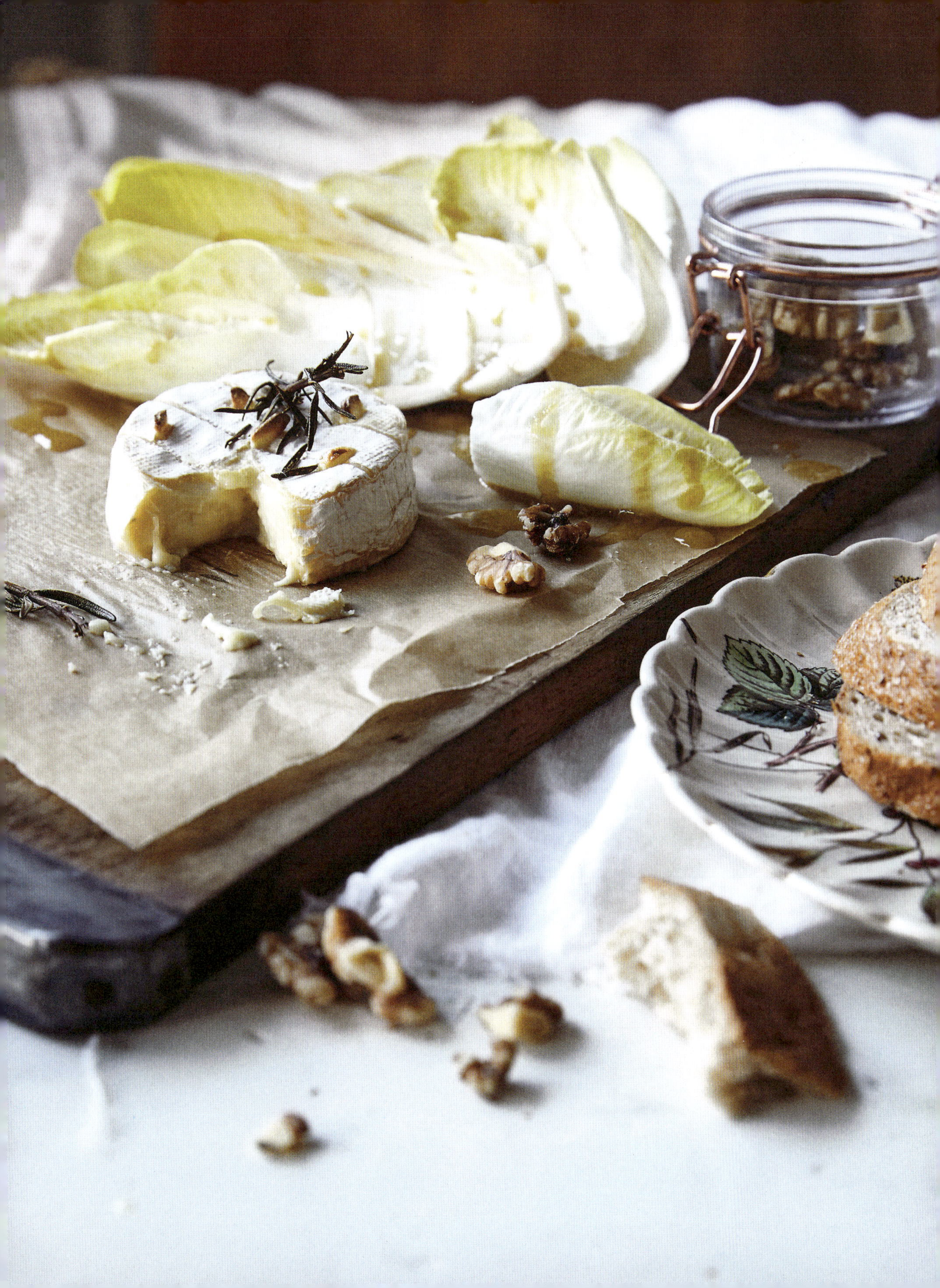

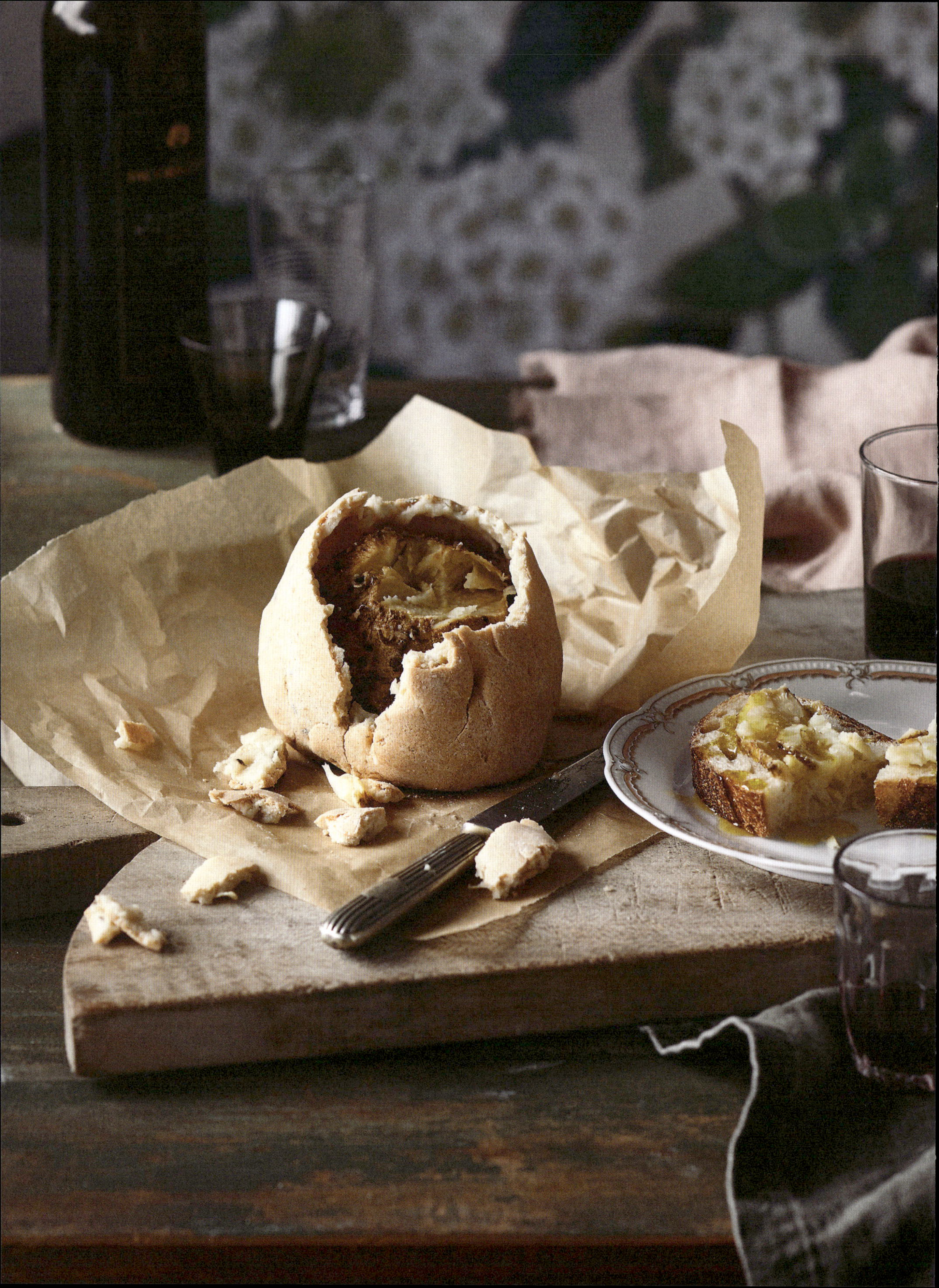

SALT-BAKED CELERIAC

SERVES 8–10

A whole vegetable – and a weird-looking one at that – might not be your obvious go-to for a drinks party, but if you take the time to slow-cook celeriac in this way, the result is more like a rich, buttery pâté than one of your five-a-day. Obviously, this is largely an autumn or winter pastime, so you will also benefit from some good house-warming side-effects. Occupational health and safety requires me to suggest that since cracking open the crust can be a bit brutal, it would be prudent to get the handling of rolling pins, hammers and oyster shuckers out of the way before imbibing too many cordials.

---

300 g fine salt
300 g (2 cups) plain flour
2–3 egg whites
a few sprigs of rosemary or thyme, leaves picked and chopped
1 whole celeriac (on the smallish side)
3–4 garlic cloves
sourdough bread and olive oil, to serve

Preheat the oven to 200°C (180°C fan). Line a baking tray with baking paper.

Mix together the salt and flour, then fold in the egg whites, rosemary or thyme, and about 100 ml cold water, just enough to bring the dough together. I use an electric mixer fitted with the dough hook to give this a workout, but you could just knead it by hand until it's smooth and pliable (you won't be eating the dough, so no need to put in too much effort!). Your dough should still crack a little when it is rolled out – if it is too wet, it might slide off the celeriac as it warms, instead of forming a hard casing for the ever-shrinking celeriac.

Trim the crazy wiggly bottom off your celeriac, cutting it severely enough to give it a flat platform base, then tidy up any long strands of green from the top. Flatten a small handful of the dough to make a disc for the celeriac to sit on and place it on the baking tray. Roll out the rest of the dough to about 6 mm and shroud your celeriac, tucking a few unpeeled garlic cloves between it and the dough. Now squeeze together the join between the disc and sheet of dough to create a seal, making sure there are no gaps. The end result is, well, odd, to say the least. Hide the poor thing away in the oven for 2 hours.

When it comes time to break the crust, your options include a fairly hefty whack with a rolling pin or hammer, or a few stab-and-twist motions with an oyster shucker. Then, using oven gloves to protect your hands, wrench away the crust to expose a crater big enough to get a knife or spoon in there to extract the treasure below. The edges of the celeriac that have been in contact with the dough will be very salty, so make sure you get enough of the inner celeriac to even out the saltiness. Spread on slices of sourdough and enjoy. The garlic is there primarily to flavour the celeriac, but should still be good to eat – mushed onto your bread with olive oil.

The happy hour

ARTICHOKES WITH TARRAGON AIOLI

SERVES 12 FOR A PARTY OR 6 AS A STARTER

Growing up on the Adelaide Plains, we thought of artichokes as weeds, their spiny leaves interfering with our important business of building cubby houses or walking home from school. Imagine our surprise when it turned out that their hearts - preserved in oil in a jar - were nice to eat! And of course, the exciting truth is that with artichokes, you can use the lot. And they make the most delicious starter or snack that can be whistled up with barely any effort, ready to be eaten messily and communally.

---

6 large artichokes
juice of 1 lemon

TARRAGON AIOLI
6 garlic cloves
2 teaspoons olive oil
235 g (1 cup) good-quality mayonnaise
½ teaspoon dijon mustard
2 teaspoons finely chopped tarragon

EVEN EASIER
Make the aioli in advance: it will keep, covered, in the fridge for a day or two. When it comes time to serve, thin the mayonnaise with a little oil if it is very stiff – the consistency should be more like a cream than a jelly.

PRESSURE-COOKER OPTION
Instead of steaming the artichokes, cook them in the pressure cooker for around 12 minutes.

For the aioli, preheat the oven to 180°C (160°C fan). Wrap the unpeeled garlic cloves in foil, drizzle over the olive oil and sprinkle with a generous pinch of salt. Scrunch the foil tightly around the garlic and bake for 12-15 minutes until soft and caramelised. When it's cool enough to handle, squeeze out the flesh from the skins, remove any green parts, then crush to a paste using a pestle and mortar (or whizz briefly in a small food processor). Combine the garlic paste with the mayonnaise, mustard and tarragon, then transfer to a small bowl.

Time to tackle your artichokes. Use a large, sharp knife to trim the stems, then cut off about 5-6 cm from the top to give you a straight edge. Pull off any obviously manky outer bits, but since we are in the business of eating the petals, don't be too over-enthusiastic here. Give the artichokes a rinse and place them stem-side up in a steamer basket. Pour a couple of centimetres of boiling water into the base of the steamer, then squeeze in the lemon juice and add a few pinches of salt. Bring the water to the boil, then steam the artichokes for 20-30 minutes, depending on their size: pluck at a leaf and if it comes out quite easily, they're ready.

To serve, have the aioli on the table, along with a big bowl for the discarded leaves, and at least one artichoke within easy reach of each guest. Eat by plucking a petal from the artichoke, hanging onto the pointy end. Dip the paler, fleshy end into the aioli, then scrape the little lobe of flesh between your teeth and eat, discarding the rest of the petal. When you get to the heart of the artichoke, the furry, spiky choke needs to be scooped out before you can trim and eat the heart. While artichoke hearts are delicious, you might want to save them for another meal, rather than de-fuzzing and chopping when you could be enjoying the company of your guests. But if you're keen, by all means go ahead and cut them into quarters before giving them the same aioli treatment as the petals.

LENTIL PÂTÉ

SERVES 4-6

This party dip has been adapted by Wendy from a meal she had at the Balmoral Bathers' Pavilion in January 1997, during what was her honeymoon, insofar as you could call sleeping on your cousin's sofa, with exquisitely meagre funds, a honeymoon. Coral-coloured lentils were served with deep-fried eggplant (aubergine), creating a dish she has thought very fondly of ever since. When you have made this pâté once, you can start thinking about how to use it in a main meal – maybe with chargrilled slices of eggplant or even a steak. Or both.

½ small brown onion, roughly chopped
3 garlic cloves, roughly chopped
1 cm ginger, roughly chopped
2 cm fresh turmeric, roughly chopped, or ½ teaspoon ground turmeric
1 tablespoon ground cumin
3 tablespoons vegetable oil
200 g (1 cup) red or orange lentils, picked over
500 ml (2 cups) vegetable stock
½ green chilli, seeds removed, very finely chopped
1 kaffir lime leaf, very finely chopped
1 tablespoon good-quality fish sauce
1 tablespoon lime juice
glug of olive oil
2 tablespoons finely chopped coriander stalks (save the leaves to garnish)
3–4 sweet, sweet cherry tomatoes, finely diced
crackers or bread, to serve

MAKE IT VEGAN
Use tamari instead of fish sauce.

Put the onion, garlic, ginger, turmeric and cumin into a mini blender or small food processor and blitz to a paste. Or you could persevere with a mortar and pestle.

Scrape the paste into a heavy-based saucepan, add the oil and cook the paste over medium heat for at least 5 minutes until fragrant, stirring all the while to make sure it doesn't burn.

Rinse and drain the lentils, then add to the pan, along with the stock, chilli and lime leaf. Bring to the boil and then turn down the heat and simmer until the lentils are soft – usually around 10 minutes. You might need to skim off the lentil froth and top up with a little water along the way.

Leave the lentil pâté to cool slightly, when it will firm up a bit more, then season with the fish sauce and lime juice: use your best judgement here, adding bit by bit and tasting until you hit the right balance. Loosen with a little olive oil and add some salt if you think it needs it. Stir in the coriander stalks and scatter over the cherry tomatoes. Chop the reserved coriander leaves and sprinkle on top.

Serve the pâté with crackers or bread.

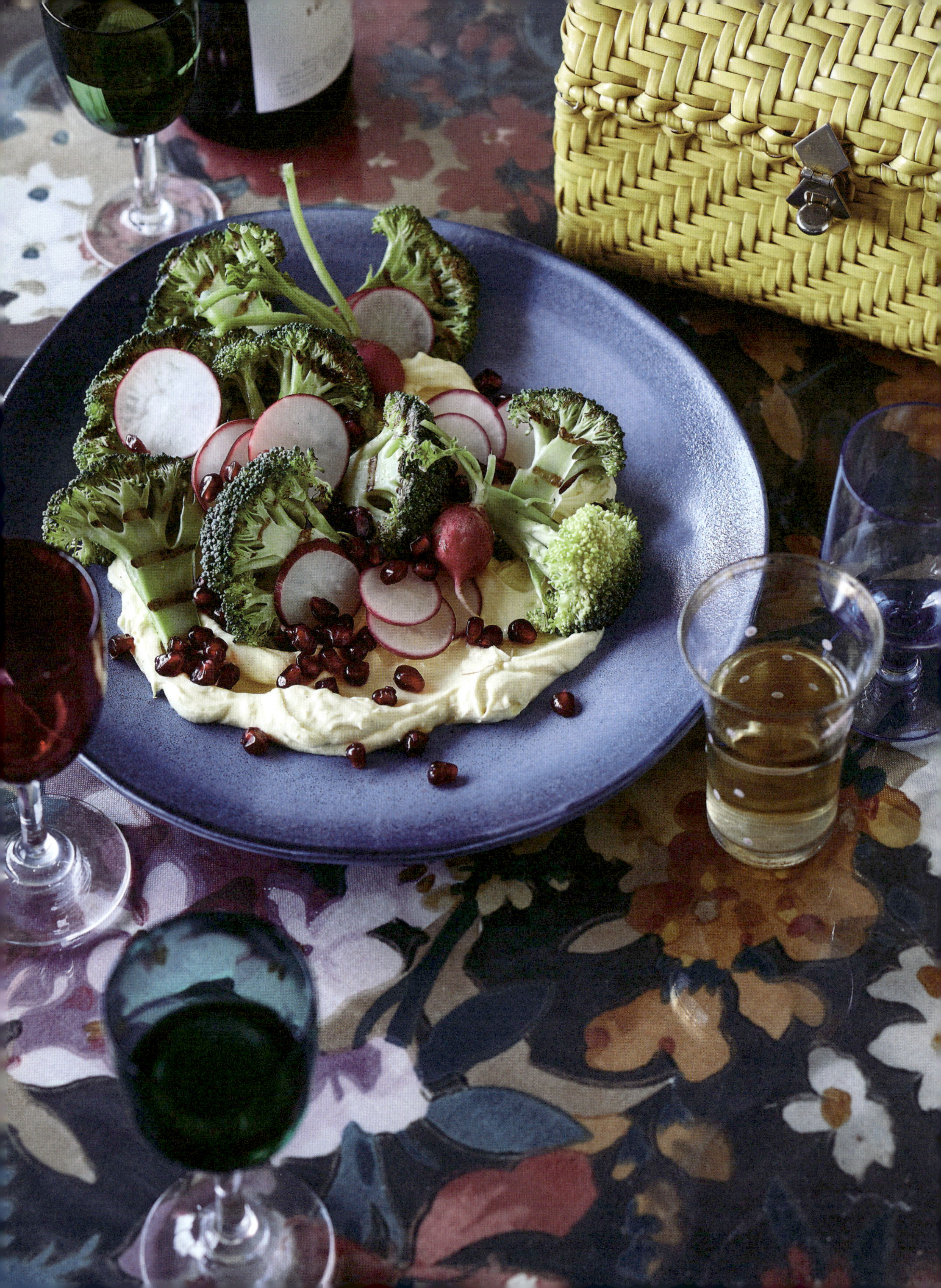

UPSIDE-DOWN SAFFRON LABNEH PLATE

SERVES 6

While some sort of dip with crudités is about the most obvious thing you could possibly bowl up at a drinks party, it can outrun obviousness if you mix up the presentation a little. If, for instance, you served your dip spread out on a shallow plate with all your dipping agents arranged on top. Here, homemade labneh coloured bright yellow with saffron wears a hat of charred broccoli, accessorised with discs of radish and some pomegranate seeds.

Don't be nervous about making labneh. It's incredibly easy. And even though this one only has a handful of ingredients, the simplicity allows the subtle taste of saffron to be enjoyed virtually undisturbed – a rare thing, and a good one.

---

1 head of broccoli, broken into florets
olive oil, for brushing
6 large radishes, thinly sliced into rounds
seeds of 1 pomegranate

SAFFRON LABNEH
500 g Greek-style yoghurt
½ teaspoon ground saffron (or 12 saffron strands, toasted in a dry frying pan then ground to powder)
1 garlic clove, finely grated or very finely chopped
1 teaspoon salt

EVEN EASIER
No time to make labneh but still want a sunny yellow dip? Grab a tub of good hummus and stir a couple of big spoonfuls of thick yoghurt and a teaspoon of ground turmeric through it. Turmeric is hysterically approved-of just now, and apparently it can do just about everything except collect your dry cleaning.

For the labneh, line a bowl with a 40 cm square piece of cheesecloth. If you don't have muslin, or you suffer from my disorder (constantly buying cheesecloth because I never have cheesecloth in, putting it in a cunning place and then being unable to find it, thus reverting for all intents and purposes to the original state of non-cheesecloth-having), it's fine to use a brand-new Chux or J-cloth. Or a clean tea towel, at a pinch.

Mix the yoghurt with the saffron, garlic and salt. Scoop the yoghurt mixture into the cloth-lined bowl, then gather up the corners of the cloth and secure into a loose bundle with a rubber band. Do not squeeze it. Tie a string around the rubber band and hang the bundle from a cupboard door handle or the kitchen tap or anywhere where it can dangle. Put the bowl underneath to collect the liquid that will drain out of it; the longer you leave it, the firmer your labneh will be. I reckon if you cut the thing down once you have about 250 ml (1 cup) liquid in the bowl, you're on track. (If you forget and leave it for ages, you'll wind up with yoghurt cheese, which is firm enough to roll into balls! A project for another day, perhaps.) Spread the labneh over a serving platter.

Cut the broccoli florets in half. Anoint with olive oil and place, cut-side down, on a hot chargrill pan or barbecue. Cook for about 5 minutes, turning halfway through, until tender and charred, then leave to cool. Arrange the broccoli and radishes over the labneh and sprinkle with the pomegranate seeds.

Acknowledgements

Thank you to my Mum, Christobel, for always being able to whip something up and for teaching me to be curious in the kitchen. Thank you to Wendy for introducing me to so many ingredients I would never otherwise have come across. Thank you to anyone who's ever come to my house and not minded the shambles, and to everyone who's cooked for me (especially those who have made something vegetarian, specially). To my friends and neighbours in 'the Commune' - where kids' dinners regularly seat a dozen and everyone seems to have the knack of stretching resources to feed everyone: You people make my life so happy.

Writing a cookbook is a complicated and magical process by which your ordinary food is made to look fabulous by employing just the right light and just the right plate. So thank you to the studio crew of Rob Palmer, Vanessa Austin and Ross Dobson, the guiding hands of Alison Cowan, Jane Price, Madeleine Kane and Aileen Lord, and of course Jane Morrow, whose enthusiasm made this book happen and the last one too!

Final thanks go to my catering affiliates, Jeremy, Audrey, Elliott and Kate: I love you, and I love cooking with you.

First of all, to anyone who has ever invited me to share a meal or a drink or even just a biscuit with them at their house: thank you, I have enjoyed every single crumb.

Thank you to my mother, Patricia Sharpe, who moved here from the other side of the world for a few months to do school runs and hold the household together so that I could test recipes and work. I am grateful for the feedback from many people on recipes and writing, especially Sophie Bevan and Rachel Westall, who are always direct but spot on with their suggestions for improvements. Cheers to my neighbours who don't mind me using their fridge and helping myself to their pantry when I forget to buy an essential ingredient. Thank you to Marie Aschehoug-Clauteaux for her relentless positivity and Sam Perkins for a lot of practical day to day help. And a special shout out to anyone who comes to my open house drinks on Friday nights - I look forward to that hour all week. Huge love and thanks to Michael Jenkins for being enthusiastic about every dish I cook and every project I embark on. It is lovely to have him and his deputy cheerleaders, Alice, Louis and Felix, on my team.

Index

A
almonds
   Bienenstich tray cake 158
   Bostock 19
   marmalade baklava 200
   Moroccan chocolate
      & almond surprise
      biscuits 164
   plumble 202
   rhubarb syrup crumb
      cake 143
Amalfi Pizzeria Ristorante
   (Adelaide) 88
anchovies
   bagna freddo with tarragon
      & pink pepper 217
   crispy-skin fish with
      rosemary & anchovy
      cream 94
   mozzarella salad with
      broccoli, anchovies
      & olives 135
   spaghetti pangrattato 54
Apollo (Sydney) 51
apricots
   apricot cobbler 197
   apricot, pistachio &
      rosewater coronet 154
artichokes with tarragon
   aioli 230
aubergines *see* eggplants
avocado salsa 173

B
bagna freddo with tarragon
   & pink pepper 217
baked camembert with witlof
   & walnuts 226
baklava, marmalade 200
banana & oat smoothie,
   coffee 24
barberry cookies, seeded oat,
   dark chocolate & 167
Bathers' Pavilion, The
   (Sydney) 231

beans
   chilli beans with lime leaves
      & avocado salsa 172
   mushrooms, white beans
      & radicchio with soft
      polenta 110
   Persian new year soup 99
   stuffed peppers with feta
      & beans 76
   see also broad beans;
      green beans
beetroot sambol 181
Bienenstich tray cake 158
biscuits, Moroccan chocolate
   & almond surprise 164
bok choy noodle soup with
   pickled eggs, shiitake & 100
Bostock 19
Bottura, Massimo 97
breads
   apricot, pistachio &
      rosewater coronet 154
   Bostock 19
   choc-hazelnut milk
      buns 32
   soda bread 40
   see also flatbreads
Brindisa (London) 51
broad beans, tagliatelle
   with lemon cream, pine
   nuts & 69
broccoli, anchovies & olives,
   mozzarella salad with 135
brownies, hibiscus 213
burgers, fuss-free salmon 78
butter
   bagna freddo with tarragon
      & pink pepper 217
   crumpets with Vegemite,
      mustard & parsley
      butter 31
   horseradish & chive
      butter 40
   lemon & pepper butter 40
   masala butter 130

C
cabbage, marinated tofu with
   soy beans & pickled 90
cacio e pepe gougères 218
cakes
   Bienenstich tray cake 158
   birthday cakes 149
   cherry ricotta bundt cake
      145
   chocolate celebration cake
      146
   citrus mascarpone layer
      cake 150
   passionfruit curd meringue
      cake 140
   pistachio Louise cake 157
   rhubarb syrup crumb cake
      143
   sticky pumpkin gingerbread
      166
   see also brownies
camembert with witlof &
   walnuts, baked 226
cannelloni, roast mushroom 97
capsicums *see* peppers
caramel
   caramel sauce 207
   salted caramel 'crack' 198
carrot, feta, olive & lentil
   salad 118
cashew curry with beetroot
   sambol, Sri Lankan
   butternut & 180
cauliflower
   cauliflower rarebit 108
   cauliflower salad with
      sherried currants, capers
      & mint 119
celeriac
   salt-baked celeriac 229
   Thai celeriac salad with
      peanuts & dried shrimp
      117
Cha Ca La Vong (Hanoi) 82
chard & cheese tart with
   poppy-seed pastry 75

cheat's piadina 28
cheese
   baked camembert with
      witlof & walnuts 226
   cacio e pepe gougères 218
   cauliflower rarebit 108
   chard & cheese tart with
      poppy-seed pastry 75
   cheese & caraway baked
      olives 224
   cheese pastry 224
   cherry ricotta bundt
      cake 145
   citrus mascarpone layer
      cake 150
   fennel & pecorino gluten-
      free crackers 225
   kefalograviera, fried egg
      & rocket rolls 51
   lemon mascarpone filling
      150
   pierogi russki 86
   smoky eggplant parmigiana
      104
   store-cupboard frittata 48
   warm goat's cheese salad
      with grapes & walnuts
      136
   see also feta; halloumi;
      mozzarella
chermoula 102
cherry ricotta bundt cake 145
chickpeas
   chickpea salad with Cuban
      mojo 128
   falafel wraps 188
   hummus 14
   mograbieh salad with
      toasted nuts 124
   vegetable & green olive
      tagine 102
chilli beans with lime leaves
   & avocado salsa 172
chocolate
   choc-hazelnut milk
      buns 32

chocolate celebration
   cake 146
chocolate glaze 146
chocolate sauce 208
hibiscus brownies 213
Moroccan chocolate
   & almond surprise
   biscuits 164
salted caramel 'crack' 198
seeded oat, dark chocolate
   & barberry cookies 167
citrus mascarpone layer
   cake 150
clafoutis, or cheat's quiche 56
cobbler, apricot 197
coconut
   coconut sambol 130
   mango, coconut &
      passionfruit pudding 211
   pistachio Louise cake 157
coffee, banana & oat
   smoothie 24
cookies, seeded oat, dark
   chocolate & barberry 167
corn
   corn-cob salad with masala
      butter & coconut sambol
      130
   fresh corn polenta with
      baked eggs & smoky
      tomatoes 38
   limey corny salmon bake
      174
   Mexican winter soup 178
coulis, quick raspberry 147
courgettes *see* zucchini
crab & nasturtium sandwiches
   171
Crabb, Christobel 171
crackers, fennel & pecorino
   gluten-free 225
crispy-skin fish with rosemary
   & anchovy cream 94
crumpets with Vegemite,
   mustard & parsley
   butter 31
cucumber salad, punched 134
curd
   lemon curd 151
   passionfruit curd 140
curries
   egg salan 179
   Sri Lankan butternut
      & cashew curry with
      beetroot sambol 180
   summer eggplant curry 109

D

Di Natale, Richard 143
dips
   bagna freddo with tarragon
      & pink pepper 217
   hummus 14
   lucky-dip padrón peppers
      with strained yoghurt 221
   upside-down saffron labneh
      plate 233
DIY crispy fried shallots 123
dressings
   herb dressing 124
   vinaigrette 136

E

eggplants
   smoky eggplant parmigiana
      104
   summer eggplant curry 109
eggs
   cauliflower rarebit 108
   clafoutis, or cheat's
      quiche 56
   egg salan 179
   egg & salmon on rye
      breakfast squares 23
   flatbread omelette with
      lime & tomato salsa 71
   fresh corn polenta with
      baked eggs & smoky
      tomatoes 38
   kefalograviera, fried egg
      & rocket rolls 51
   poke-bowl buffet 187
   prawn omelette with oyster
      sauce 59
   shiitake & bok choy noodle
      soup with pickled
      eggs 100
   store-cupboard frittata 48
   Turkish scrambled
      eggs 20
Estia (Adelaide) 51

F

falafel wraps 188
fennel
   fennel, ginger & tomato
      braise 55
   fennel & pecorino gluten-
      free crackers 225
   fennel, walnut & sun-dried
      tomato pappardelle 49
   salmon & fennel pie 81

feta
   carrot, feta, olive & lentil
      salad 118
   prawn saganaki 67
   store-cupboard frittata 48
   stuffed peppers with feta
      & beans 76
fish
   crispy-skin fish with
      rosemary & anchovy
      cream 94
   poke-bowl buffet 187
   turmeric fried fish with
      noodles 82
   see also salmon
flatbreads
   cheat's piadina 28
   falafel wraps 188
   flatbread omelette with
      lime & tomato salsa 71
French mushroom, kale &
   polenta soup 65
fresh corn polenta with baked
   eggs & smoky tomatoes 38
frittata, store-cupboard 48
fuss-free salmon burgers 78

G

garlic, roasted 15
Gillard, Julia 108
ginger, red lentil & tomato
   soup 68
gingerbread, sticky pumpkin
   166
gingernut ice-cream
   sandwiches 207
glass noodle salad with
   prawns & pink grapefruit
   122
glass potatoes 193

GLUTEN-FREE RECIPES
artichokes with tarragon
   aioli 230
bagna freddo with tarragon
   & pink pepper p217
baked camembert with
   witlof & walnuts
   (variation) 226
carrot, feta, olive & lentil
   salad 118
cauliflower rarebit 108
cauliflower salad with
   sherried currants, capers
   & mint 119

chickpea salad with Cuban
   mojo 128
chilli beans with lime
   leaves & avocado salsa
   (variation) 172
clafoutis, or cheat's quiche
   (variation) 56
corn-cob salad with masala
   butter & coconut sambol
   130
crispy-skin fish with
   rosemary & anchovy
   cream 94
egg salan 179
egg & salmon on rye
   breakfast squares
   (variation) 23
fennel, ginger & tomato
   braise (variation) 55
fennel & pecorino gluten-
   free crackers 225
French mushroom, kale &
   polenta soup 65
ginger, red lentil & tomato
   soup 68
glass noodle salad with
   prawns & pink grapefruit
   122
glass potatoes 193
gluten-free shortcrust pastry
   14
heart-starter plum jam 27
hibiscus brownies
   (variation) 213
hot-smoked salmon
   with pea-green salad
   (variation) 184
lentil pâté 231
limey corny salmon bake
   174
lucky-dip padrón peppers
   with strained yoghurt 221
mango, coconut &
   passionfruit pudding 211
marinated tofu with
   soy beans & pickled
   cabbage 90
Mexican winter soup 178
mozzarella salad with
   broccoli, anchovies &
   olives (variation) 135
mozzarella salad with spring
   veg & lemon-infused
   oil 126
mushrooms, white beans
   & radicchio with soft
   polenta 110

pistachio Louise cake
    (variation) 157
plumble (variation) 202
poke-bowl buffet (variation)
    187
potato salad with samphire
    & lemon 127
prawn omelette with oyster
    sauce (variation) 59
prawn saganaki (variation)
    67
punched cucumber salad
    134
roasted & raw vegetable
    salad with zhug 114
roasted thyme peaches 205
salmon & mustard rice
    paper rolls 46
shiitake & bok choy noodle
    soup with pickled eggs
    (variation) 100
smoky eggplant parmigiana
    (variation) 104
Sri Lankan butternut
    & cashew curry with
    beetroot sambol 180
sticky pumpkin gingerbread
    (variation) 166
store-cupboard frittata 48
stuffed peppers with feta
    & beans 76
summer eggplant curry 109
Thai celeriac salad with
    peanuts & dried shrimp
    117
toffee & orange panna cotta
    210
tofu larb 107
turkish scrambled eggs
    (variation) 20
turmeric fried fish with
    noodles 83
upside-down saffron labneh
    plate 233
vegetable & green olive
    tagine (variation) 102

Gordon, Peter 78
gougères, cacio e pepe 218
Gough, Karen 154
granola, St Niklas 25
grapefruit, glass noodle
    salad with prawns
    & pink 122
grapes & walnuts, warm
    goat's cheese salad
    with 136

green beans
    crispy-skin fish with
        rosemary & anchovy
        cream 94
    hot-smoked salmon with
        pea-green salad 184

H
halloumi
    chickpea salad with Cuban
        mojo 128
    halloumi, lime & rocket
        spaghetti 45
harissa 14
heart-starter plum jam 27
herb dressing 124
herb sauce 76
herby salad 189
hibiscus brownies 213
honey
    Bienenstich tray cake 158
    mandarin & honey
        madeleines 162
    marmalade baklava 200
    puffy pancake with honey
        & orange syrup 36
horseradish & chive butter 40
hot-smoked salmon with
    pea-green salad 184
Howard, Janette 226
hummus 14
Hunter Works, The
    (Sydney) 84

I
ice cream
    gingernut ice-cream
        sandwiches 207
    snowball sundaes 208
Ivy, The (London) 31

J
jam, heart-starter plum 27

K
kale & polenta soup, French
    mushroom 65
Kazen (Melbourne) 46
kefalograviera, fried egg &
    rocket rolls 51
Knott, Kate 184

L
labneh plate, upside-down
    saffron 233
larb, tofu 107
Lawson, Nigella 166
lemon
    lemon curd 151
    lemon-infused oil 15
    lemon mascarpone
        filling 150
    lemon & pepper butter 40
    tagliatelle with lemon
        cream, pine nuts
        & broad beans 69
lentils
    carrot, feta, olive & lentil
        salad 118
    chilli beans with lime leaves
        & avocado salsa 172
    ginger, red lentil & tomato
        soup 68
    lentil pâté 231
    old-fashioned vegetable
        pasties 190
Levantine (sardines) 60
Liaw, Adam 171
limey corny salmon bake 174
lucky-dip padrón peppers
    with strained yoghurt 221

M
madeleines, mandarin
    & honey 162
mango, coconut & passionfruit
    pudding 211
marinated tofu with soy beans
    & pickled cabbage 90
marmalade baklava 200
masala butter 130
mascarpone layer cake,
    citrus 150
mayonnaise 15
meringue cake, passionfruit
    curd 140
Mexican winter soup 178
mograbieh salad with toasted
    nuts 124
mojo sauce 128
Moroccan chocolate &
    almond surprise
    biscuits 164
mozzarella
    cheat's piadina 28
    mozzarella salad with
        broccoli, anchovies &
        olives 135

    mozzarella salad with
        spring veg & lemon-
        infused oil 126
    smoky eggplant parmigiana
        104
mushrooms
    French mushroom, kale
        & polenta soup 65
    mushrooms, white beans
        & radicchio with soft
        polenta 110
    roast mushroom cannelloni
        97
    shiitake & bok choy noodle
        soup with pickled eggs
        100

N
nasturtium sandwiches,
    crab & 171
noodles
    glass noodle salad with
        prawns & pink grapefruit
        122
    Persian new year soup 99
    shiitake & bok choy noodle
        soup with pickled eggs
        100
    turmeric fried fish with
        noodles 82
nuts, mograbieh salad with
    toasted 124

O
oats
    coffee, banana & oat
        smoothie 24
    seeded oat, dark chocolate
        & barberry cookies 167
    St Niklas granola, 25
old-fashioned vegetable
    pasties 190
Oliver, Jamie 78
olives
    carrot, feta, olive & lentil
        salad 118
    cheat's piadina 28
    cheese & caraway baked
        olives 224
    mozzarella salad with
        broccoli, anchovies
        & olives 135
    slow-roasted tomato
        pappardelle with olive
        tapenade 88

237

vegetable & green olive tagine 102
omelettes
    flatbread omelette with lime & tomato salsa 71
    prawn omelette with oyster sauce 59
orange panna cotta, toffee & 210
Ottolenghi, Yotam 38

P
Palermo peppers on toast 96
pancake with honey & orange syrup, puffy 36
pangrattato, spaghetti 54
panna cotta, toffee & orange 210
passionfruit
    mango, coconut & passionfruit pudding 211
    passionfruit curd meringue cake 140
pasta
    fennel, walnut & sun-dried tomato pappardelle 49
    pea risoni with parmesan & pepper 52
    roast mushroom cannelloni 97
    slow-roasted tomato pappardelle with olive tapenade 88
    tagliatelle with lemon cream, pine nuts & broad beans 69
    see also spaghetti
pasties, old-fashioned vegetable 190
pastry
    cacio e pepe gougères 218
    chard & cheese tart with poppy-seed pastry 75
    cheese pastry 224
    gluten-free shortcrust pastry 14
    old-fashioned vegetable pasties 190
pâté, lentil 231
pea-green salad, hot-smoked salmon with 184
pea risoni with parmesan & pepper 52
peaches
    peach-leaf vanilla slice 142
    roasted thyme peaches 205

pecorino gluten-free crackers, fennel & 225
peppers
    lucky-dip padrón peppers with strained yoghurt 221
    Palermo peppers on toast 96
    stuffed peppers with feta & beans 76
Peris, Nova 200
Persian new year soup 99
pesto 15
piadina, cheat's 28
pie, salmon & fennel 81
pierogi russki 86
pine nuts & broad beans, tagliatelle with lemon cream 69
pistachios
    apricot, pistachio & rosewater coronet 154
    pistachio Louise cake 157
Plibersek, Tanya 224
plum jam, heart-starter 27
plumble 202
poke-bowl buffet 187
polenta
    French mushroom, kale & polenta soup 65
    fresh corn polenta with baked eggs & smoky tomatoes 38
    mushrooms, white beans & radicchio with soft polenta 110
potatoes
    glass potatoes 193
    old-fashioned vegetable pasties 190
    pierogi russki 86
    potato salad with samphire & lemon 127
    salmon & fennel pie 81
potted prawns 223
prawns
    glass noodle salad with prawns & pink grapefruit 122
    poke-bowl buffet 187
    potted prawns 223
    prawn omelette with oyster sauce 59
    prawn saganaki 67
pudding, mango, coconut & passionfruit 211
puffy pancake with honey & orange syrup 36

pumpkin
    ginger, red lentil & tomato soup 68
    Sri Lankan butternut & cashew curry with beetroot sambol 180
    sticky pumpkin gingerbread 166
punched cucumber salad 134

Q
quiche, clafoutis, or cheat's 56
quick raspberry coulis 147

R
radicchio with soft polenta, mushrooms, white beans & 110
rarebit, cauliflower 108
raspberry coulis, quick 147
rhubarb syrup crumb cake 143
rice paper
    rice paper crisps 107
    salmon & mustard rice paper rolls 46
ricotta bundt cake, cherry 145
risoni with parmesan & pepper, pea 52
roast mushroom cannelloni 97
roasted garlic 15
roasted & raw vegetable salad with zhug 114
roasted thyme peaches 205
rosewater coronet, apricot, pistachio & 154
Ryan, Alice 193

S
saffron labneh 233
salads
    carrot, feta, olive & lentil salad 118
    cauliflower salad with sherried currants, capers & mint 119
    chickpea salad with Cuban mojo 128
    corn-cob salad with masala butter & coconut sambol 130
    glass noodle salad with prawns & pink grapefruit 122

herby salad 189
    hot-smoked salmon with pea-green salad 184
    mograbieh salad with toasted nuts 124
    mozzarella salad with broccoli, anchovies & olives 135
    mozzarella salad with spring veg & lemon-infused oil 126
    potato salad with samphire & lemon 127
    punched cucumber salad 134
    roasted & raw vegetable salad with zhug 114
    Thai celeriac salad with peanuts & dried shrimp 117
    warm goat's cheese salad with grapes & walnuts 136
salan, egg 179
Sales, Leigh 171, 184
salmon
    egg & salmon on rye breakfast squares 23
    fuss-free salmon burgers 78
    hot-smoked salmon with pea-green salad 184
    limey corny salmon bake 174
    poke-bowl buffet 187
    salmon & fennel pie 81
    salmon & mustard rice paper rolls 46
    smoked salmon with soda bread & special butter 40
salsas
    avocado salsa 173
    tomato salsa 71
salt-baked celeriac 229
salted caramel 'crack' 198
sambols
    beetroot sambol 181
    coconut sambol 130
samphire & lemon, potato salad with 127
sandwiches, crab & nasturtium 171
Santo, Elsa 174
sardines 60
    Levantine 60
    sardines with spaghetti, currants & mint 62

Scandi 63
Virgin Mary 62
sauces
  caramel sauce 207
  chocolate sauce 208
  herb sauce 76
  mojo sauce 128
  nuoc cham sauce 82
  tomato sauce 104
  white sauce 104
  yoghurt mint sauce 188
  zhug 114
  see also dressings; salsas; sambols
Scandi (sardines) 63
seeded oat, dark chocolate & barberry cookies 167
shallots, DIY crispy fried 123
shiitake & bok choy noodle soup with pickled eggs 100
slow-roasted tomato pappardelle with olive tapenade 88
smoked salmon with soda bread & special butter 40
smoky eggplant parmigiana 104
smoothie, coffee, banana & oat 24
snowball sundaes 208
soda bread 40
soups
  French mushroom, kale & polenta soup 65
  ginger, red lentil & tomato soup 68
  Mexican winter soup 178
  Persian new year soup 99
  shiitake & bok choy noodle soup with pickled eggs 100
soy beans & pickled cabbage, marinated tofu with 90
spaghetti
  halloumi, lime & rocket spaghetti 45
  sardines with spaghetti, currants & mint 62
  spaghetti pangrattato 54
Sri Lankan butternut & cashew curry with beetroot sambol 180
St Niklas granola 25
sticky pumpkin gingerbread 166
store-cupboard frittata 48
Storer, Jennifer 205
stuffed peppers with feta & beans 76
summer eggplant curry 109
sundaes, snowball 208

T
tagine, vegetable & green olive 102
tagliatelle with lemon cream, pine nuts & broad beans 69
tapenade, olive 88
tarragon aioli 230
tart with poppy-seed pastry, chard & cheese 75
Thai celeriac salad with peanuts & dried shrimp 117
toffee & orange panna cotta 210
tofu
  marinated tofu with soy beans & pickled cabbage 90
  poke-bowl buffet 187
  tofu larb 107
tomatoes
  cheat's piadina 28
  fennel, ginger & tomato braise 55
  fennel, walnut & sun-dried tomato pappardelle 49
  flatbread omelette with lime & tomato salsa 71
  fresh corn polenta with baked eggs & smoky tomatoes 38
  ginger, red lentil & tomato soup 68
  prawn saganaki 67
  slow-roasted tomato pappardelle with olive tapenade 88
  smoky eggplant parmigiana 104
  tomato sauce 104
Turkish scrambled eggs 20
turmeric fried fish with noodles 82

U
upside-down saffron labneh plate 233

V
vanilla slice, peach-leaf 142

VEGAN RECIPES
coffee, banana & oat smoothie (variation) 24
French mushroom, kale & polenta soup 65
ginger, red lentil & tomato soup (variation) 68
glass noodle salad with prawns & pink grapefruit (variation) 122
glass potatoes 193
heart-starter plum jam 27
lentil pâté (variation) 231
lucky-dip padrón peppers with strained yoghurt 221
mango, coconut & passionfruit pudding 211
marinated tofu with soy beans & pickled cabbage 90
mograbieh salad with toasted nuts (variation) 124
Palermo peppers on toast (variation) 96
plumble (variation) 202
poke-bowl buffet (variation) 187
potato salad with samphire & lemon 127
punched cucumber salad 134
roasted & raw vegetable salad with zhug 114
roasted thyme peaches (variation) 205
spaghetti pangrattato (variation) 54
Sri Lankan butternut & cashew curry with beetroot sambol (variation) 180
Thai celeriac salad with peanuts & dried shrimp (variation) 117
tofu larb 107
vegetable & green olive tagine 102

vegetables
  mozzarella salad with spring veg & lemon-infused oil 126
  old-fashioned vegetable pasties 190
  roasted & raw vegetable salad with zhug 114
  vegetable & green olive tagine 102
  see also specific vegetables
vinaigrette *see* dressings
Virgin Mary (sardines) 62

W
walnuts
  baked camembert with witlof & walnuts 226
  fennel, walnut & sun-dried tomato pappardelle 49
  warm goat's cheese salad with grapes & walnuts 136
  white sauce 104
Wong, Penny 82
wraps, falafel 188

Y
Ying Chow (Adelaide) 90
yoghurt
  lucky-dip padrón peppers with strained yoghurt 221
  upside-down saffron labneh plate 233
  yoghurt mint sauce 188

Z
zhug, roasted & raw vegetable salad with 114
Zulfiqar, Jennifer 179

Published in 2018 by Murdoch Books, an imprint of Allen & Unwin

Murdoch Books Australia
83 Alexander Street, Crows Nest NSW 2065
Phone: +61 (0)2 8425 0100
murdochbooks.com.au
info@murdochbooks.com.au

Murdoch Books UK
Ormond House, 26-27 Boswell Street, London, WC1N 3JZ
Phone: +44 (0) 20 8785 5995
murdochbooks.co.uk
info@murdochbooks.co.uk

For Corporate Orders & Custom Publishing contact our business development team
at salesenquiries@murdochbooks.com.au

Publisher: Jane Morrow
Editorial Manager: Jane Price
Design Manager: Madeleine Kane
Editor: Alison Cowan
Designer: Aileen Lord
Photography: Rob Palmer (except pages 13 and 234, bottom, by Elissa Linder)
Styling: Vanessa Austin (except pages 13 and 234, bottom, by Cynthia Inions)
Food Preparation for Photography: Ross Dobson
Production Director: Lou Playfair

Text © Annabel Crabb and Wendy Sharpe 2018
Design © Murdoch Books 2018
Photography © Rob Palmer 2018 (Elissa Linder pages 13 and 234)

All rights reserved. No part of this publication may be reproduced, stored in a retrieval system or transmitted in any form or by any means, electronic, mechanical, photocopying, recording or otherwise, without the prior written permission of the publisher.

ISBN 978 1 76063 194 9 Australia
ISBN 978 1 76063 453 7 UK

A cataloguing-in-publication entry is available from the catalogue of the National Library of Australia at nla.gov.au

A catalogue record for this book is available from the British Library

Colour reproduction by Splitting Image Colour Studio Pty Ltd, Clayton, Victoria
Printed by C&C Offset Printing Co Ltd, China

MEASURES GUIDE: We have used Australian 20 ml (4 teaspoon) tablespoon measures. If you are using a smaller European 15 ml (3 teaspoon) tablespoon, add an extra teaspoon of the ingredient for each tablespoon specified.

The publisher would like to thank the following for their help with the photography for this book:
Aura Lifestyle, Bonnie and Neil, Dulux, Emily Ziz, Maison Balzac, Mud Australia, Sparkk, TeraNova tiles, Wedgwood.

The paper in this book is FSC® certified. FSC® promotes environmentally responsible, socially beneficial and economically viable management of the world's forests.

St Nikolas grande P 25
coffee Smoothie P. 24
Boshca P 19
Plum Jam P 27